Joie de Vivre

Also by Harriet Welty Rochefort

French Toast

French Fried

Joie de Vivre

Secrets of Wining, Dining, and

Romancing Like the French

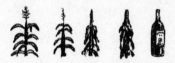

Harriet Welty Rochefort

Thomas Dunne Books

St. Martin's Press

New York

THOMAS DUNNE BOOKS.
An imprint of St. Martin's Press.

JOIE DE VIVRE. Copyright © 2012 by Harriet Welty Rochefort. All rights reserved. Printed in the United States of America. For information, address St. Martin's Press, 175 Fifth Avenue, New York, N.Y. 10010.

www.thomasdunnebooks.com
www.stmartins.com

ISBN 978-1-250-00456-7 (hardcover)
ISBN 978-1-250-01796-3 (e-book)

First Edition: October 2012

10 9 8 7 6 5 4 3 2 1

This book is for Philippe, husband and helpmate *extraordinaire*

And our children and grandchildren, my *joie de vivre*

Contents

Acknowledgments

This is the place to thank, first and foremost, my husband, Philippe, without whom this book—and my richly textured life in France—would not have been possible. Not only did he literally take over the household chores to give me precious time to write, but he patiently endured my questions and doubts, skillfully edited and formatted draft after draft of the manuscript, and graciously agreed to be interviewed for some of the chapters.

Next I would like to thank my editor at St. Martin's Press, Anne Bensson, and my agent, Regula Noëtzli. They share a rare quality: in addition to being first-rate professionals, they promptly and courteously answer e-mails. I appreciate that *politesse*.

So many people helped me with this book that it's impossible to list them without inadvertently leaving out some names. I hope those omitted will forgive me. If they let me know who they are, I'll be happy to stand them to an espresso in a Paris café! Thanks go to all those interviewed in this book, whether named or anonymous. All were more than generous with their time; many of our interviews ended up in long lunches and gab sessions. I am grateful for their observations and insights.

Special thanks go to Judy Fayard, Sarah Federman, Dorie Laurent, Janet Lizop, Marcia Lord, and my sister Miriam Trangsrud Welty, for reading all or parts of the manuscript and for their gently proffered and always astute constructive criticism. Others who lent a helping hand: Elaine Aragon, Barbara Cassasus, Sarah Colton, Isabelle Desormeau, Lynne Dills, Persis Gouirand, Judith Kaplan, Stanislas Kraland, Angenette Meaney, Florence Rosenberg, Nancy Sayer, Jan Tabet, Vivian Thomas, and "the Martha Cook 3": Clare Drews, Denise Padden, and Meril Yu. Sandra Messier at Le Cordon Bleu was most efficient and kind in dealing with my various requests. Great gratitude goes to my French family and my American family, who are always there for me.

When all is said and done, only one person takes responsibility for the content of these pages. My viewpoint is, of course, subjective, and my opinions my own. I truly think the French possess *joie de vivre* and hold secrets to the good life. My hope is that you'll discover a few of those secrets—and have a moment of *joie* as you read this book.

Joie de Vivre

Introduction

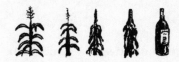

The first time I came to France I was stunned—everything looked so small. The cars, the bridges, the narrow streets, the portions of food, even the people. . . .

But that initial impression gave way to a stronger one. After all, many European countries looked tiny. No, France was special because of something else, that *je ne sais quoi,* an ambient style that permeated the simplest of things. I didn't need to attend an Yves Saint Laurent fashion show to know that Frenchwomen are elegant—I just had to look around me. I didn't need to eat in three-star restaurants—I feasted on savory French fare in the most modest bistros. I didn't need to study philosophy—all I had to do was stop by a café near the Sorbonne and imagine what all those earnest professor and student types were discussing over their wee black espressos. That they were so alluring in their slightly worn clothes and artfully arranged woolen scarves only added to their charm.

I have to admit, about two minutes after arriving in France, I fell in love with the French, their style, their intensity, their self-possession, their flair, their *joie de vivre*. I later fell in love with a man who possesses all these qualities in every pore of his very French soul. I figure that if I could remain married for almost forty years without getting bored, something exciting must be going on. And there is, every single day. The sparkle springs from my spouse, but equally from living amid his compatriots with their matchless French panache. I love their talent for finding joy in the moment without wondering what's next. I love the flair they put into every element of their lives, such as:

- *Pastries.* German desserts are delicious—and heavy. French pastries are so light and airy they make you want to weep.
- *Scarves.* Whether Hermès or *ordinaire,* the scarves Frenchwomen wear are not too perfectly knotted or tied, but somehow exactly right.
- *French gardens.* The senses come alive in France's flowers, in its gardens and public parks. From the well-known and beloved Jardin du Luxembourg to the off-the-beaten-track, handkerchief-size Parc de Belleville in the working-class east, the green patches of Paris are lavished with care. City gardeners are the unseen geniuses of the City of Light.
- *Kissing.* The French kiss publicly—yet they're alone in the world. In what other city could the famous Doisneau photo *Le Baiser de l'Hôtel de Ville* have been snapped? That it turned out to have been staged—with a couple who were lovers in real life— makes no difference. It's an eminently romantic photo in an evocative and emblematic setting.
- *Charm.* French charm ranges from "reserved" to "explosive." For the latter, think French actor Jean Dujardin, who won the 2012 Oscar for Best Actor in

The Artist. With his free and easy style, high spirits, devastatingly radiant smile (and adorable French accent), he's the portrait of exuberant, natural French allure and *joie de vivre*. You can't underestimate the power of charm. It's what's kept me in this country for decades. I live with a "charming" Frenchman every day (his captivating "charm" is the "reserved" variety—nice too!).

- *Rudeness.* Yes, the French put flair into their rudeness! But here's the encouraging news: they have changed. Tourists expecting the worst from the "rude French" are instead startled and gratified by their kindness. The thing is, though . . . when the French— and particularly the Parisians—decide to be ill-mannered, they elevate it to an art form. Actually, for them it's a game. They love nothing better than a nice little (or big) clash. So when they are coarse, gruff, or brusque, naturally it's done with great thought and totally on purpose. For them, confrontation is *fun*. I kid you not.

Ah, the French. France without the French wouldn't, couldn't, be France. That's my opinion.

Others—actually quite a few others—maintain that France would be perfect if the French would do everyone a big favor and vanish from the face of the earth.

My reply to that is, yes, then it would indeed be perfect, perfectly . . . boring.

Why are the French so different from everyone else in the world? Because they've got flair, panache, brio, élan, style. Because they put joy and pleasure at the top of their life priorities and not down there somewhere after duty and toil. Because they celebrate the moment.

Am I the only one who's noticed this? Hardly. Scores of

Francophiles, famous and not so famous, have praised the French art of living, their *savoir-vivre* and *joie de vivre*. In "Baguettes and Briefcases: The Art of Living," Lilianne Milgrom writes (for *Bonjour Paris*), "From the moment I stepped out of my loft in Ivry, it was clear that I had left the United States behind. The French have an undeniable knack for the Art of Living, a certain enjoyment and appreciation of life's small pleasures which I find irresistible." Now ninety-five years old, Olivia de Havilland, the gentle Melanie of *Gone With the Wind,* has lived in Paris since 1953. She told *Madame Figaro* magazine that her decision to begin a new life in Paris is one she has "never had the occasion to regret. The list of what I love about the French is endless: their vivaciousness, their independence, their love of life, food and wine, and their conversation . . . French is like music to my ears."

Les Français truly are singular in the way they live, act, and think. More than any other nationality, the French are concerned with form and style, appearance and presentation (right down to sheets and tablecloths, which many still iron, or get ironed, if they're lucky enough to have a cleaning lady). More than any other nationality, they exude a lightness of being that is a veritable art form. Life is serious, yes, but why be ponderous?

Eva Joly, a well-known Norwegian-born French magistrate, member of the European Parliament, and candidate for the Green Party in the 2012 French presidential elections, told a French daily that her best memory of France as a young *au pair* was the discovery of "the way of life, the interest in food, in appearance, in culture. It was exhilarating. . . . We were entitled to take a deep interest in our shoes. In my country, that would be indecent. This explosion of happiness has never ceased. When I'd shop rue Mabillon with my mother, she would say, 'You live like kings.'"

Her thoughts on the French penchant for pleasure were echoed by an Argentinean student who theorized, "The French are hedonists, devoted to wine and cheese. *And convinced that that's what life is all about.*" (Italics mine.)

Pleasure or fun? "Fun," commented a pundit in the *International Herald Tribune,* "is different than pleasure. . . . You don't feel fun; you do a fun thing." He contrasted it with pleasure, which comes with "being" and which has to develop on its own.

Pleasure is that little French secret. The French know all about pleasure. They know how to enjoy the moment. Most of all, they don't actively seek pleasure or think it's their due. "Pleasure," one wise Frenchman told me, "isn't something you look for. When it comes, it comes, unbidden."

This *is* a country where a well-known magistrate can embark on a quest for the right pair of shoes in the exact color to go with her outfit, and the strolling and comparing and time taken is not considered futile or frivolous. It *is* a country where you can stand for long minutes in front of a *pâtisserie* ogling a perfect *mille-feuille* nestling among the *religieuses* and *tartes normandes,* a *mille-feuille* that you may not buy but are simply happy to contemplate because it's so beautiful. It most assuredly *is* a country where you can guiltlessly indulge in all kinds of activities that might be considered "fluff" in other places. But to you, if you're French or almost French, a more than passing interest in food and wine and shoes and how things look and smell and taste is what makes life worth living. It's as if a secret voice is constantly whispering, "Go ahead, it's all right to enjoy the moment." In France you won't find waiters strolling by with startling regularity to ask you if you're still "working" on your meal. Working? For my husband and for any self-respecting French person, this is a contradiction in terms. How can you "work" on a meal, which by definition is a moment of pleasure?

* * *

The way the French think about life and the way they act isn't always easy to explain to foreigners. How those French mix it all up! That's why so many books try to decipher their often puzzling behavior. One of my favorites is *French Ways and Their Meaning* by the famous American novelist Edith Wharton, who lived in France for many years and understood the French well. Although published in 1919, the tome is timeless. If I cite Wharton so many times in this book, it is because I find her description and analysis of the French character true, insightful, and profound.

"The French," she writes wryly, "have never taken the trouble to disguise their Frenchness from foreigners." The phrase speaks volumes about how enigmatic the French seem to others, but most assuredly not to themselves. On the contrary, the French are perplexed by all the interest in them when all they are doing is being . . . French.

For foreigners, the French are a delight or a disaster, rarely anything in between. They are paradoxical, embodying contradictory traits. For example, the same person can possess exquisite manners and be horribly rude. And they act out their emotions. One day the guy at the cleaner's will joke and smile; the next, he's down at the mouth and looks as if he's going to commit suicide. In the beginning I thought I might have done something wrong. I hadn't; he was showing his mood to the world. The French truly wear their hearts on their sleeves. They can be prickly and oversensitive. At a cheese shop I ventured to ask if a Brie was creamy (I wanted to avoid the cardboard inside of an unripe Brie) and got One of Those Looks from the cheese vendor. *"Mais bien sûr,"* he huffed. I wanted to say. *"Exchoozay frigging moi,"* but instead I smiled and departed with my cheese—which, I must admit, was indeed perfect.

If people have such strong love-hate opinions about the

French, it's because they are hard to ignore. The national French fowl, after all, is the rooster. That barnyard bird crows loudly, forcing the world to sit up and pay attention. Luigi Barzini in *The Europeans* wickedly observed, "The brilliantly plumed cock is the first to announce the dawn of a new day to everybody, dominates his immediate world, seduces and fecundates all the unresisting hens, destroys his rivals, and crows triumphantly from the top of the dungheap." Take that, you galling Gauls!

"It's hard to be French," sighs my Gallic mate. He should know. (Note: the French are drama kings and queens. They are often ironic or use nuances, and unlike the rest of us, *they* all seem to know when something isn't to be taken literally.) In the beginning I took my dear partner's every word to the letter—until I finally wised up and realized that 98 percent of the time he was kidding, exaggerating, or putting me on. Once I figured out that little detail, I loosened up and had a lot more fun—too bad it took me about three decades.

Natives of other nations may be more reliable, more predictable, more steady, but none can compete with the French for the sheer intensity with which they lead their lives and go through their days, whether in dining, drinking, romancing, or taking to the streets to demonstrate. As I write these words—but I could write them in ten years and it would be the same—the French are in the midst of a major showdown with the government in a ten-week-long strike, the result of which is traffic congestion, gas shortages, snarled metro and bus and plane schedules, and garbage piling up on the pavement in some cities. And guess what? Seventy percent of the population approves of the strikers.

The reason for the strike: opposition to a reform in the retirement system, but also and perhaps mainly to French president Nicolas Sarkozy, who is a sterling example of what happens when the famous French flair isn't tempered by *savoir-vivre* (the art of good manners, which he singularly lacks). Sarkozy daringly challenged powerful French taboos with audacious slogans such as "work more to earn more," an idea that might be logical to the rest of the world but that's anathema to the French (well, not all of the French, it just sounds that way). In 2008 that catchphrase, among some of the president's other shocking one-liners, ended up on a Sarkozy voodoo doll complete with a handbook providing instructions for putting a curse on the president and twelve pins to plant in *la poupée.* Sarkozy's lawyer sued but lost. A French appeals court, however, ordered the doll's marketer to print a notice saying that stabbing or pricking the doll would harm the personal dignity of the president. (Talk about boosting sales . . .) As for dignity, in speculating on why, after three years as president, Sarkozy had yet to take on the decorum of the office, the left-leaning French weekly magazine *Le Nouvel Observateur* observed that he had "made the French insecure with his agitation and his aggressive behavior . . . , his *sans-gêne,* his disdain for good manners, and, in short, his absence of *savoir-vivre.*" *Mon Dieu.*

If you searched the world for the polar opposite of Charles de Gaulle, you would get Nicolas Sarkozy. De Gaulle was tall, with an imperial stance. He abhorred spending government money so much that when he invited his grandchildren to dine at the Élysée Palace, he paid for their meals out of his own pocket. His wife, Yvonne, was so plain vanilla the French called her Tante Yvonne (Aunt Yvonne), and she mainly stayed out of sight. There was not one iota of *nouveau riche* about de Gaulle, who was dignified, formal, and even intimidating. Skip to Sarkozy: he is short, but so was Napoléon. From the minute Sarkozy became president, he committed a series of faux pas: he donned Ray-Ban aviator sunglasses that made him look like a mafioso; he cruised on a millionnaire friend's yacht (in a country where conspicuous consumption is the ultimate taboo, definitely not the thing to do); and, *horreur,* he thumbed his nose at the anti-American French contingent by whisking his family off on a vacation to the States. And that was only a warm-up. He consulted his cell phone during a private audience with the pope—talk about tacky—and made his love life so public that everyone was relieved when he finally divorced his second wife, remarried, settled down, and announced his third wife's pregnancy, making him the first French president to have divorced, remarried, and become a father while in office. His Socialist successor, François Hollande, one-upped him by being the first French president not married to his partner. To his credit, Sarkozy abandoned the Ray-Bans and gave up some of the other *nouveau riche* accoutrements. By then, though, the damage had been done. For while the tolerant French were initially mystified by, haltingly accepting of, and even faintly fascinated by Sarkozy's down-to-earth style, the day he directed a few choice words (*Casse-toi, pauvre con,* which means "Get the f—— out of here, ass——") to a simple citizen who had publicly insulted him, the grace period was over. The French love good repartee and will forgive a lot—but not a president who cannot or will not remain above the fray. It's hard to do, but Sarkozy managed to shock the largely unshockable French.

When I first came to France to live, I didn't know much about the French other than that they in general, and one Frenchman in particular, had conquered my imagination. I wanted to know more about the way they acted, lived, and thought. I couldn't have found a better living classroom than I did with my husband, his family, and his friends. As I grappled with cultural differences, I vacillated between total admiration and total incomprehension. My thoughts on that perplexing period of time resulted in my first book, *French Toast,* in which I celebrated the maddening mysteries of the French. That book was cathartic, a toast to the French and, frankly, to myself for discovering that that there was much, much more to celebrate than castigate. In my second book, *French Fried,* I embarked on a joyful and savory trek through the world of French cuisine, from my Périgourdine mother-in-law's kitchen to an initiation into champagne tasting at the Ritz with Gérard Margeon, one of France's foremost sommeliers.

After examining some of the conundrums of French life in the first book and exploring the world of French cuisine in the second, I decided in this third quest to take a closer look at the famous French *joie de vivre.* What exactly is it? Where can it be found? Does it really exist or is it a figment of screenwriters' imaginations? It does indeed exist. *Joie de vivre* was the first thing I noticed about France. Like all tourists, I marveled at the monuments, but above all, I was genuinely struck by the ambient vitality, the buzz and bustle. All those French people looked as if they were having such a good time. And they still do.

I knew, though, that I was on tricky ground with the subject of *joie de vivre.* Frankly, if you live in Paris, as I do, and take the metro every day, you might start to wonder where exactly that *joie de vivre* is. It's certainly not underground. You might also wonder why the French are reputed to take so many antidepressants. Are they depressed? Pessimistic? And if so, how does pessimism jibe with *joie de vivre*?

At heart the French would like nothing more than to enjoy life, and they've got a social structure that allows them to do so in a way the rest of the world envies. But France is a country with a long history, of feasts but also famine, peace but also wars and invasions. So in every French person's mind is this knowledge that although things may be good now, bad may be lurking around the corner. Polls show the disconnect between how the French see the outside world and how they see "their own world." They are pessimistic and worried about life in general (you would be too if you watched too much French TV news, a real downer), but are quite happy with their own personal lives.

No wonder they sometimes look glum—even though they're not.

I asked a young Frenchman about this paradox one day. His mournful response: "We haven't had any good news since France won the Soccer World Cup in 1998." I tried hard not to laugh. "Come on," I pleaded, "surely something pleasant has happened since then." He shook his head, desperately trying to recall some joyful event. I would have felt terrible except that it was a beautiful spring day and we were sipping Perrier on the terrace of a café on the place Gustave Toudouze in the ninth arrondissement. The fellow was young, healthy, good-looking, employed, with a fine educational background, and a nice girlfriend. He told me he was working hard on renovating a little house he and his father had purchased nearby. And I thought, *How French this all is.* He was lamenting the bad state of life in France in general when his life in particular was dandy, even enviable. I don't know about you, but I can think of a lot of people who would love to be under the age of thirty and renovating a house they've bought in one of Paris's most sought-after neighborhoods. *Non?*

My secretly happy interlocutor was proof personified that the ambient French pessimism about the state of the world doesn't dent their personal *joie de vivre,* the joy they get from their work, their holidays, their food, their wine, and their families. They may sigh over a lack of *savoir-vivre,* the art and rules of social etiquette that enable people to live together in a civilized way, but judging from the plethora of books and businesses coaching the French on how to act, they aspire to it. Whoever would have thought that the French, the

masters of *bonnes manières*, would have to relearn them—
Louis XIV would turn over in his tomb. As for *savoir-faire,*
the art of doing things well, with expertise, not to worry:
France is known throughout the world for its creators and
artisans and the talent and standards of perfection that go
into the fabrication of everything from Baccarat crystal to a
perfectly aged cheese to a sumptuous haute-couture dress.

Joie de vivre, savoir-vivre, and *savoir-faire* have most definitely not deserted France. *Au contraire.* I am convinced
that if foreigners flock to France as their number one tourist
destination, it's because in addition to the museums and
monuments, they're intrigued and entranced by the famous
French lifestyle. As one young American observed, wide-
eyed, "All those people on the café terraces are talking to
each other, not sitting there separately watching a TV screen.
They're deep into their conversations. And they're not only
chatting, but laughing, frowning, flirting, disagreeing, and
even embracing in full view of all."

Can some of this French way of living be transposed? We
Americans may never get the five legal weeks of paid vacations and the other perks the French have, but we certainly
can take a few tips from the French on the art of living. Hey,
joie de vivre is free!

Joie de vivre is both simple and revolutionary. It's simple
because a moment of *joie de vivre* can be lunch with a girlfriend. How easy is that? It's revolutionary because for work-
driven, vacation- and long-lunch-deprived Americans, it almost
requires brain surgery. Why? Because to make that lunch a
moment with a French touch it has to be just for fun, no rush,
no agenda.

One of the secrets of the French *joie de vivre* is that although people are serious about their work, they are every
bit as serious about their lives. There's no "I'm too busy" to

see a friend, to shop, to stroll, to delight in some serendipitous pleasure even in the midst of the busiest day, even if for a wee moment. The French have a great capacity for putting top priority on their life, not their work. That's one reason the French have us stymied: How can they knock off for all those vacations and be as productive as Americans, who have so few? My French husband would say, "Because we're smarter," but joking aside, it's fairly simple: when the French work, they work. And when they play, they play. Maybe that's because they aren't plagued by the Protestant work ethic, which makes work the road to salvation. Forget it!

We may not have their vacation time, but to put some *joie de vivre* in our lives, a pretty table with a linen tablecloth and a bouquet of fresh flowers will do. I grew up in the Midwest but had several "French touches" in my life, starting with a French family in our town who settled there after World War II. The restaurant they opened, the Normandy Inn, featured French antiques they brought over with them from their family home in Le Havre (which had been requisitioned by the Nazis) and savory homemade French food that convinced me early on that France was for me. It must have influenced my mother as well. One day I came home from school for lunch to find a table for two she had set up in the corner of our dining room with a place card on which was written *Chez Doris* (her name). I was delighted. We were zillions of miles away from France, in the brutal winter of Iowa, and there we sat having a stylish French moment. So trust me, if you can "go French" in Iowa, you can go French anywhere. Aesthetics travel!

One last point on *joie de vivre* hit me while dining at a neighborhood restaurant in Paris with my husband on a Saturday night. The place was tiny, with red-checkered tablecloths and little red candles on the tables, a sprinkling of eclectic works of art on the walls, none by anyone even remotely known, good comfort food, a warm atmosphere—and bad-news music blaring from a bad-news radio station. The waiter kindly turned it down, but it was still there, and I realized that my husband didn't care and that I soon didn't either. I remarked then that maybe this is what makes up *la joie de vivre*—focusing on the good, not the bad. Time and time again, I've seen or been in situations where something's off, but the French by and large simply ignore it. They prefer to get on with enjoying what's right. An example? Let's take creature comforts. My American self wants to be at the right temperature, have air-conditioning when it's too hot, lots and lots of heat when it's too cold—now! Most of the French people I know, starting with my husband, don't seem to be as obsessed with this as I and many of my compatriots are. Another example: when something's broken, I want to fix it—immediately. My French husband finds my inability to accept situations as they are most amusing. Okay, I'll probably never change, but it did occur to me that this tolerance of things the way they are, this understanding that nothing's perfect, and the ability to accept that rather than rebel against it, is a major component of *joie de vivre*. "No civilised race," writes Edith Wharton, "has gone as unerringly as the French toward the natural sources of enjoyment."

I give many speeches on the cultural differences between the French and the Americans and see that not only is the fascination with the French a constant, but that a lot is left to say. The cultural chasm is indeed vast, but it is bridgeable. Trying to get to the heart of that indefinable French soul, that French *joie de vivre* and *art de vivre,* is not easy. After all, the French are impossible and intriguing and impossibly intriguing. They cook and drive and flirt and insult each other with exuberance. They never let up.

I might find another country where I don't have to wonder

so much about people's emotions and moods or have to be constantly on my toes to figure out what's going on, but how I would miss the savors, the serendipity, the surprises that each day brings. Maybe that's what attracted me to France and the French. Somehow I knew I'd escape *ennui*. And I did.

Romance, French Style

*A hot late afternoon in July. My "kind of" French boyfriend—
let's call him Jacques—suggests we have a drink at Le Select,
that famous café on the boulevard Montparnasse frequented
by Picasso, Man Ray, Fitzgerald, and Hemingway and featured in Woody Allen's* Midnight in Paris. *How romantic
can you get? He wants me to meet a friend of his, he says.
"Fine." I beam. "I'm always up for meeting new people." I
didn't know it then, but I was part of a setup that was to
change my life.*

What I didn't know when I accompanied Jacques to Le Select was that he and his pal had already made a gentleman's
agreement. If his friend and I liked each other and wanted to
go out together, Jacques would "accept" (understatement:
he'd be deliriously happy). The reason: Jacques was not into
commitment and was eager to go on to the next girl. I was
toast. (I'd be tempted to say "French" toast. . . .) Neither
Jacques, nor I, nor the friend I was casually meeting could
imagine that this encounter would result in a Franco-American

courtship, marriage, a stepson and two sons, and five grand-children.

But I'm getting ahead of myself. If, in writing about ro-mance *à la française,* I start close to home, what could be more natural? I grew up in a small town in Iowa, and the chances I'd have a romance in Paris starting in a famous café in a magical and historic setting were frankly not high—until I decided upon graduating from the University of Michigan to purchase a one-way ticket to Paris (brilliant move!).

Romances That Start in Cafés

In the early seventies, it was a cinch for an American to find a job in Paris, and I did—several, in fact. When I wasn't work-ing (mostly as a secretary, which was worse than unfortunate for my bosses, who practically paid me to leave), I was doing more important things, such as hanging out in cafés and meeting people. Now, *that* was *joie de vivre.*

The fateful meeting Jacques arranged at the café was no more than one casual *rendez-vous* among others. I took one look at his *ami* and had two thoughts: (1) this isn't going to be fun, and (2) what a pity—he's good-looking. That was true. He was slim and handsome with blue eyes and good features, and nicely dressed in a blue blazer and tan chinos. But what a dark look. Jacques, I grumbled to myself, had done some seri-ous miscasting, thinking he could join Ms. Open Smiley Face with Mr. French Frown. I reminded myself to give him a big piece of my mind next time around. For immediately after making the introductions, Jacques departed, waving a cheery good-bye. I didn't know the good-bye was forever, and I didn't know I'd been set up. All I knew as his compatriot and I set-tled down on our wicker chairs was that I'd give the whole ordeal no more than fifteen minutes—maximum.

One hour later we were still there, and the Gloomy French Scowler had me chortling and chuckling at almost every word that came out of his mouth. Was it what he said or that his droll remarks were so out of sync with the expression on his face? Deadpan humor, I decided. I have a weakness for it.

We decided to prolong the evening and repair to the next-door pizzeria for dinner, where during dessert we discovered a mutual love for chocolate. That settled it. Funny, good-looking, loves chocolate. And a gentleman. He picked up the bill, escorted me home, opened the car door (I may be a feminist, but I like attention!), and didn't make any moves, the way most of the other fellows I went out with would have. I wondered why. . . . A few days later he crossed town to bring me a record player, trudged up six flights of stairs, and still made no advances. I began to see a strategy: he *wanted* me to wonder. Clever, I thought. I have a *definite* weakness for clever.

I soon found that Philippe (by now he had a name instead of the French Frowner or the Guy from the Café. In fact, he had a long one, Philippe Jean Pierre André) is opinionated. He has a point of view on everything, which he articulates clearly with nary a shred of political correctness. *So* refreshing. To add to this, not only did he not mind my disagreeing with him, he encouraged it. He taught me, among other things, that sparring is stimulating and fun when you do it without getting nasty and personal. An art form, one might say. Very French.

So, as you can see, this was hardly one of those film romances where two people meet, their hearts instantly go pitter-patter, and they walk off into the setting sun. What did happen was that I put off a trip to Argentina (my après-Paris fantasy at the time) and stayed to go out with my new boyfriend, whom I greatly preferred to the "now toast" Jacques. Not only did the *faux* curmudgeon make me laugh, but he turned out to be a walking encyclopedia. "What's that monument?" I'd ask, and he'd tell me when it was built, under what king, for what reason, and supply the whole historical context as he did so. *And* he wasn't pedantic! I could cast more praise his way, but I don't want to make anyone jealous (he's a great cook, he helps me in the kitchen, he offers me flowers and not only for anniversaries, he's the most considerate person I've ever met, he's . . .). Okay, okay, I'll stop, but not before saying that he never did become a bore, and the combo of the deadpan face and what one friend called "quiet wit" has never ceased to fascinate, frustrate, mystify, and amuse me.

Oh, yes, he can still summon the scowl.

A dear American friend of mine met her French husband in a café as well, and it was, she tells me, love at first sight. "I was sitting on one of those long banquettes at the Café Danton reading an Agatha Christie. I'd been in Paris for nine months working as an *au pair,* but I was lonely. I looked up and saw a guy sit down three tables away. He kept glancing at me, and I thought, 'Oh, no, another one trying to pick me up.'" Then, she continued, the man, who had on "a rusty-brown shirt in terrible taste," stood up, came to her table, and asked her what she was reading. The shirt may have been unsightly but she found its owner handsome with "incredible eyes and an appealing deep voice." He turned out to be French (up to then most of those interested in her hadn't been), they started talking, he invited her out to dinner in one of those ten-franc places that existed at the time. "We hit it off immediately—it was definitely a *coup de foudre* [love at first sight]." Of course, this being France, the story had a hitch. As things progressed, she learned that he was (unhappily) married. You might think that at this point she threw something at him and trounced off, *mais non.* She was, she says, too deeply in love to care. He must have been as well—three

years later he divorced, they married, and they are still together forty years later.

Meeting in a café, whether you're being introduced or
whether you happen to strike up a conversation with someone and it goes from there, is hardly uncommon. Even
though their number has plummeted from two hundred
thousand in 1960 to forty thousand today, cafés are a French
institution *par excellence* and, pre-Internet, *the* place to go.
After the war, many writers, the most famous of whom were
Sartre and Simone de Beauvoir, frequented cafés simply because they were warmer than their freezing apartments. In
Saint-Germain-des-Prés, the café scene was lively, with students shuttling back and forth between the numerous spots.
Hélène Véret, former photo editor at *Life* magazine, remembers, "The Flore was too expensive and too intellectual, so a
lot of us went across to the street to the Royal Pub—which
now houses Armani." She also recalls that in the provincial
town she grew up in, young girls didn't go to a café alone.
The first time she and her friends went to one, she says, "We
were so proud. We got all dressed up in white gloves and felt
rather sinful."

Whether for a setup or by serendipity, cafés, bistros, and
brasseries can be incredibly romantic places to meet. Why?
Because you're in one of those "you never know what can
happen" scenarios. One recent night, Philippe and I returned
to the Select, as we do from time to time, where I watched a
pickup attempt play out in front of us. A beautiful young,
blond French girl dressed in black with high black boots
strolled in. She didn't seem to be looking for anyone, chatted
with the waiter, ordered a glass of wine, and sat alone on the
banquette serenely and self-confidently. She wasn't conventionally pretty but had something drop-dead attractive and
intriguing about her. One of the two young men at the adjoin-
ing table couldn't keep his eyes off her as he chatted with his

friend, and finally, when he could no longer resist, he approached her. She talked to him briefly, smiled, and the conversation finished just as her boyfriend walked in and sat down. The disappointed suitor nodded to her as he left, and I couldn't help wondering if those two might not see each other again. That's what I like about the French and romance—you never know. Anything is possible.

In one of my favorite French films, *Le Vieux Fusil,* Clara, played by Romy Schneider, dines in a *grande brasserie* with Julien, a surgeon, played by Philippe Noiret. The film tells the story of a tragedy loosely based on the 1944 massacre by the SS of the inhabitants of the village of Oradour-sur-Glane in the Limousin, but before the unspeakable disaster unfolds, the flashback of their first meeting shows Julien, impeccable in a well-cut suit with a flower in his buttonhole, and a resplendent Clara, in a stylish hat with a black veil and black outfit that accentuates her perfect figure. The bespectacled Julien is clearly overwhelmed by Clara's beauty. The café scene is the prelude to their romance, marriage, and a moment of *joie de vivre* and happiness before the brutality of war changes everything.

The French Kiss

Cafés, as I said, are perfect places for budding romances, but almost anywhere in the French capital will do. Paris is a made-to-order setting for love and kisses.

Robert Doisneau, whose photos of Paris and its people are emblematic, captured *the* French kiss at the Hôtel de Ville in a picture that has become the symbol of "romantic Paris." Nothing's changed since he snapped that photo. Take a stroll around town: you'll see couples kissing on bridges, in cafés, in parks, on buses, on billboards . . . even in cemeteries. I had never deemed a graveyard a locus for romance but had to reconsider after practically smashing into a couple locked in each other's arms, embracing among the tombs in the vast and poetic Père Lachaise Cemetery in the east of Paris.

Our son David and his girlfriend, Rachel, were featured on one of those three-meter-high billboards in the metro kissing in front of the "new town" of Marne-la-Vallée, where the Disneyland Paris theme park is located. Obviously the city fathers, when cogitating on promoting their town, thought a handsome, young romantic couple would be just the ticket, and David and Rachel were only too happy to oblige. How hard is it to be paid to kiss? And do several takes? It was probably one of the most fun jobs either of them has ever had. As for me, what a strange and wonderful feeling to see a member of the family plastered all over the Paris metro.

Some Americans—maybe other nationalities as well—are surprised by what they call PDA (public display of affection). It's one of the easiest things to catch on to in this culture, as the renowned humorist Art Buchwald attested in his memoir *I'll Always Have Paris,* in which he wrote about courting his future wife, Ann: "Ann and I walked through Paris late in the afternoon, late into the night, and early in the morning—stopping every few feet to hug and kiss. Not one person objected, and even the gendarmes nodded their approval." Doing what he did in Paris—kissing his beloved on the steps leading into the metro or "better still, rubbing her back at the Sacré-Cœur overlooking all of Paris"—would, he wrote, have been considered inappropriate behavior in New York City, and, as for Los Angeles, "the only place you could steal a kiss was when you were stalled in traffic on the freeway. In Paris, the citizens positively approved of open displays of affection at any location." I have a book called *The Best Places to Kiss in Paris* and, after reading it, concluded there's really no place *not* to kiss in this city (well, maybe in church, unless you're getting married. The authors do, however, suggest *behind* a church, in the cloister of Saint-Séverin—if you try and succeed, let me know!).

The French kiss all the time and everywhere. Grandparents kiss children, children kiss each other, straight men kiss. Friends give each other *la bise,* a brief, light peck on the cheek whose number depends on whether you're from the capital or the provinces (or other factors, none of which anyone can figure out). Deep in the provinces, it's four kisses, two on each cheek. In Paris, it's often one perfunctory kiss on each cheek. And some people, I can't figure why, give three kisses. Maybe a compromise? More formal and less common, the *baise-main* is a gentle skimming of the skin as the man bows slightly and takes the hand of the married (not unmarried), gloveless (no gloves for a kiss) woman. A *baise-main* can take you by surprise. Suddenly your hand has been lightly lifted, and by the time you understand that the gentleman is rendering a brief homage, it's over. Who practices the *baise-main*? Mostly people from traditional backgrounds, and mostly men "of a certain age." My husband doesn't do it. My sons wouldn't even consider it. Some women find it positively feudal. I like it.

Do you know how to say "French-kiss" in French? It's *rouler une pelle* (literal translation: "roll a shovel"!). Well, you get the idea. Hardly romantic—and vulgar in French. I asked my husband why. He couldn't give me a reason but confirmed the coarseness of the expression and added, smiling roguishly, "The point is not to say it, but do it. It's the only way to kiss." *Voilà.*

We Americans may have a hard time figuring out the *bise* or the *baise-main,* but the French have a hard time figuring out our back patting, which looks every bit as strange to

A Romantic Day in Paris

In the morning:
Have a cup of tea in the Musée de la Vie Romantique, rue Chaptal.

Or get a view of Paris as you sit on the terrace facing the Bateau-Lavoir in Montmartre.

In the afternoon:
Take a boat down the Canal de l'Ourcq for an incredibly romantic view of old Paris and the locks.

At night:
Listen to a Chopin concert in la Roseraie de Bagatelle.

Or take two glasses (real glass, not plastic) and a bottle of champagne or a bottle of Loupiac and foie gras. Go to the quais near the Institut du Monde Arabe. Stake out a nice spot, place your drinks and food on a pretty tablecloth, and watch the Bateaux Mouches glide by.

them. In her brilliant chapter "Conversation" in *Cultural Misunderstandings,* Raymonde Carroll writes about the "patting on the back, against which the French body rebels." For Carroll, the back pat at the end of an embrace between two persons of the opposite sex is a clear signal that their relationship is "not a sexual or romantic one." All of which is rather dreadful to the French. "The back patters don't really connect, or only with the upper part of the body. They're physically close but take the utmost care to turn their heads so their faces don't touch," one clearly mystified Frenchman observed.

Love in the City of Love

Sex is sex everywhere, but in Paris there's the added quality of romance. Everywhere. All the time.

Before coming to France, I'd caught a few glimpses of French romance. One of them was the French film *A Man and a Woman,* by Claude Lelouch, which I viewed as a student at the University of Michigan. In this "foreign" film, everything was indeed new and different to me. As I sat in the dark cinema watching Anouk Aimée, with that becoming stage name, high cheekbones, and expressive dark eyes, opposite Jean-Louis Trintignant, playing a sexy race-car driver, chimes went off in my brain. Such romance. Such beauty. *I've got to get over there as fast as I can.* Another time, in San Francisco, I spied a French couple at a table in a restaurant. They were carrying on a low conversation and were totally oblivious to everything else going on in the room. They'd pulled around them an invisible bubble. *That* was French, and something I had never observed with any American couple in similar circumstances. How could they remain so private in public? I wondered. I knew I'd have to go see for myself.

When I finally got to France, I wasn't disappointed, for it is *the* country of romance, where a new encounter can happen anytime—at a red light, on a street corner, at the grocer's, in the metro, in the park. This was a revelation for me all those years ago and recently for Ann Lawson, a twenty-year-old student on a semester in Paris. Seated in the Luxembourg Gardens doing homework one afternoon, she was complimented by "at least four or five" different French fellows. "They told me I had beautiful hair, a nice smile, and then went their way without asking for my phone number or anything," she marveled, noting, "This would never happen at my college in the U.S." She admitted that she finds this whole new scene "very enticing. After you hear compliments like that, you want to keep on hearing them."

She most probably will, for in Paris love and romance are in the air and everywhere—including in the metro. In pre-Internet days, there might be a look of mutual appreciation, maybe even a *coup de foudre* before the object of desire would disappear in the crowd. With the Internet, the chances of finding that person have improved, and if the number and success of search sites say anything, it's that French people of all ages are having a *coup de foudre* almost every day. I checked out two sites, croisedanslemetro.com (crossed paths in the metro), which, as its name indicates, is only for the metro, and dilelui.com (tell him or her), which gives the frustrated searcher a stab at finding the vanished person whether the chance meeting was in the metro, the TGV, the airport, the bakery, the theater, or the shopping mall.

Messages range from brief—"Our eyes met. Contact me"—to the more elaborate, such as "It was a little after 18h15. You are tall, with blue-green eyes. You were reading *Le Monde* standing up, with your back to the pole before sitting down in front of me. I was reading a book in Italian, listening to my iPod, and my phone rang. You looked at me discreetly, then stared until a fat tourist came between us and prevented us from continuing. I saw you doing everything to try to catch my eye, but you were bothered by the tourist's big paunch. I smiled, then became intimidated, and started reading again. I got off at Nation, saw you looking at me once again, then left. I am tall, slim, brown haired. I would love to see you again."

That's the metro; romance is also in the office—big-time. One recent poll showed that fully one-third of office workers have gone beyond being colleagues. I asked a French friend and my niece, both of whom work in large companies, if this presents problems. Do the couples hide the relationship or register it with HR to avoid sexual harassment charges? They both laughed. "No, thank God!" My niece told me that the big guessing game at her office is to try to pick out the couples. On one occasion, a young woman became pregnant, and, my niece noted, "Strangely, at about the same time, a young single man transferred to another department." When the baby was born, he resurfaced, they got married, and *then* they went to HR—to announce the news and get all the benefits that come in France with having a baby. My niece concluded, "Who's going with whom is above all a subject that has everyone talking and which is quite amusing." I'd wager that a French person would have a *real* hard time adjusting to an American office situation in which the threat of sexual harassment and the necessity of spelling out relationships dampen the pleasure of spicy conjecture.

A Certain Vagueness

In France *vague* is the name of the game when it comes to love and romance. You never know who's with whom, and even if you think you do, you may be wrong. If there's one thing the French love when it comes to love, it's mystery.

A French friend told me about a Parisian dinner party where she was seated next to a distinguished older man and woman. "I talked to them for three hours and didn't figure out until after I left that they must have been married for the past forty years!" she exclaimed. That's not unusual: many times in France you'll go through an entire evening with people you don't know, and when you leave, you'll realize that you don't even know their names, not to mention how they might be "related." Are they boyfriend and girlfriend, husband and wife, sister and brother, ex-husband and wife? You don't know and they aren't telling.

This "discretion" or "secrecy," this French tolerance and, yes, even desire for gray areas, starts early on. As Debra Ollivier pointed out in *What French Women Know,* when little French girls pluck daisies, they don't say, "He loves me, he loves me not." Rather, they chant, *"Il m'aime un peu, beaucoup, passionnément, à la folie, pas du tout,"* spelling out the whole range of human emotions from loving a little, a lot, passionately, to the point of craziness, or not at all. At a tender age, they already know there are not two but several degrees and shades of love.

There are also many ways to be together. Two French university students who are now "just good friends" told me that when they were a twosome, they didn't tell anybody. They recalled that on a trip to Turkey with a group of friends, no one knew they were together. On purpose. For the young woman, not telling the world that they were a couple was a mixture of propriety and pride. The secrecy wasn't restricted to their pals. "I never would have told my parents who I was going out with because it might not have worked," the young woman said.

So how, I asked them, do you know who's with whom, if they're a couple, married, or available? "It's not easy," the two friends replied, almost in unison. "There might be minidetails; you might talk more to one person than another or be seated next to him. But it shouldn't be obvious."

Why? Because the French value their private lives. It's well known that the sex lives of the powerful are considered private—but so are the sex lives (and lives in general) of everyone else. When you are invited to a French person's home, you're confined to the living room because the rest is considered off-limits. In the same way the French only open parts of their home, they only open up parts of their lives—and that's even with their best friends. There's no "need to know" or "need to tell" in the air. You don't have to announce that you're going out with so-and-so, or that you've been married for X number of years, or that your husband was married twice before. In the States, you might go to a gathering and know not a soul, but you'd soon get filled in as to who is with whom. That doesn't happen in France. I've been at many a party where I could absolutely not figure out how the people I met were connected to one another. I finally stopped trying. Who cares, anyway? (I'm becoming French. . . .)

Here's what Anne Sinclair, whose private life became fodder for the international media after her husband, Dominique Strauss-Kahn, was arrested on charges of sexually assaulting a chambermaid in a New York hotel, replied to a journalist at *Elle* magazine who asked her if she was still in love after all she'd been through: "It's none of your business."

She was replying to the journalist but also, one felt, to the moralizing French and American feminists who criticized her for not condemning or leaving her husband. Every couple has its internal workings, she noted. And the arrangement two people have together is their business, no one else's.

As far as spelling things out and "the conversation" in which the woman sounds the man out on "where they are" and "where they stand," it doesn't happen early in the game, if at all, probably because any Frenchman who gets the feeling he's getting an ultimatum would flee. It may come later, not labeled as such, when a couple's been together a long time and are deciding to live together—or not.

All very, very subtle—and very, very French.

Sex—On s'amuse

Francis I was one of the favorite kings of France. He was tall, six feet six inches, handsome, a patron of the arts and letters, and a friend of Leonardo da Vinci's. He built or added on to a dozen castles, including Fontainebleau, Blois, and Chambord, and adored *les fêtes,* food, wine, and women, for whom he possessed an "immoderate" love. In addition to his wife, Claude (whose only gift to French history is the name of a small green prune, the Reine Claude), who gave him seven children, François had two official mistresses and a bevy of pretty young things around him all the time. His motto was "a court without women is like a garden without flowers."

The French find love, romance, and sex vastly amusing. They have "always been a gay and free and Rabelaisian people," observed Edith Wharton in *French Ways and Their Meaning.* "They attach a great deal of importance to love-making, but they consider it more simply and less solemnly than we. They are cool, resourceful and merry, crack jokes about the relations between the sexes, and are used to the frank discussion of what some tactfully called 'the operations of Nature.'"

Not only do they find sex one of the greatest inventions, but they don't bother to hide their interest, which can some-times shock more puritan peoples.

When it comes to sex, they say, "Yes, we can," and go for it. While we Americans shower and brush our teeth before making love, chew on breath mints before going to a party, and generally avoid any odor that smacks of strong or raun-chy, the French gaily consume garlic, don't always roll on the deodorant, and think that a good wash before lovemak-ing is not very sexy. Remember Napoléon's writing to Joséphine: "Don't wash, I'm coming." As a famous Frenchman commented in a *French Toast* interview, "We like the jungle smell."

Louis-Bernard Robitaille, the Paris correspondent of the Canadian newspaper *La Presse,* recounts in his hilariously astute book *Ces impossibles Français* the following anecdote,

which illustrates the difference between the French attitude
to sex and the North American one. At a dinner party in the
seventies he shocked the American hostess, a high school
teacher married to a Reuters journalist, by mentioning that
the last interview the famous Italian reporter Oriana Fallaci
had with Fidel Castro was in *Playboy.* The hostess immediately cut him off by saying she didn't read *Playboy.* Robitaille's rejoinder: "In Paris, the women at that table would
have not only asked to see the interview, but probably to leaf
through the magazine with an expert and not very indulgent
eye to make comments on the bulging breasts in the photos."
All Frenchwomen? No way to know, but some of the Frenchwomen I know would most assuredly have had the reaction
Robitaille describes.

I've got legions of anecdotes of my own that show how
truly freed up Frenchwomen are when it comes to sex and
discussions of sex. That includes what we call off-color jokes,
and if you disapprove of them, you'd better not attend French
dinner parties. Imagine that you're at an American (or British
or Australian or Swedish) dinner party and a Frenchman tells
the story about a famous phrase uttered by the womanizing
King Henri IV, who never washed and chewed on garlic all
day long. He is said to have remarked, "Until I was forty, I
thought it was a bone."

I was at a French dinner party where the Henri IV story
was told. The Frenchmen and Frenchwomen all laughed. I
confess I didn't get the joke (but I never get jokes, so count
me out), and the other American woman present remained
stone-faced. Fortunately, she didn't do what one American
friend of mine did one evening, which was to throw a glass of
water in the face of a man who had told one dirty joke too
many at the dinner table. Why did you do that? I asked her. "I
was the only American with a group of French. I was fed up

and wanted to bring a halt to the incessant tasteless jokes they all found funny." She used the only means available but told me later she realized she had gone too far. You may be saying, No, *he* had. But we're in France, a country where talking about sex is not a taboo, so guess what? *She* was the one people thought strange because her reaction was so out of proportion, so inappropriate in a French setting, where when you don't like what's going on, you find a subtle way of expressing it. And not to worry: even and especially when there's a change of tone or expression or a verbal dart, the person gets it immediately. You don't have to bring out the big guns. Lamented my water-tossing friend, "I should have used my wit like Frenchwomen do." (I felt for her—the French verbal dexterity is an art form that takes years for foreigners to attain and some never do.)

I recounted the anecdote to a Frenchwoman who has never been to the States and doesn't speak English for what I hoped would be an authentically French reaction. Like the tolerant soul she is, she understood that my friend was upset and offended by the jokes. However, picking up a glass of water and throwing it in the offending party's face when at the table? *Mon Dieu!* No Frenchwoman, she mused, would even think of doing that. It would spoil the meal! I asked her what a Frenchwoman *would* do should a man be telling a dirty joke, or worse, several. "That happens regularly," she stated matter-of-factly. "Men are like children. If they have an audience, they'll keep going. You need to give them limits. You either say gently but firmly, 'Okay, *ça va,*' which means 'Okay, that's enough now,' or you make him understand he's gone too far by not participating or even turning your back." Basically, she said, the Frenchwoman would do everything to avoid overt hostility. Bad form!

Anyway, in a country where naked men and women (or

parts of naked men and women) don't shock, no one gets too upset over things that would make most Americans apoplectic. At the end of a meal in a Thai restaurant in Paris with an American friend one day, the waiter brought us each a teeny cup of sake. At the bottom was a raised glass into which one could gaze and see, for the women, a naked man with penis in full view, and for the men, a naked woman in a provocative position. My friend did a double take and said, "You would *never* see this in the States. And if you did, rather than seeing it as a joke, you'd get extremely upset, politically correct reactions." When I told the anecdote to Philippe, he wryly said, "Make sure you tell your readers you're talking about an Asian restaurant, not French." Come to think of it, even though the French have no hang-ups about nudity, I've never seen such a thing in a French restaurant . . . but the point of the story is that nudity in itself is not shocking. Unlike my astounded American friend, a French person would look at the bottom of the cup and either laugh or yawn. Ah, those worldly French!

The French take sex, body parts, nudity, as a matter of course, and not too seriously. Remember when Janet Jackson accidentally revealed a breast at the 2004 Super Bowl and everyone went ballistic? Jackson issued an apology to anyone who may have been offended. The same thing happened to French actress Sophie Marceau at the 2005 film festival in Cannes. She laughed and shrugged it off. No apologies.

Catherine Millet, the author of the bestselling *La vie sexuelle de Catherine M.,* simply went back to her day job as the respected editor of an art magazine once the book, in which she recounted her active sex life, was published. *Active* is an understatement, but that wasn't a problem. I'm fairly certain that a woman in the States writing a book recounting her sex life in grippingly graphic detail would have a harder time. In France, Millet wasn't judged. If readers criticized the book, it wasn't because of the juicy sex or because they thought it "immoral." It was because they either found it "boring" or didn't believe her!

In France a well-known politician can attend partner-swapping evenings without any journalists reporting on it even though they are perfectly informed (it's a free country, isn't it?). There's a high tolerance in France for behavior that would get a philandering American or British politician on TV making a public confession, upright, forgiving wife by his side. (The French are as mystified by these "confessions" as we are about their telling off-color jokes in mixed company—with both sexes cracking up.) A cardinal of the Church can, and at least one did, die in the arms of a prostitute—and people found it funny, not shocking. (The worldly-wise French know that even the "purest" of the pure can succumb to temptation.) Huge billboards in the metro show ads of seminude women in scanty underwear. Hardly anyone gets upset. I say *hardly* because, depending on the ad, some feminists aren't amused. But it's safe to bet that the vast majority find nothing shocking, distasteful, or prurient in them. I've also seen ads of men in their underpants and they weren't boxer shorts. Equal opportunity!

Any one of the above examples would be greeted by disapproval or scandal in an "Anglo-Saxon puritan country." But then, France is not an Anglo-Saxon puritan country.

To take a recent example, each summer French newspapers try to put in as much entertainment in the form of games and special features as they can since it's a slow season for news, not to mention a slow season for journalists, who are massively on vacation. The national Sunday newspaper the *Journal du Dimanche* ran a series called *"Correspondances amoureuses,"* in which it published excerpts from the love letters of famous public figures. Some of the letters were touching, some romantic, some sweet. And some, such as the ones between Henry Miller and Anaïs Nin, were sizzling hot—for a Sunday newspaper.

Since sex in France is a "simple" thing and "less solemn," it's not always about things that shock. However, there are degrees of "less solemn." Try to imagine this off-the-charts story recounted by the weekly satirical newspaper *Le Canard enchaîné*: "A sixty-three-year-old woman retiree and her lover were arrested by police in the streets of Carcassonne. The lover, whose penis was outside his slacks, was attached to the woman by a little chain she had put around his testicles. In court, the couple justified themselves by explaining, 'We did it for fun, we were having such a great time.'" The prosecutor, who could hardly keep a straight face, asked for "an extremely severe punishment of a ten-euro fine with suspension" . . . and destruction of the chain.

What's Sexy?

As for sex being a "simple" thing, "Sex," muses an American friend who's married to a Frenchman, "is about the little things here. Just having a cup of coffee can be sexy." "Sexy" in France can be a smile, an atmosphere, a secret look between two people who don't know each other—yet. Sexy in France can be beautiful legs shown off by high heels. Sexy can also be what's not revealed, as opposed to what is. And sexy can be something that's "off," something that makes the person interesting and intriguing. Perfectly aligned white teeth and the blond, tanned California look doesn't translate into "sexy" in Parisian terms. Anne-Marie Lecordier, a *Parisienne* image consultant and former *chef de cabine* on Air France, smiled as she recalled her many travels to the States, which she loves, and the comments of a French steward friend as he checked out the California girls. "Did you see that one?" he would say.

"She's got fake nails, fake boobs, and talks too loudly." Of the three, the last was definitely the worst point for, as Anne-Marie explained, "In France, well-mannered people are shocked by loud conversations." Add to that the impeccable hair, the piano-key teeth, the "everything perfect" look, she said, and you don't get the Frenchman's idea of sexy. "For a Frenchman it's not conceivable. There's not enough subtlety."

Hear ye, hear ye, all you women looking for a French boyfriend or husband. *Having everything right is a turnoff.* That's really great news when you think about it—to be sexy and attract a Frenchman, you don't have to be perfect or conform to the current idea of what that is. On the contrary, something quirky, something funny, a flaw, will get him interested. Don't say I didn't tell you.

Crimes of Passion

Love, romance, and sex can be pleasurable, light, and amusing. And love, romance, and sex can be sad, dark, and dramatic. A popular French song written in 1784 laments that the pleasure of love lasts only a moment, whereas the *chagrin* (sorrow) of love lasts forever: "*Plaisir d'amour ne dure qu'un moment, chagrin d'amour dure toute la vie.*"

Sometimes that *chagrin* can go so far that terrible crimes are committed. In France an estimated 150 to 200 crimes a year are considered crimes of passion. Juries now judge these crimes severely, but up until 1975 the penal code stipulated— are you ready?—that "in the case of adultery, the murder committed by the husband on the wife, as well as the accomplice, at the moment he surprises them in the act in the conjugal home, is excusable." Note that it was the murder committed by the husband on the wife and not vice versa. Fortunately, times have changed.

I've never heard revenge-fantasy songs in France, such as "Before He Cheats" by Carrie Underwood (that doesn't mean there aren't any—it simply means I haven't heard them), in which the wronged party swears she'll slash the tires of her lover's car so he'll think before he cheats. From what I've seen, the wronged Frenchwoman would be more likely to work things out with her mate or go off and have an affair of her own. Or get a divorce. And rather than slash the tires, she'd probably smile sweetly and put a killer dose of sleeping pills in his Bordeaux.

It seems to me that almost every time I read the newspaper there's some story about a passionate crime in which the wife has poisoned the husband or the husband has strangled the wife. This happens in other countries, but somehow, in this romantic country, it is jarring. *Oh, well,* I tell myself, *the French are nothing if not a passionate people.* But at least these days husbands can't get away with murder. Perhaps because of increasing woman power? In a seismic shift, seven out of ten divorces in France are now instigated by women.

Foreign Women Look at Frenchmen

What's so special about Frenchmen? Why do foreign women succumb to their charms and even end up marrying them?

For American Jennifer Jourlait, who married her French boyfriend, "Marc's Frenchness was definitely an attraction. He was only a couple of years older than I but so much more worldly and mature than anyone I had dated before . . . plus he was a real man who was *not,* I repeat, *not* afraid to wear pink or purple and didn't own a baseball cap. He was the antithesis of the typical college 'dude'—knew how to drink responsibly and well, preferring wine to beer. Imagine that." Speaking of drinking, one young American woman dating a

Frenchman learned that "the French know and care more about what they eat and drink. I made the mistake of bringing a subpar bottle of wine to a dinner party once—from then on, he chose the wine." She laughed, adding that he was also horrified that she practically lived on frozen food.

My friend Elizabeth Mudd Beguerie, now married to her French boyfriend and the mother of two young children, told me, "When Jerome first started to court me, it was just that, he courted me. American men have a hard time remembering that opening doors, buying flowers, pulling out chairs, and thoughtfulness go a long way." What impressed her the most, she says, was "the fact that he treated me like a lady in such a sophisticated way. He would write me love letters and poetry, but it seemed so second nature to him that I didn't question it. Frenchmen are in touch with their feminine side without being the slightest bit cheesy or less manly." She added that she also loves her French partner's "self-deprecating humor" and his "adorable" accent. "My favorite example," she said, "was when he told me he loved the 'bitch.' It wasn't until I made him describe the 'bitch' that I realized it was the 'beach'!"

Not only are Frenchmen not afraid to show their "feminine" side, one young American told me, but she found that "in this man-oriented culture, Frenchmen aren't afraid to step back and let the women lead" and "they know the right thing to say." Her idea that a true macho wouldn't want to be seen with a taller woman was turned on its head by the image of France's most famous power couple, Nicolas Sarkozy and Carla Bruni. Even with his two-inch elevator shoes, Sarkozy is still a full three inches shorter than his five-foot-eleven wife. (Well, you've got to give him credit for *something*. . . .)

Kathryn Gaudouen, one of my American journalism students at the Institut d'études politiques, more commonly known as Sciences Po, met her future husband at a party Philippe and I gave for both my students and his fellow history students at the Sorbonne. Kathryn well remembers that night and especially a few "French things" that happened, particularly *la bise* that a "cute, well-dressed Frenchman" tried to give her before she pulled back because she felt he was breaking her personal space. To prove it was a cultural misunderstanding and that she wasn't snobbish, she stuck with him the whole evening. And, she concluded in an understatement, "I guess it worked." As the evening rolled on, Hadrien was obviously totally captivated by the charm of the blond, blue-eyed, French-speaking Kate, and Kate by the charming Frenchman. So captivated that the two, who carried on a long-distance courtship, married in the States four years later.

In the beginning he seemed "so French" to her, she told me. At our party, she remembered, "My fork dropped off my plate. Immediately, Hadrien handed me his own and went into the kitchen to find another for himself, also bringing the dirty fork with him to put in the sink. I knew I was in France when he did that because no American man would have . . . it's more likely an American would have picked it up, blown on it, and said, 'Here—good as new.' "

I laughed as I thought of all the mixed stereotypes the two cultures entertain about each other. Since we Americans are so hygiene conscious and the French are said to be less so, you'd think the behavior would go the other way, with the American picking up the fork to clean. But since I have a French husband and he would, and has done, exactly the same thing, I know that the fetching of whatever has been dropped is about more than hygiene. It's a quick Gallic reaction, a combination of gallantry, attentiveness, and charm. Can I imagine a Frenchman letting the lady pick up her own fork? Not unless he was what the French call a *goujat* (boor), and you wouldn't want him anyway.

As for Philippe's Frenchness, he wasn't exactly wearing a beret or carrying a baguette when we met, but was he ever French! In France, family is important, and unlike in the

States, where everyone scatters, French families often live in proximity, which is why I was almost immediately introduced to and welcomed into his. I couldn't understand a word they were saying for the first couple of years, but that's all right—I could get in that kitchen and watch what my future mother-in-law was cooking up, I could check out what Philippe's well-dressed sister-in-law was wearing and when (for example, no apron in the kitchen and yet no spots on her fashionable clothes, as I point out in *French Toast,* something that still today remains a mystery to this American klutz), and I could admire his tall, stylish, and slim French aunt who, dressed in black from head to foot with only one large, stylish gold brooch, was the embodiment of Parisian chic. His father, Henri, was a prince of a man who possessed an old-fashioned gallantry that his son fortunately inherited. I'm a feminist, but I appreciate his opening doors for me, taking my arm, jumping up from the table to get me whatever I need, showering me with flowers and compliments. Believe me, after all the inattentive loser boyfriends I had (oh, how I hope they're reading this), it was a sea change. Philippe introduced me to some unbelievable French food, including *pied de porc* (pig's foot) and every raw-milk cheese he could find, and took me to the Basilica of Saint-Denis to "meet" the kings and queens of France, most of whom are buried there. It was a freezing-cold day and I complained, but he wasn't having it. "You Americans always think of your comfort," he said, laughing, putting his arm around me and steering me to contemplate the majestic Renaissance tomb of Francis I.

Wedding Bells

Have you ever noticed that when you don't really care about what happens, it happens? If I'd come to France to hook a

Frenchman, it would never have come about. Being nonchalant about the whole thing, I ended up in a serious relationship. Go figure. And who could be as nonthreatening as I? No conversation about "where we stand"—but day-to-day pleasure. No conversation about "Shall we live together?" We did. Then, gradually, one thing led to another, until one day we actually found ourselves discussing marriage, a subject on which my significant other was extraordinarily relaxed, and for a good reason. He knew that to accomplish that act, one of us (shall we say the most interested party?) would have to trek to the *mairie* (city hall) to get all the necessary papers. Since he had witnessed me desperately trying to fill out French social-security and other such administrative forms and knew I was beyond hopeless when confronted with any kind of official paper, he was 99 percent sure that once he told me about the *mairie,* he'd hear no more about marriage, weddings, parties, and the whole lot.

How wrong he was. I was more motivated than he thought. The evening after our discussion I had all the papers in hand. All we had to do was fill them out. . . . Forty years later, I remain convinced that he married me out of sheer shell shock.

So it was that we stood before Monsieur le Maire in the city hall of the fifth arrondissement in front of the Panthéon on a sunny, crisp November day and tied the knot. (In France, you are obligated to marry in a civil ceremony at city hall. After that, you do what you want. It can be a religious ceremony or nothing at all. The two events are totally separate.) We hosted a lunch for our immediate families in a private salon at the Coupe-Chou, a fifteenth-century restaurant in the Latin Quarter, where we spent the entire time interpreting, for his family spoke no English and mine no French. Later in the afternoon, my new *belle-mère* and *beau-père* hosted a champagne party in their vast apartment on the boulevard de

Vaugirard for family and friends. It was simple, elegant, and undoubtedly one of the most stress-free weddings in the history of weddings.

Whether a long religious service and a reception and dinner in a castle or a brief civil service followed by a dinner party on a boat floating down the Seine, weddings in France are an occasion for pleasure and panache. My friend Dorie Denbigh, a former fashion reporter, who married French tennis businessman Jacques Laurent, turned up at the *mairie* in the fashionable sixteenth arrondissement in a dress that Japanese designer Issey Miyake had made especially for her. Depending on where you live in Paris, the ceremony takes on different tones. When I lived in the upscale neighborhoods of the sixteenth district and Neuilly, the weddings, even the civil service at the *mairie,* were quite proper, with everyone conventionally dressed (although I'd hardly say that an Issey Miyake dress is conventional—that exquisite creation was definitely an exception).

Our current apartment in the trendy east of Paris is quite close to the *mairie* and right on our way to the rue des Pyrénées, where we shop for food, so on many Saturdays we find ourselves smack in the middle of a wedding party. Since the neighborhood is multiethnic, that can be Arab women belting out the traditional *youyous,* smart-looking Frenchmen and Frenchwomen in all kinds of creative garb you'd never see in the wealthy west of the city, Africans in colorful turbans that match their dresses. As for children—and this perhaps is true all over the city now except for the most conservative families—many times one of the babies or children present is the offspring of the couple getting married. That was the case for David and Rachel, our youngest son and his wife, whose Hannah was nineteen months old when they stood before Madame la Maire. In my day, you lived together, married, and then had children. The growing trend

these days is living together, then children, then marriage—
maybe.

Marrying a Frenchman

It's one thing for a foreigner to have a romance with a Frenchman. It's totally another to marry one. As I've said when
commenting on my own marriage with a Frenchman, everything gets mixed up. If I were married to an American whose
behavior mystified me, I'd know it was because of our different personalities and backgrounds, especially if he came from
a big city in the East and I came from a small town in the
South or Midwest. When an American marries a Frenchman,
those factors are amplified: small town, big town, of course,
with, added to that, cultural differences involving the way we
think and act and "are" that are major.

Sometimes the differences are subtle, sometimes they are
as big as an elephant. Sometimes they're positive, sometimes
negative. What I've noticed, and many Americans married to
Frenchmen notice, is that their French partners are particularly attentive to details. Of course some Frenchmen aren't
that way—ask any woman who's divorced one or is in an
unhappy relationship. This being said, the Frenchmen who
do pay attention pay attention to everything: how the dinner
table looks, how the food tastes, what you said you liked in a
store window that suddenly pops up a few months later as a
gift, how you look not only when you dress up, but all the
time. That's because they're French; they pay attention to
those things in general. Aesthetics are ever present.

I may have gotten lucky, but my husband has always encouraged me to keep my American side, my American con-
nections, and my American spirit. He didn't need to encourage
me to keep my American accent—there's nothing to be done

about that. He's been supportive in every way. The "French" part of that is that he doesn't "suggest," he tends to "order," so we have nice arguments about that (see chapter 4, on disagreements). I want "consensus," he doesn't function that way. But as far as support is concerned, I couldn't have asked for more. I write this with apologies to all those women who found themselves with egotistical, inattentive, selfish Frenchmen. I guess Kathryn and I, and a few other people I know, got the best.

That doesn't mean there's no effort to make, on both sides. If you marry a Frenchman, you will need to know how to play his game. Thirty-seven-year-old Iranian Leyla Lebeurrier, by her own definition a strong-minded lady, confessed, "I often give the impression that my husband has made a decision, especially in front of other people." Believe me, she is not alone. Frenchwomen, as I learned early on, may know tons more than their husbands, have made a decision he claims as his, and sit through a tall tale that has little connection with reality. My husband, for example, multiplies most figures by three for the sake of a good story. I inwardly gasp at his daring but say not a word—I learned in France that interrupting would spoil the fun. Unlike American wives, French wives don't feel the need to set their husbands straight, especially in public. Feminists will hate this, but for me that means they truly have more confidence in themselves as women. They are also polite and considerate of their husbands' male pride. Why shoot the guy down?

Three of Us in This Marriage—Him, Me, and Our Cultural Differences

In case you're thinking of marrying a Frenchman (or Frenchwoman), two pieces of advice. First, to meet one and keep him or her interested, you must play the game of hard to get. Anything that's too easy lacks mystery, challenge, and is no fun for them. Second, once you've hooked your Frenchman or Frenchwoman, know that the going may get rough because you don't understand each other's reaction to the same things. This is one thing if you're seeing each other occasionally. When you live together, the cultural differences are daily.

Here's an example. On one stifling day in Paris, I open two windows in the insane hope of getting a cross breeze going.

It's not long before I get the Typical Reaction.

"What's going on in here? Do you want us to get pneumonia or TB?" my husband yells, genuinely horrified, as he rushes about shutting the windows.

In the early days of our marriage, I would have been riled, wanted to argue. *Chez moi aux États-Unis,* I would tell him, we don't get pneumonia or TB from open windows, we get a frigging *breeze.*

Now I'm much wiser on this score. (I took a few tips from Frenchwomen.) I smile. I know that this is one of those innumerable Franco-American marital disputes that is never going to get resolved. For my husband, a breeze is not a breeze. It's a draft. For my mother-in-law as well, come to think of it. Every weekend for years we'd trot off to the family country home, where, ensconced in my favorite chair, I'd start relaxing after opening the front door and the back *justement* to get some airflow.

You would have thought I'd wished a plague on their house.

Much fluttering. Some good-natured lecturing. *"Mais, ma petite fille,"* my mother-in-law explained, surely thinking that my own mother had shirked her duty, "don't you know that you could get a terrible cold or worse?" (We're talking ninety-degree heat here.) Okay, I'm not fighting that battle any longer, and I do allow that it could be this particular family and not all the French, especially because my husband did actually have tuberculosis as a young adult and spent a year in a sanatorium, so maybe I should let them off the hook. That's another challenge of a bicultural mariage: Is the person doing what he's doing because he's French or because he's himself?

Nor do I get my dander up when I spill a glass of red wine on a white tablecloth and my husband acts as if I should go to court for the crime.

As usual, I ask myself if this overblown reaction is typical of all French husbands or just my French husband. I thought it might be my husband's particular behavior until I compared notes with a dear friend who's been married to a Frenchman as long as I have.

"He drives me crazy," she told me. "Every time I break something, whether it's inexpensive and easy to replace or, God forbid, *porcelaine de Sèvres*, I get the 'You Americans are so clumsy' act."

What's *that* all about? we asked each other, and concluded it could be several things: (1) A question of space. After all, the United States is seventeen times the size of France, which explains why we Americans are so klutzy when on tiny turf. (2) A different attitude toward consumption: as American wives, our attitude is clearly "break something, spill something, no big deal." Buy a new glass, wash the tablecloth. French husbands find this intensely irritating. Why not be more careful? (3) We agreed this is the most plausible explanation: because they can have their hissy fit with their American wife in a way they couldn't if their wife was French—the French wife would totally ignore their "show."

You'd think that after all these years I'd have the way my

dear French partner thinks, acts, and reacts completely and totally figured out. Not at all.

But you know what? It's not a one-way street. He can't figure out my behavior any better than I can figure out his.

One day I screwed up my courage and asked him to give me a list of five to ten typically American things I do that exasperate him.

"I'll tell you if you make me a really good dinner," he promised.

How's that for being French?

We dined, the dinner was good, and he never did answer my question.

Why?

La galanterie française—which is why I married him in the first place all those years ago.

Interview with Philippe

HWR: *What would you advise a foreign woman who wants to marry a Frenchman?*

PHR: She should not expect him to change and he shouldn't expect her to.

HWR: *What? You mean I haven't become French? I speak French all the time!*

PHR: Uh . . . your French is perfect, *chérie*. It's fabulous and makes all the Frenchwomen jealous [I told you he was gallant], but there are still some *différences*.

HWR: *What differences? I suppose you'll say that when you yell and gesticulate and are generally going bonkers, you're just being French and having fun, whereas as an American I think I'm living with a nutcase—although, come to think of it, I'm actually starting to enjoy the histrionics . . .*

PHR: *Et voilà!* You've become a little bit French after all!

Small Is Good: *Les Petits Plaisirs*

A minuscule espresso, a petit piece of chocolate, a morsel of sharp cheese, a half-filled glass of wine: the French prefer tasting and sipping to gorging and guzzling. Small is good.

Small Size, Large Size

In France, small things procure big joys. In fact, *la joie de vivre* is composed of many small and simple pleasures: a stroll on the banks of the Seine, a tiny taste of dark chocolate with your wee espresso, a *petit verre de rouge* (little glass of red wine). Small is good!

When I came to France, I discovered small. It seemed that everything was diminutive, and the word *petit* was everywhere. I go on a *petit tour* around the block to drink a *petit café*. Then I may do a few *petites courses* (small errands) before I wend my way back to my definitely *petite* home sweet home. On the way I might sample a piece of *fromage*, but it

won't ruin my appetite, samples being *petit* (as in thumbnail).
Time for dinner? The meat or fish and accompanying vegetables barely fill, and certainly don't overlap, the plate. My
wineglass is not filled to the brim.

Do you wonder why the French aren't fat? Here's the answer: portions are *petites*.

In America I hop into a huge car, drive for miles, do some
mega-errands, fill up the roomy trunk with groceries, and return to my sister's large house with its three-car garage and
put the food away in a giant kitchen with a monster refrigerator that makes ice. At the grocery store, I'll take samples
that compared to the tiny ones offered in France look as if
they'd feed my entire family for a couple of days. When I go
to a restaurant, there's so much food left over, the waiter asks
if I'll want a box (I don't). My large glass of wine will be
filled close to the top. If I drink Coke, even the small size
looks huge to me, and the minute I finish, the waitperson
rushes to the table to give me a free refill.

In America, "big," even supersize, is what we're all about
and what we like. That's normal; you can tuck all of France
into the state of Texas and there will be plenty of room
(about 20 percent!) left over.

The French have big as well, such as *grand* and *grandeur*
used in phrases like *la grandeur de la France* or *grand reporter* or *grand patron, grandes écoles* or *grand prix. Grand*
is above us, awe-inspiring, sometimes puffing up with importance whatever it is that is thus described, whereas *petit*
is *sympathique* and down-to-earth. Babies, for example, are
très petits, and when you particularly like someone, they are
suddenly transformed into *petit* or *petite.* My mother-in-
law always referred to her Swedish neighbor as *"la petite
Suédoise"*—even though at five feet ten inches the lovely
woman towered over her. *Petit* is not always *sympathique.* A

mec, for example, is a "guy." However, if you call someone *un petit mec,* it is definitely not nice. You've just labeled him "pathetic." Got to be on your toes when it comes to these *petites différences*!

A word before continuing. In keeping with the theme, this chapter will be . . . *petit.*

Petites Boutiques

I once asked an American friend who often comes to France what she liked to take back with her, what for her was typically French. She replied that unfortunately these days you can find almost any French product in the States. However, she reflected, there's something you can't find and have to be in France to experience, and that is "the French experience of shopping in the little stores. Every time I look at my *santons,* the figures that go into the Nativity scene, I remember the fun I had shopping for them in Provence and the boutique where I found them." She says she has all sorts of items from all over France, and that the pleasure is in the quest. "You can't duplicate the shopping in those tiny places, the experience of searching, and the joy of coming upon a special object unexpectedly."

Another American friend and I met in the Marais one afternoon for a drink. Before parting, we wandered in and out of the numerous boutiques near the Metro Saint-Paul, starting with the Red Wheelbarrow bookstore, with its tightly packed high shelves and shelves of books in English, and moving on to antique stores, stores selling marvelous hats, stores selling items you don't need but want to have so artfully are they presented. "Do you do this in L.A.?" I asked her. "Never," she replied. "First of all, there's no time, and secondly"—she looked down the ancient street lined on both sides with dozens of tiny tantalizing places to stop in and shop in—"we don't have this."

The only problem with *petites* boutiques is that they are sometimes so itsy-bitsy and so teensy-weensy you have to be exceedingly careful, especially if you're a clumsy American like me. In a booth at the flea market I once broke two crystal glasses when my handbag accidentally hit them. I briefly entertained the thought of running hysterically into the street and disappearing into the crowd, but since the noise made my guilt obvious, I owned up and apologized profusely. That time I got off the hook—the owner realized she'd put the glasses and tray in a perilous position. Generally, though, the rule is that you pay for what you break. So, dear reader, beware of pint-size places! I now clutch my handbag as close to me as possible and in a *petite* boutique pretend I'm walking through a minefield, not a store.

Les Petits Détails

Details are very French. It's that tiny touch that makes the difference. Over coffee, a French friend told me she hadn't slept all night because she was worried about a problem at work. It's true that her hair could have used a shampoo, and she had circles under her eyes. But she was dressed elegantly and casually with a gorgeous necklace that flattered her face and an understated but valuable watch. Even though it might have been a bad-hair day and a bad day in general, if she ran into a client in the street, she had no apologies to make. She was "put together" thanks to a few well-planned details.

The simplest French table will have pretty place mats or a jacquard tablecloth and a bouquet of flowers. The tomato salad is rid of its seeds and doesn't go to the table unless it's got a sprig of parsley. And speaking of salads, the homemade vinaigrette or mayonnaise is not hard to make and is a detail that transforms an ordinary dish into a delight.

Details count!

Un Petit Coup de Fil, un Petit Moment, une Petite Fête

Philippe says that when he speaks English, sometimes his phrases come out "funny." He'll say, "Okay, I'll give you a little phone call," which is the French equivalent of the English "Okay, I'll call you." But it's not the same: "a little phone call" is the translation of *un petit coup de fil*, which is friendlier, has a warm ring to it. We'll also spend *un petit moment* together or have ourselves *une petite fête*. The *petit moment* and the *petite fête* convey a special intimate moment, just the two of us doing something we've concocted together.

Les Petits Fours

I have this thing about *petits fours*: I love them. The literal meaning of *petit four* is "small oven." The main thing to know about these Lilliputian-looking savories is that they are sweet or salty, and either miniature appetizers or, if presented in great quantity and variety, a stand-up meal (kind of a French version of tapas). Most buffets feature them—but there are *petits fours* and *petits fours*. . . . The best memory of *petits fours* I have was when Philippe's company organized a private evening at the Pompidou museum for the top management and their wives. We had the museum to ourselves, and after a private tour of the artworks with our own personal curator (imagine!), we drank champagne and feasted on the most exquisite sweet and salty *petits fours* I've ever tasted. I believe that night they were from Dalloyau, but they could have been from Lenôtre—both *pâtisseries* specialize in making *petits fours* for such events. I read that Napoléon was behind the creation of the *petit four*. He was tired of sitting at the table and wanted a simpler way to be among his guests. Thank you, Mr. Bonaparte!

Almost every French bakery has an assortment of *petits fours* and mini-*viennoiseries* that present three main delights: they're a delight for the eye, they're a delight for the taste buds, and they're a delight for the figure because you can have your taste of sugar without ingesting your calories for the day. When I want a taste of a *pain au chocolat* or a *pain aux raisins* but not the whole thing, I opt for the minisize pastries, about the size of my thumb, as opposed to the normal ones, which are about the size of my hand. In one bite I get the pleasure (the taste of the butter, the chocolate melting in my mouth) without the pain (of added kilos). How's that for *joie de vivre*?

Le Petit Beurre

Speaking of small things to eat, *le petit beurre* is a simple butter cookie you can buy in any grocery store. Invented in 1886 by Louis Lefèvre-Utile, the "real" or *véritable petit beurre*, which has many imitators, is still produced today in Nantes with the *B* of *petit beurre* right in the middle of each biscuit. It's an enormously popular cookie, which can fit into the palm of your hand, and often the first one given to a child. It's always fun to see if the tot bites right into it or goes at it methodically corner by corner. We gave one to Hannah, our only Parisian granddaughter, and waited to see her plan of attack. She grabbed it, took a quick look, and immediately went for the corners. Now, what would we have done if she'd gone for the center? What would that have meant? Nothing! Watching Hannah happily munching on her *petit beurre* was just one of those *petits plaisirs*.

Un Petit Coup de Rouge

Whether red wine or white wine, in France the glass is filled to no more than two-thirds, and if you're serving wine at home, that's what to do for some logical reasons: maybe the guest doesn't like wine, maybe the guest doesn't like that particular wine, maybe the guest wants to have a little of each wine, but a big glass at each course would end up being too much. In addition to that, filling a glass to the brim is considered . . . vulgar. As far as getting buzzed, I've been at dinner parties and cocktail parties where we all have a lot to drink but no one gets drunk. Maybe because the glasses are small and it's embarrassing to ask for twenty refills? The idea is to taste and savor the wine, not swim in it. Of course, young people everywhere like to get soused, and French young people are no exception. However, many of them have had a taste of wine at home with their parents, so the idea of drinking as rebellion is not as firmly anchored as it is in the United States, which had Prohibition. French young people aren't angels, to be sure, but maybe because France is a wine culture, they respect wine more. In France you don't see the kinds of spring-break scenes you see when U.S. college students let loose in Cancún. . . .

Un Petit Noir

"What would you like to drink?" In a café, *un petit noir* is the response you'll most often hear. It's a wee cup of black coffee, strong and black. No milk. If it had milk, it would be *un petit crème* or *une noisette*. Served in a china cup, it's the total opposite of the huge ersatz coffee mixtures that rushed office workers in the United States carry in their cardboard containers as they stride to work. Sometimes, *le petit noir* isn't even all that good. I've had better coffee in Italy. The whole point of *le petit noir*, though, is that you don't drink it on the run. You drink it sitting down and can make it and the lounging, thinking, and dreaming last for hours. Think of it: two euros may seem expensive, but if you can occupy a table on the terrace of a café in the heart of Paris watching the world go by for an hour or two or more, it's definitely a bargain!

Mon Petit Lapin, Mon Petit Chou, and Other Petits Animals and Vegetables

If someone calls you his *little rabbit* or *little cabbage*, feel flattered. These are terms of endearment. My father-in-law called all of us *mes petits agneaux* (my little lambs). My son calls his son *mon petit loup* (my little wolf).

Only certain animals and vegetables qualify, though. For example, I've never heard anyone say *mon petit cochon* (my little pig) or even *mon petit chien* (my little dog). But you can call a little girl *ma petite chatte* or "little kitten." A cabbage (*mon petit chou*) is a common term of affection, but I've never heard anyone called *ma petite tomate* (my little tomato). As for fruits, even though they're sweet and good, you never hear anyone referred to as "my little banana" or "my little apple." *C'est comme ça* (that's the way it is).

La Petite Robe Noire

The classic black dress is always spoken of as the *little* black dress, not the black dress. Because it's referred to as *la petite robe noire,* it takes on a positive connotation. The *little* doesn't mean it's insignificant. On the contrary, it's a must. Sexy and chic at the same time. Only the clever French could transform a simple piece of somber clothing into a universal emblem.

Petits Plaisirs

In his book *La Première Gorgée de bière et autres plaisirs minuscules* (The first sip of beer and other minuscule pleasures), Philippe Delerm writes about many of the pleasures that make up French life, ones we all too often take for granted. I loved his comments on the once-a-week treat French people indulge in on Sunday. If you ever pass a bakery on Sunday, you may wonder about those long lines of people. The story goes that a Russian paper featured a picture of one saying that there was a bread shortage in Paris. On the contrary, those patient people are waiting for their weekly indulgence in a sweet. (In traditional French families, dessert during the week is fruit and/or a yogurt.) As Delerm writes, and as I know from experience, deciding which cakes and what kind (small cakes? one big one? fruit? chocolate?) is one part of the pleasure. The next is watching the bakery lady carefully place the selection in a white cardboard package and tie it up with a ribbon. Delerm writes lovingly about the pleasure found in what might seem a long, drawn-out process. It is a ritual, the contrary of zipping out to find any old cake in two minutes.

Had I grown up in Boston or New York or any American

city, I might have had trouble slowing down to enjoy *petits plaisirs*, but growing up as I did in a Midwestern town of five thousand or so souls where the pace is slow, I had no problem. I love sitting on café terraces watching the world go by, I love going into stores just to look, I love all our vacations (and this being France, they are numerous), I especially love the French attitude toward time. You don't always have to rush; there are moments when you can and should slow down. It did, though, take some adjustment, I must admit. Early on, when I thought I needed to purchase an object missing from my kitchen or bathroom, I had to have it *right now*. *Très américain.* Once, when I was in frustration mode about something I didn't have and "needed" to get, Philippe said, "I don't know what the fuss is all about. I'd rather contemplate what I don't have. Not having it and wanting it is even better than when you finally get it." I almost fell on the floor in the face of such a revolutionary thought. For me, the getting is the point!

Gradually, though, I found I could savor moments, and didn't *necessarily* need to possess what I liked or have it immediately or ever. (This all sounds too good to be true— maybe I should add that since everything in France is so expensive compared to the States, for pragmatic reasons I began opting for one or two *objets de désir* instead of the several I'd have in the States.) In any case, pleasure, I found, is more often than not wrapped up in the immaterial. Here's a personal *petit plaisir:* when Philippe was still working, he would call me or I'd call him at the office a couple of times during the day. What struck me about those calls was that he took the time out of a busy executive schedule and never once cut me off with an "I'm too busy to talk." (Hey, maybe talking to me was a *petit plaisir!*) In contrast to that, I was shocked when I contacted a couple of old friends when in New York and found myself relegated to arranging drinks and dinner with them via their "assistant." Too busy for a *petit* one-minute conversation with *moi*? Whoa!

The German occupation and the disaster it wreaked in France surely had something to do with a heightened appreciation of life. Now rather dated, *Encore un que les Boches n'auront pas* (another one the Nazis won't get) was an expression often used during World War II to invoke the idea that while the Germans might have overrun the country, they couldn't rob the French of minute moments of pleasure.

Une Petite Promenade

Here's pleasure: After a doctor's appointment, instead of hopping on the closest metro and going directly home, I decided to walk. Not fast, and not particularly with a purpose. It was a "wander walk" whose only goal was to eventually end up at the École Militaire metro stop from where I was deep in the heart of the fifteenth arrondissement. I struck out, passing the pastiche Ricardo Bofill buildings on the Place de Catalogne and the back of the nondescript Gare Montparnasse. Most of the neighborhood, especially the rue du Commandant Mouchotte on which the Sheraton Hotel is located, looks as if it could be in Detroit. Surely no one's idea of a picturesque *petite* promenade.

But that's the thing about small pleasures and the *joie de vivre*. Even in places that aren't particularly attractive or your idea of Paris, there's always something to see. In addition to that, for me Paris holds specific memories in certain places, and the fifteenth arrondissement, where all of Philippe's family lives, is one of them. As I headed toward Pasteur, I found myself directly in front of the building on the boulevard de Vaugirard where my in-laws lived for forty years before downsizing and moving to an apartment not far away. I remember how amazed I was at my mother-in-law's concern about finding a good butcher or baker in the new neighborhood, which to her was like a new continent. (She did.)

As I stood in the street gazing first at the wrought iron-work on the entry door and then up five floors to the windows of their former apartment, the memory snatches came fast—of my vigorous seventy-year-old father-in-law bounding up the stairs two by two instead of taking the old-fashioned elevator; the elegant Haussmannian apartment with its high ceilings, spacious entry hall, and three capacious main rooms looking over the street; a long, long hall that led back to the kitchen and bathroom and two bedrooms, one for my husband, one for his sister. I remember many things about that apartment, notably that the wallpaper got changed regularly since my father-in-law, being in the business, liked to test his products. I also had an image of my stepson, at age three, accidentally tripping over a valuable Chinese vase, which miraculously remained intact. And how could I not summon up all the savory family meals prepared by my mother-in-law? Standing there, I could almost smell the *pot-au-feu*.

I even remembered my first lesson in French hospitality. Martine, my future sister-in-law, had invited me for dinner one night when Philippe was out of town, and I decided to get my hair done to look nice. Unfortunately, it took much longer than I thought, and since this was before the days of cell phones, I couldn't warn her I'd be late. In the end, I showed up at nine-thirty. She and her husband, Alain, had waited and were exceedingly gracious—even though both had to work the next day and starting a meal at that hour was most probably not on their top ten list of amusements.

I remembered champagne flowing at our wedding reception in that apartment and chuckled to myself as I remembered my mother-in-law waking me up one morning to announce that Philippe had been arrested and I was to go get him out of the police station. *What?* He'd been driving his sister's car with no identity papers and had gone down a one-way street the wrong way, where he ran right into a police van filled with *flics* (cops), who were only too happy to apprehend him for breaking every law in the book. But someone was in a good mood that day—by the time I reached the station, he was ready to go and everyone shook hands (or is that my memory embellishing things?).

I started remembering so many stories that I decided to move on or I'd still be there hours later.

As I walked away, dodging traffic, I had one final flash. It was a photo of my father-in-law's automobile, a luxury Talbot, parked on the boulevard in the late 1940s. What was so unusual about the photo? In those days when few had cars, it was the only one in the street!

Down the boulevard Pasteur and on to the avenue de Breteuil I strolled, with the view of the rounded, golden dome of the Invalides in front of me. School had let out and conservatively dressed mothers walked and chatted with their children. In the central area, young people lolled on the grass, and old people sat on park benches enjoying the afternoon sun. I took a left and ended up at the École Militaire. A stop for coffee at the appropriately named Les Terrasses, and then I descended into the metro. It was a beautiful day and the *petite promenade* was definitely a *petit plaisir*. I hadn't thought for one second about what I had to do when I got home. In France, where you're surrounded by beauty, you can have moments like this every day, strolling or sitting or contemplating. They do wonders for the morale. *La joie de vivre!*

And now, *au revoir*. I'm happy to have spent this *petit moment ensemble* (this little moment with you).

Interview with Philippe

HWR: *How does it feel to be a citizen of a small country?*

PhR (climbing onto a chair to look impressively *grand*): We don't enjoy it. We want to be big. That's why we're arrogant. It's the ruse we found to forget that we're small.

HWR: *Talk about complicated!*

PhR: Not really. When you're *petit*, you have to be smart.

Savoir-Vivre: Life as an Art Form

Style and élan, *panache,* savoir-faire *and* savoir-vivre. *Form and content: in France, how you do things is as important as what you do. The importance of the lightness of being. The meeting as a (free) art form.*

Figuring out what's in a Frenchman's mind is a gigantic, almost insurmountable task. I know—I've been trying to figure out my husband's and his compatriots' brains and behavior for several decades. And I've barely scratched the surface.

What is it in their history, traditions, education, that makes them the way they are? What's important to them?

And who are "the French" anyway? A Corsican is not like a Breton, and a Norman is not like an Alsatian, and a Parisian is not like anyone else at all. In spite of their differences, though, they share certain ways of thinking and doing things that for the rest of us are decidedly "French."

After approximately fifteen thousand days of living among and observing the French (starting with my *very* French husband), I came to a few personal conclusions to share with you. Many were initial impressions, which remained. For example, the first time I came to France, I instantly remarked that life seemed to be carried on at a different, a higher, a more intense pitch. The French looked so involved in what they were doing. They looked each other in the eyes (and still do in this Internet age, which is nothing short of remarkable). In brief, they were totally engaged with life.

The second impression, which I formed after a few years of living in France, was that the French manage to take the simplest, most ordinary event or occurrence and elevate it to an art form. In other nations workers stage strikes, but in France strikes are a veritable pageant, a street show. In other nations people give formal dinner parties, but none can rival the French dinner party, which is a ceremony governed by an incredible number of written and unwritten rules. The inhabitants of other countries eat roast chicken, and so do the French (*poulet rôti* is a Sunday favorite because it roasts on a skewer outside the butcher shop and all you have to do is buy it), but in France there's *poulet Basquaise, poulet à l'estragon,* and *poulet au vin jaune et morilles,* to name but three of an infinite variety of preparations. Other nations have presidents, but how many have leaders who construct entire monuments to mark their "reign": the Pompidou museum; Mitterrand's (horrible, in my opinion) Bibliothèque Nationale and Opéra Bastille; Giscard d'Estaing's transformation of the Orsay train station into the Musée d'Orsay. Last but not least, other nations have waiters, but the French have the Haughty Waiter; if he didn't exist, the French would have invented him.

Somehow everything in France seems larger-than-life. There's passion and reason, balance and imbalance, total predictability and total unpredictability. The pastries are lighter and the cabdrivers more sullen. The men are seductive, the women, especially in Paris, harder to figure out. No one smiles, it would seem, but then someone does and it's as if the sun has come out. The Eiffel Tower winks at you, and the buildings of different epochs remind you that you're just passing through, one person in a continuum. It's against this backdrop that the French go about their lives, lives I'm convinced they'd find boring if they hadn't devised all kinds of complications and ingenious rules to keep themselves on their collective toes. Only the French could have come up with *savoir-faire* and *savoir-vivre,* knowing how and what to do and how to live.

As for *joie de vivre,* the French wisely know that it's a state of being. Some people were born with it, others have it some of the time, some never do (how sad). They also know that *joie de vivre* doesn't come about in some musical-comedy context where everything is perfect. *Joie de vivre* happens whenever people are passionately tussling with real life, and you can experience it in the oddest situations. Here's what happens when you stick around Paris long enough. Rather than being disturbed by Parisian skirmishing and squabbling, bickering and battling, you begin to find the whole thing rather brilliant, kind of like a *pièce de théâtre.* You discover yourself either smirking or smiling as you watch an argument that once upon a time would have made you uncomfortable or find yourself actually going head-to-head with a person who has ticked you off, something that in your civilized "other" life outside France, you would never, ever have dared. The first time you volley off what to you is a nasty response, you think that thunder and lightning will open up from the sky and you'll be swallowed up. Or that the person you've insulted will get out his gun. When nothing happens, you re-alize that the Parisians thrive on disputes, and if you can hold your own in one, well, you're now part of the scene. Welcome! Outside Paris, people get their *joie de vivre* from qui-eter and less contentious lifestyles. (They're normal!) Which is why I love to get out of the capital every six weeks or so . . . after which I'm ready to rejoin the fray. It's safe to say that the French (the Parisians, mostly, but the Marseillais aren't bad either) have elevated the dispute to an art form. When done well, it's like fencing, a sport the French are remarkably good at—I wonder why . . . ?

Below is my admittedly eclectic selection of what to me makes the French so French, and some of the ways in which they elevate "life" to "art."

Art and Aesthetics

The words of Salvador de Madariaga, written in the 1930s, ring true today: "If passion is the first instant in the creative process, the second or form-giving phase is controlled by the intellect; in its narrower and more concrete sense, the word 'art' means precisely the form-giving power of the intellect moved by aesthetic emotion. France is therefore the country which excels in Art."

Art and the love of aesthetics can be found everywhere in France, in castles and cathedrals, in flowers and fashion shows. Art is everywhere: if you want to find "art" in France, you don't need to hit a museum. To see French ingenuity in art, all you need to do is visit the gardens at Versailles and marvel at how the walkways and the promenades were designed not only to give King Louis XIV a harmonious view but a perfect place to stroll amid fountains that, water being scarce, were turned on as he passed and off as soon as he was out of view. (Oh, to be a king!) That was the king, but you can see the talent for, interest in, and love of staged displays as you walk down any street. Every time I trek off to my morning yoga class, I pass by the Printemps department store, where an entire window is devoted to Ladurée macaroons; the centerpiece is composed of two tempting triangles of the delicacies, one green, one pink. I can buy the macaroons, and sometimes I do, but I can also simply admire the art that's gone into the window dressing. And how I do. (It kind of messes up my concentration for yoga, though—those pistachio macaroons keep floating into my mind when I'm supposed to be meditating. . . .)

Stanislas de Quercize, CEO of Van Cleef & Arpels on the Place Vendôme, invited French philosopher Michel Serres, professor at Stanford and the Sorbonne, member of the French Academy, and one of France's most original thinkers, for a tour of the famous jewelry house. As Quercize told *Le Figaro*, Serres, whose father was a roadworker, suddenly stopped watching the specialized jewelers as they chiseled precious stones, and proclaimed, "Messieurs, you are not working." There was a glacial silence. Then he added, "This isn't work, it's *de l'œuvre* [art]." What a *French* story, I thought. Only in France would a French CEO see the value of inviting a prominent French thinker to visit the workshops; only in France would the two then hold a discussion on whether jewels are "accessible" to all. Serres's opinion: "I don't have jewelry of this sort, neither does my wife. . . . I am not the owner of the *Sonate à Kreutzer,* but I listen to it, and that suffices for my pleasure." In other words, beauty is for everyone.

In France the attention to aesthetics extends to the simplest things. When you go to the bakery, even if you buy only one little cake, you walk away with a prettily tied package. In the flower shop, the salesperson always asks, "Is it for you or *pour offrir?*" Even if the bouquet or single long-stemmed rose is not "to offer," but to bring home, it will carefully be wrapped in transparent plastic with the seal of the flower merchant and a bow. The French love flowers and give them to each other on almost every occasion. They give them to celebrate happy events, such as birthdays and anniversaries and Valentine's Day, when the lines outside the flower shops almost equal the lines you normally see outside the *bou-langerie*. And they give them for sad ones as well. Within a radius of one kilometer where we live, next to the Père Lachaise Cemetery, there are at least ten floral shops. You quickly learn which flowers are for tombs (chrysanthemums, for example—don't offer them when invited to dinner), but these stores are by no means restricted to flowers for funerals. There are red and white and pink geraniums to brighten up the windows of city apartments, jasmine for good smells, exotic lilies of the valley. There are shops where you can compose your own arrangements, and shops where it's done for you, and you don't have to go to a fancy shop in a fancy neighborhood to procure a beautiful bouquet. The neighborhood I live in is what the French call *populaire*, or "working class," but you wouldn't know it from looking at the flower shops. Léa and Christophe Cocozza, the young owners of La Roseraie flower shop, have an assortment of flowers and plants for every budget. Christophe wakes up at dawn to get the flowers at the central market outside Paris in Rungis; Léa then arranges them, beautifully, in artful bouquets. She seemed surprised when I asked her if people bought flowers not only as gifts, but for themselves. She said she has customers who buy a bouquet of tulips or roses for their home every week just for the pleasure. Flowers are everywhere, for everyone.

Everything at the Maison Legeron, an establishment that has been making flowers and feathers since 1727, is "done by hand," says Bruno Legeron, whose great-grandfather bought the firm in 1898; it has been in the family ever since. "The only thing we don't do," he joked, "is raise our ostriches down in the basement." There are no birds in the basement, for sure, but there are bird feathers galore, whether from pheasants, black guinea fowls, swans, or others, all of which are carefully stored in plain, oblong cardboard boxes lining the walls from floor to ceiling. Ostrich feathers notably are classified according to quality and labeled *très très belle, très belle,* and *belle.*

On the day I visited the atelier, Bruno, age fifty-five, was dressed in jeans and a tracksuit top, over which he wore a black apron adorned with huge safety pins holding down various roses and feathers. He certainly looked "modern," but the atelier, which contains many small rooms spread over several floors, looked as if the computer age had passed it by. Bruno is proud of doing things the old-fashioned and collegial way (workers in the atelier all have specialities but pitch in to help each other when there's a rush, he says). Pointing at an antiquated cash register where the amounts are still in French francs, Bruno joked, "That's my computer." After the war, Bruno explained, hundreds of firms made flowers and feathers for ladies' hats. Then came the automobile and, notably, the demise of *le chapeau.* Now only three houses are left in France, of which the Maison Legeron is the only family-owned one, furnishing handmade flowers out of leather, silk, latex, and velvet for designers from Dior to Jean Paul Gaultier to Jimmy Choo and ostrich feathers for the Lido and the Folies Bergère, to name but a few of the firm's prestigious clients.

As Bruno talked, I gazed up at the ceiling. Hanging over our heads were rows and rows of enormous white silk peonies, which Legeron had created for a Cartier window display. I was filled with both a sense of history and admiration for the exquisite craftmanship I had witnessed during the visit—as well as a fleeting but powerful desire to own a drop-dead gorgeous, two-meter, black-and-white boa made of top-quality ostrich feathers that I gently fingered on my way out the door. But then, who *wouldn't* want to possess a hand-made creation with more than a century of French *savoir-faire* behind it?

Form—the Way You Do Things

There's a reason you won't hear French people saying, "Whatever." "Whatever" means "I don't care" and implies that the means to the end aren't that important.

In France, the means, the form, the manner, the presentation, are, on the contrary, all-important.

As Sanche de Gramont, the French scion of an aristocratic family who became an American citizen, writes in *The French: Portrait of a People*, "Every situation is either legislated or determined by usage." He goes even further: in this country, which "has an almost Oriental sense of decorum," form is important for its own sake. He's joined in that opinion by Salvador de Madariaga, who declared in his book *Englishmen, Frenchmen, Spaniards* that "France is the teacher of the world in matters of form and of composition."

When I first arrived in France, I had no idea that if you left off the *monsieur* or *madame* when greeting someone with a *bonjour*, you were not only being incomplete, but impolite. The polite form is *Bonjour, monsieur* or *Bonjour, madame*.

I figured that if even a simple *bonjour* required a profound knowledge of French etiquette, I was in deep trouble. Actually, being a foreigner absolved me of my many mistakes—I wasn't *supposed* to know all the things the French know from the day they're born. I wasn't French so wasn't held to their standards.

Gradually, though, I learned a few things about form by example or osmosis. I discovered for myself that in France presentation is not incidental, but capital. The kings may be long gone, but customs that started in the court, and the respect for rules and protocol, are still present in France today.

French flair, style, and panache imply some kind of freedom.

But form is ever present, and style and panache are played out within its boundaries. Form is not some abstract concept; it governs daily life, from the *baise-main* to the *bise* to the handshake to the use of the formal *vous* and the informal *tu*. I never realized how the universal *you* in English facilitated life until I started speaking French. V*ous* and *tu* can be veritable nightmares. When I started going out with Philippe, I asked him, since he was divorced, if he now called his ex-wife *vous* instead of *tu*. After he stopped laughing, he told me that it's not because you're divorced that you stop addressing your ex the way you always did, in this case as *tu*. (Well, how did I know?)

Every foreigner discovers that knowing when to use *tu* and *vous* is beyond complex. Do you call a friend's mother *tu*? Do children address their parents as *vous* or *tu*? Do your daughters-in-law call you, the in-laws, *tu* or *vous*? There's no blanket answer to any of these questions. The use of *tu* and *vous* depends on each family and each particular relationship. In formal families, parents and children address each other with *vous*. My mother-in-law called me *vous,* and I did likewise with her. That did *not* mean we didn't like each other. She chose to call me *vous* and I followed; we both appreciated the distance given by *vous*. However, her sister, Philippe's aunt, who was much more casual, immediately called me *tu*. And that was fine as well. My three daughters-in-law address Philippe and me as *vous* because we're older and inspire fear (just kidding). I call each of them *tu* (but can get away with it because I'm American and don't know anything—also just kidding). Philippe addresses each of them with *vous*. Are you still with me? Yes, it's complicated—and that's only for families. With new acquaintances, it's best to start off with *vous* even if you rapidly slip into or mutually agree on *tu*. Most young people instantly use the informal *tu* among themselves. This being said, no matter what the age, look for telltale signs that signal you've committed a faux pas. If you nonchalantly use *tu* and your interlocutor's smile starts to freeze, it's time to revert to the formal *vous*—fast.

It's all so abstruse—except for animals. No animal is a *vous*. That one at least is easy.

Learning about form starts early in France. At school children are taught to sit up straight, write with an ink pen (in *French Toast* I shared the story of how our youngest son, in spite of a coordination problem, was *made* to write with an ink pen, no ifs, ands, or buts), form their letters perfectly, and not write or draw outside the lines. When they get older, essay writing is important. Regarding content, one of the most common criticisms of student papers is *hors sujet* ("off the subject"), meaning that the person has strayed from the strict confines of the assignment at hand. It's not good to be *hors sujet* in school, which, I concluded in a flash of insight one day, might explain why once the French get *out* of school and into, say, a business meeting, they go totally wild and become the world champions of off the subject. As for form, students are taught to write tightly with a thesis, antithesis, and synthesis. You can tell *énarques,* the graduates of France's top school, which include French presidents, cabinet members, and top-ranking business executives, by the way they speak in perfectly formed paragraphs with points and subpoints. (You want to stab them as they pour forth their well-wrapped-up arguments. Sometimes what they're saying is rubbish, but it's said so *well.* . . .)

The way you address people is important, both orally and in writing. Children are taught to say *bonjour* to adults, and not to omit the *monsieur* or *madame*—otherwise it's not quite as polite. (Maybe because adding the gender shows they are actually looking at the person?) That initial *bonjour,* that acknowledgment of the presence of the other, follows them through life. (I am not saying that the *bonjour* makes the French warm and fuzzy. I am saying it makes them polite.) I got so used to the French way of greeting and being greeted when entering a shop or a room that when teaching a group of international students at Sciences Po, I was shocked by their total indifference. I, the teacher, walked in the room and they continued talking to each other, while tapping on the keys of their computers or their cell phones. (Multitasking apparently didn't include glancing at the person who had entered the room). *"Hello,"* I would vociferate, and even then hardly anyone would look my way. Let me tell you that they lost points with me on that one! In France, one of the worst things you can do is to ignore the other person, which is why French parents spend a lot of time making sure their little ones say *Bonjour, monsieur* or *Bonjour, madame* and look the person in the eyes. Frankly, in the beginning, when I saw Philippe's parents and aunts making the children repeat those magic words, I thought it was ridiculous, that they were producing parrots. Now that I see the difference a greeting makes, I get their point—and am amused to see our sons going over the *bonjour* routine with their children, just as their grandparents and we did with them.

Learning and repeating *Bonjour, monsieur* and *Bonjour, madame* is nothing compared to learning the proper forms to use when writing (fortunately, if you're a foreigner, you won't have to do this). It's so complicated that even though I speak fluent French, whenever I write a note in French, I pass it by Philippe for inspection. I don't want to write anything grammatically incorrect or, especially, offensive, which is easier to do than you might think. As Edith Wharton, that wise lady, noted, "No one knows more than the French about good manners: manners are codified in France, and there is the possibility of an insult in the least deviation from established procedure." For example, if you write to a higher-up, you don't send your "salutations," you send your "respects." If the higher-up writes to you, he or she will not send respects (natch). I found this all so Byzantine that I finally made up a chart of French signatures from the most neutral and frequent to the most affectionate. They range from *cordialement* (an Americanization—it didn't exist twenty years ago) to *avec mes pensées très affectueuses* (with my very affectionate thoughts). There's also the Terribly Respectful and pompous *je vous prie d'agréer l'hommage de mes sentiments respectueux* (I beg you to accept the homage of my respectful best wishes), a phrase you'd address to the archbishop of Paris. (I doubt I'll ever have to use that one.) I figured that with those three under my belt I wouldn't get into any major trouble. I didn't really need to worry. Many French people now simply opt for *sincèrement,* the catch-all *cordialement,* or, on e-mail, the boring *bien à vous* or nothing at all.

Form goes beyond handwriting and the correct saluations. Form is also in knowing the order of things. You have to know not only to greet people by saying *Bonjour, madame* or *Bonjour, monsieur* but how to go on from there, especially if you are making a request. The way you present yourself may make the difference between getting what you want and not getting it.

An American friend of ours found this out when visiting a museum outside Paris for research on World War II. He immediately went to the desk and asked for the desired material. After all, that's what he was there for, right? Right in the States. In France, a few little matters of "form" must be taken care of before getting to the point.

For starters, in that museum, which was in a far-flung Parisian suburb and staffed by volunteers, you don't begin with what you want. You first state *who you are.*

Watching the scene and seeing the reaction of total noninterest, Philippe stepped in and did things the French way.

"My friend," he explained, "is a prestigious university

professor in the U.S. and is seeking this material for a book that he is writing on the French Resistance."

Suddenly everything changed. A university professor from America! Working on the French Resistance! They gave him everything they had.

So, I asked Philippe, why didn't they do that from the get-go?

"Because," he explained, "this is a tiny museum with hardly any means staffed by a skeleton team of volunteers. Knowing that someone needs something is not enough. They need to know the importance of the person's mission. For them, some American standing there demanding material might even seem threatening or domineering. Once they knew whom they were dealing with, they were gracious and generous. In France, you have to size up every situation before you proceed."

I told you that nothing's simple in this country! And if you don't keep your eyes open and ears tuned for the unseen and the unspoken, you'll miss a lot of what's going on. That's because the French don't like to go at things point-blank.

The Art of the Enigmatic

If there's one thing that can drive an American, a German, or a Swede straight up the wall, it's lack of clarity. Where are we going? What are we doing? Has the game plan been spelled out? We of the northern cultures love the clear-cut, the unambiguous, the definitive, and the specific.

Not the French. The French may be world experts on form, but conversely they are comfortable in situations that are vague, and ill at ease in situations where all is spelled out to the letter. They love the unclear, the implied, the inferred, and the enigmatic. Part of this is because for the French, explaining things point by point is an insult to intelligence: it means, quite simply, that the person you are talking to is unable to figure things out. I can't tell you how many parties, social occasions, school affairs I've been to in France where no one knows what's going on and that's just fine. Either everyone knows because of customs or codes or, well, they'll figure things out. For example, dinnertime. What time shall we come for dinner? I once asked my sister-in-law in my first days in France. Oh, anytime, she replied airily. I pressed her: Anytime? You mean six? She was secretly horrified but equably suggested that anytime from eight on would be great. Why didn't she say that in the first place? Because for her no civilized person in his right mind would eat before eight. And note the "anytime *from*" in her phrase. Translation: don't you dare show up right at eight, and certainly not before! Recently we were invited to a birthday party, except we didn't know it was a birthday party. By some miracle we found out in extremis and showed up with a hastily chosen present. Other guests obviously knew more than we did and had gone in together on a group gift, a golf club. No problem, we figured. Forewarned is forearmed and we hadn't been forewarned. The people giving the golf club knew the fellow well; we didn't. Everyone was free to do his or her own thing (if, that is, they had ferreted out the initial information, which was that it was a birthday!).

Another example: signs. When I had an operation in a French clinic, I was pleased by the cleanliness and hygiene, the courtesy and efficiency of the personnel, the professionalism of the medical team, the work of the ophthalmologist, who's been our family doctor for almost forty years, and his anesthetist, who in addition to being serious and competent is a nice person to look at as you gently phase out (sexist remark? I can say that: this is France). Filling out the satisfaction form,

I criticized only one thing: the "welcome." When you arrive at the clinic, you see a sign saying *accueil* (reception) and a waiting room. But you don't know whether you're to sit in the room waiting to be called or to first go to the not-so-welcoming *accueil,* where a rather forbidding lady is sitting. So you ask, and depending on who answers, you may get lucky and get the right information. In that particular case it turned out that you first went to the *accueil,* signed in, and then waited in the waiting room. Guess what: a simple sign would end confusion and solve the problem.

But that would be taking people for fools.

A French Free Art Form: The Meeting (La Réunion)

You may wonder (I certainly do) how anyone in his or her right mind could make a link between *joie de vivre* and a French meeting, whether a town hall meeting, a business meeting, co-op meeting, or any other gathering where people get together to decide things. Oops. First error. A French meeting is not held to *decide* anything. Once you get this straight, you can relax and enjoy the fun. But never, never think that you are clustered together with the sacred purpose of coming out of the room with a resolution (or two or three).

At a co-op meeting, I silently fumed as my fellow owners veered wildly, insanely, even flamboyantly, away from each and every point on the agenda. At discussion point seven out of twenty, which had already taken two hours, I started checking out the room for sleeping accommodations since I figured the meeting might turn into an all-nighter. Finally I spoke up: "I have two questions. One, what are we doing here? And two, when we leave, what will we have decided?" Utter silence as heads turned my way. I had finally managed to get their attention. It was only for a second, though, to contemplate this daft American from another planet where you go in to a meeting and come out with a plan of action. *Quelle idée.* That's no fun. A meeting is to *discuss*.

Now, here's where the *joie de vivre* comes in. Remember what I told you about how the French love to disagree? The key word there is *love*. The French do not shy away from controversy. They love it, relish it. Bring it on! If the French can't arrive at decisions by the end of a meeting, it's because they're so busy contradicting each other. It's a bucketload more fun than having to reach some boring old agreement.

In our second home, an apartment in the west of France, our neighbors embrace any pretext to host a party. Each year before the annual co-owners' meeting, one or another will hold an elegant *cocktail dinatoire,* a kind of a combination cocktail/noshing hour (which is not an hour but three or four) where the champagne and every other liquid known to man flows and is drunk from real glass glasses, and plates and plates of fabulous food keep coming and coming and coming on real china plates. The first time I was invited to one of these evenings, I thought it would be a drink and peanuts and good-bye. Oh, was I wrong. This is *France.*

The very French thing about the above is that at that annual co-owners' meeting the friendly guy you saw at the party the night before is transformed into a drill sergeant, and the same people who were yukking it up over drinks are now at each other's throat. During the long, long gathering, you think at certain moments that these dear neighbors may even come to blows. (In America, at this point, they probably would.) Then, three, four, five hours later, it's all over. After shouting, turning red in the face, insulting their neighbors in the worst way, even resorting to veiled threats, the "meeting" (at which no decisions have been made other than to call another one, shoot me in the head) is blessedly over. The same people who had come close to murdering each other smile, shake hands, give each other *les bises,* and gaily make a *rendez-vous* for another party.

We have always rented apartments and only became owners ten years ago, so for most of my life in France, I was spared these co-owners' meetings, but I'd heard all the horror stories. Now I have to attend them, and I admit that every single time I am amazed, dumbfounded, flabbergasted. However, I finally understood something about the Dreaded Meeting: it's a free art form in a rule-bound country. Do your thing! You've got to hand it to the French, who, I finally concluded, surely invented *la réunion* as a way to blow off steam and nothing more. They get their *joie de vivre* out of all the histrionics. They love being up and down, furious one minute, happy the next. They adore drama, and a "meeting" is high drama played out behind closed doors. What more could one ask for?

As an American I can think of one thing: *Get me out of there!*

The Art of Serendipity: The Nonpursuit of Happiness

As Edith Wharton observed so astutely, "The Frenchman . . . is not afraid of anything that concerns mankind, neither of pleasure and mirth nor of exultations and agonies. . . . The French . . . have no idea that life can be evaded, and if it could be they would not try to evade it. They regard it as a gift so magnificent that they are ready to take the bad weather with the fine rather than miss a day of the golden year."

That might sound a tad grandiloquent but she's got a point. Perhaps if the French have so much *joie de vivre,* it's because they're not looking for it. There's no idea that happiness is something that can be pursued, or even that if pursued would be found. Joy is where you find it. It may turn up, and it may not. And when and if it does, it may or may not stay. Americans have the "pursuit of happiness" inscribed in the Declaration of Independence, and so naturally we think it's out there, something we can grab, and are disappointed when it eludes us. As my friend Debra Ollivier, an American who lived in France for ten years and now lives in Los Angeles, remarked, "Americans are unhappy because they spend so much time trying out all the recipes for happiness and they don't work."

She recounted a conversation she had with French friends that she said would never have happened in California. One friend was lamenting about how she so loved her partner but that he was a difficult, complicated man. To which her friends replied, "But you must go all the way with this to the very end no matter how much it hurts." Debra laughed and said, "That was just so remarkable. In California, the friends would have been wary of complexity and suggested that he's no good for her; they would have put the emphasis on protecting herself." The lack of pragmatism, the willingness to plunge into a situation that may be enriching and passionate but may also turn out to be painful, is a form of *joie de vivre*. As Debra sagely observed, "You can still have *joie de vivre* and not be happy."

Happiness in suffering? It does indeed sound very French.

The Art of Lightness

This is what I admire most in France and what, in my opinion, is a field in which the French excel. Those who don't admire this trait call the French "frivolous." Those who do call them "brilliant."

In French, *lourd* means "heavy" or "not subtle." *Lourd* is a stein of beer, an English pudding, a boring monologue, a point-blank statement, a bear hug. *Léger* (light) is a glass of sparkling champagne, a delicate pastry, a clever conversation, an allusion, a *bise*. Needless to say, the French prefer *léger* to *lourd*.

Regarding conversation, the French expression *inutile d'insister* means literally that you don't need to be insistent (translate: boring), that we got the point the first time around, *merci*. There's nothing worse from a French conversational point of view than a laborious explanation. On the other hand, if you manage to collect your thoughts and put them together in a few scintillating sentences with a *bon mot*, you've arrived. If you're at a French dinner party or cocktail reception and a guest brings up a heavy-duty and controversial topic, you'll be surprised to see how fast the host or hostess changes the subject without anyone's noticing it's happening. It's not that serious isn't good, it's that serious is a downer at a party.

Behind the lightness, behind the success of a creation, whether it be a Dior dress or a sublime concoction invented by a great chef, is plain hard work, but—and this is the French genius—*it doesn't look that way*. What the French do superbly is work thoroughly and meticulously, strive for perfection, then make the final result appear as if all was simple. Which it most decidedly was not, but that's not the point. Analyzing, discussing, belaboring, or harping on all the sheer hard labor that went into the final product would mar its perfection, *n'est-ce pas*?

My mother-in-law and sister-in-law may be in the kitchen for hours, but when they serve the meal, they make it look as if it were effortless—and we're talking several courses. When a dish doesn't turn out the way it was supposed to, they don't make a drama out of it. They make their guests feel at ease, even when it's hard. How I admire them! One day a friend showed up with his old and horribly stinky dog, which, unfortunately, came to the table with us. I felt sorry for the dog (who, man or dog, wants to get old?) but thought I'd pass out from the odor. My sister-in-law, gracious as usual, said not a word, and the pooch remained next to his master during the entire meal.

Philippe and I have a little controversy about this: I'm of the Anglo-Saxon mind that "a man's home is his castle." In the days when people were still massively smoking, we'd have arguments about whether I could "suggest" guests smoke outside or whether I could "ban" them from smoking inside. He said clearly that you don't invite people to your home to tell them what they can and can't do. I said that in my home, I'm the one who makes the rules about what can and can't be done. We never did come to an agreement on that one, but fortunately the antismoking movement struck France and it's now a truly surprising exception to have a guest who wants to light up. My sister-in-law, however, is definitely not of the Anglo-Saxon school. In her house, the guest is king or queen. Even I have to admit that it makes for a "light" and pleasant environment.

To end this little reflection on light is good: Sugar rots your teeth and makes you fat, right? And you feel really, really bad when you break down and lunge at that forbidden sweet you've been yearning for . . . except that you needn't and shouldn't feel that way in France, where that perfect *Paris–Brest,* that marvelous *mille-feuille,* that extraordinary éclair, that tantalizing *tarte aux pommes* on a paper-thin crust, are presented so beautifully, in such reasonable sizes. They're dainty and delicate and light. So feel no guilt as you let one slide down your throat. You are participating in an enlightened aesthetic experience!

The Art of Philosophizing

Here's a chicken-and-egg dilemma. Are the French interested in philosophy because they have to take an obligatory year of it plus an essay test on the *bac* before they can get out of *lycée,* or do they have to take this year and the exam because philosophy is such a part of French culture? On the *bac,* candidates, who are all of seventeen or eighteen years old, are asked questions like the following: "Can a scientific hypothesis be proved?" "Is freedom threatened by equality?" "Does self-control depend on a knowledge of one's self?" Heady stuff, and remember, they've got to write an essay on it. Multiple choice it is not!

The French fascination for philosophy doesn't stop with graduation. France may be the only country in the world where philosophers are called upon to comment on events on the nightly news or write regular columns in newspapers and magazines. It's as if Kant were writing a weekly column for the *Des Moines Register* and the readers couldn't wait to hear what he had to say. (I'd take the example of a current philosopher in the United States, but offhand I can't think of one, whereas I have many names on my lips when it comes to France.) In France, philosophers are listened to, taken seriously. Sartre was almost a rock star (imagine), but a new generation is equally listened to. With his Byronic look and open white shirts, Bernard-Henri Lévy is all about image, but you've got to give him credit for drawing attention to the role of philosopher as concerned citizen. I mean, being a "philosopher" is his *job.* In France, people actually heed the words of philosophers. One, Michel Onfray, stirred up a mega-debate that went on for weeks when he went out on a limb and attacked Freud. The Freudians went ballistic, *naturellement,* but what I found interesting was that the ensuing feud made for hot copy in the main newsmagazines, not only the philosophical or specialized journals.

Speaking of philosophy, what do you do on Sunday morning? Stay in bed? Go to church? Mountain hike or bike? Only the French could combine Sunday-morning coffee with philosophy, *n'est-ce pas?* Almost seventeen years ago, Marc Sautet, a French professor of philosophy at the Sorbonne, started giving Sunday-morning talks at the Café des Phares at the Bastille, which rapidly became known as the Bistrot Philo. Although Sautet died in 1998, the tradition remained. Every Sunday from eleven a.m. to one p.m., those who might wonder why we're on this earth and what life is all about hop out of bed to attend the philosophy session. Waiters scurry back and forth as the *prof du jour* philosophizes to a rapt audience. Watching the scene, I couldn't help but think that perhaps part of the French *joie de vivre* comes from knowing that they're only part of a much bigger picture. And all that with *café* and croissants!

The Art of Playing with the Truth

When the French accuse Americans of being "puritan," they may be referring to our obsession with the truth. As inhabitants of an old country and a Catholic country (your sins are pardoned, you can go now), the French tend to be cynical about this matter of "truth" and perhaps more realistic about human behavior. Who doesn't play with the truth or try to?

Cheating on taxes is almost a civic duty here (hard to accomplish, though, when you're a salaried worker). If you're a politician, you play with the truth constantly, and when you don't, your colleagues think you're somehow not quite right. Cheating on your wife goes along with this, and when, many years ago, Socialist Michel Rocard went on TV to say he was divorcing his wife to remarry, the entire (macho) National Assembly almost dropped dead from surprise and shock. Oh, well, the legislators said, shaking their heads, he's a Protestant. That explains everything. (In France, Protestants, most of whom were massacred or chased out of France centuries ago, have the reputation of being upright, honest, austere, formidable, and boring.)

It isn't as if everyone cheats—there are honest people around. But cheating is accepted as, well, something people do. Students cheat on exams, men cheat on their wives, wives cheat on their husbands, salespeople give back the wrong change (strangely, always in their favor), and, as I said, almost everyone who can cheats on his or her taxes. *Cheating* may be too big a word. Let's say that in most cases people make little "arrangements" with facts or other people and/or with their conscience. A man waters his entire yard by pumping from a river on village property that no one has the right to use. Many people construct additions and annexes to their homes that are totally illegal. They do it anyway, knowing that no bulldozer will come in to tear them down. It will take years for the authorities to get anything done, and in the meantime they'll enjoy their additional living space.

Then there's cheating on the state, another activity that's easy to do in a country where almost every category of worker has some kind of "privilege." If France's ports aren't as active as Rotterdam, Anvers, or Barcelona, it's because the dockers in Marseille are constantly on strike. Crane operators at the port work only twelve hours a week and regularly go on strike for . . . earlier retirement. There's fraud on family allocations, social security, unemployment. France is not a country like Sweden or Denmark where public spending is rigorously or regularly controlled, so it takes a long time for abuses to come to light. As for the journalists who courageously denounce all the cheaters and the "privileged," they themselves benefit from an automatic, not negligeable (in 2011, 7,650 euros) deduction on their revenue before taxes.

The main thing about cheating is that you condemn everyone else for doing it. What *you* do, of course, is entirely legit. Or, as former minister and entrepreneur Bernard Tapie, who was accused of lying in a financial case, told the court, "I lied but it was in good faith." Is this *joie de vivre*? Sure it is, for the people who pull it off!

The Art of Spending Time—Speeding Up and Slowing Down

In France, as almost everywhere else, time is of the essence. French time is not Germanic time, though, or American time or northern time, nor is it Italian time or Spanish time. Sometimes it's one, sometimes it's the other. "Figuring out French time is like trying to catch a trout with your bare hands," wrote Polly Platt in *French or Foe*. Catch as catch can. . . .

The French slow down to eat but speed up to order from the menu. They drive like furies on the road but wouldn't think of saving time with drink holders in the car. They invented the fast train but love nothing more than to *flâner* (stroll).

In the fast lane: you can post a letter at night in Paris and it will arrive the next morning in Dijon. You can hop on a TGV (fast train) on a cold, rainy day in Paris and three hours later, after a comfortable ride through magnificent countryside, be in sunny Marseille on the seaside. At the end of a meal, the waiter comes to your table with a machine that will process your payment automatically and you don't even have to sign. You can buy a thousand-year-old château at a candlelight auction for the price of a pocket-size studio in Paris in the time it takes the wick of the short stub of a candle to flicker out.

But when it comes to slow time . . . arm yourself with patience. You can enter a bar, and if the guy behind it is chatting with a customer about the races or real estate, he'll keep talking. In some restaurants, you can cool your heels twenty minutes before a server comes to your table. You can twiddle away an entire morning or afternoon in a business meeting and come away from it with no result. And if invited to a French dinner party, know you'll be at the table for at least a couple of hours if not three or four.

An author, freelance book editor, and translator, our son David often goes to cafés to work. As we walked up the avenue de Clichy one day, I asked him which café he had been in. He indicated a rather ordinary-looking one but quickly specified that he has several cafés: one for rush work, one for slower projects, one for meeting friends, and one for dreaming. I laughed, because I too have my different cafés: one for the morning, one for coffee after lunch, one for afternoon tea. They each have a different atmosphere. One thing I've noticed that is a real pleasure: many times I hit my coffee time wrong, arriving at the café at eleven-thirty a.m. when the waiters are setting up the tables for lunch. I always offer to leave, but they always dismiss it with a wave of the hand: don't worry, there's plenty of time! I call that understanding of dawdling *joie de vivre*!

Know that in France time is not money. Since we lived in the *province*, a term used in France to denote any place outside Paris and its suburbs, for three years and have a home near the seaside resort of La Baule, I'm used to "provincial time," but in the beginning, what a shock. I now know that if I don't get all my shopping done by noon, I'll have to wait until two p.m. at best, and in some cases three or four p.m., for the stores to reopen after lunch—and this is at the height of the tourist season. Where have all the store owners and salespeople gone? To lunch or the beach, *bien sûr*. And it's not only the provinces. In my neighborhood in Paris, you wouldn't think of foraging for food for dinner after one p.m. or before four p.m. unless you go to the supermarket. Why? Because the small shopkeepers, even in Paris, have locked their doors and put up a sign saying they'll be back around two or three. The noon break is sacred in France, and if you don't believe it, try to get a plumber to come at *midi*. It isn't going to happen. If perchance he's already there, don't expect him to stay to finish the job during lunchtime. He'll either finish before or, if not, come back later. In this respect, the French truly are on "slow time." The French twist is that those shopkeepers absolutely do not care about the euros they lose by knocking off in the middle of the day. I told you: those French aren't materialistic!

Joie de vivre? It's not what you buy, it's how you "spend" your time. The French know that and take full advantage of even the tiniest of pleasures, whether cultivating a garden or slowly sipping a glass of wine. What's the rush?

Stephanie Novak, a twenty-two-year-old student who spent six months in Paris, told me that she admires the French philosophy of life and attitude toward time. "I feel that for the French life is happening right now, not after they finish their to-do list." And painter Liba Stambollion, who has lived in France for twenty years, told me, "I learned in France how to enjoy myself by watching others and asking myself why I wasn't enjoying myself. Here was a chance to really just live. Before, I'd eat anything to survive while I continued working. Now I'll take an hour for lunch and enjoy the pleasure with no guilt."

The Art of Barricades and Boundaries

As Edith Wharton observed, "The French are kind in the sense of not being cruel, but they are not kindly, in the sense of diffused benevolence, which the word implies to Anglo-Saxons. They are passionate and yet calculating, and simple uncalculated kindliness—the vague effusion of good-will toward unknown fellow beings—does not enter into a plan of life which is as settled, ruled off and barricaded as their carefully measured and bounded acres." That's why you shouldn't be offended when you don't get a smile from a total stranger, whether it's the guy selling you a newspaper or the person in front of you on the metro. Why should they smile at you? You are one of those "unknown fellow beings." Over the centuries, the French have devised all kinds of rules that enable them to live with each other even though, as you may have surmised from Wharton's words, they'd basically like to be left alone. Why do you think all French houses have high fences? To keep people out!

Want to live easy and "do your thing"? France may not be the place for you. That "ruled off" and "barricaded" life is composed of and governed by (mostly unwritten) dictates that enable the unruly French to live with each other (almost) harmoniously. The rules enable them to approach each other and keep their distance. From the flowers you offer to the way you set your table to the way you sign your letter, etiquette is there to smooth the way.

The Art of the Table and Some Rules

Nowhere are the rules that govern life in France so apparent as around the dinner table. The times they are a-changin', but still today the French sit down to regular meals with a variety of food. You'll now see the French lining up for sandwiches for lunch, but it's still rare to see the French eating outside regular mealtime hours. Philippe used to say he could spot the non-French by the time they were eating. If we saw people eating a meal in a brasserie at four p.m., he'd get a horrified look on his face. "But they didn't have lunch!" he'd exclaim. And then he'd worry, "If they're eating now, how could they possibly be hungry for dinner?" This kind of consideration is *not* a problem in most other countries. The French person, though, has an inner clock.

There aren't that many rules governing family meals (depending on the family), other than the Big One, which is that you eat what's served and don't leave the table during the meal.

It's when you go to a dinner party that you start to see the written or unwritten rules. But first, what dinner party? Basically, traditional parties for traditional people. French young people are much more informal and loose (and broke) and wouldn't be giving the kind of party I describe when talking about the "rules." Nor, probably, would "trendy" or "in" French people. That leaves the bourgeois, the staid middle class, of which there are a few dinosaurs around. Since I've attended many of these kinds of dinner parties, I can only conclude I'm a dinosaur. The point, though, is that these dinners do exist, and if you go to one, you'll initially be astonished at how complicated things can get.

Let's say you come from a country where being invited to dinner means going to the place around six p.m., taking a casserole, and dressing casually. The meal may be a buffet, it may be a barbecue, it may consist of many different dishes eaten at the same time on the same plate. Guests mill around the house and freely wander in and out of the kitchen to help out.

Now, let's take a Parisian dinner party. You're invited for eight p.m. but you wouldn't dare show up right at eight. *Eight* means somewhere between eight and eight-thirty—8:15 is acceptable, 8:20 is better, 8:30 pushing it, and 8:45 late—but the French hostess, being nothing if not courteous, will never let on. If you push it to the hilt and come around ten o'clock, which I swear I have witnessed, the host and hostess will be put out but won't say a thing because nothing must disturb the evening. (You might not get invited back, though . . . at least not for a good while.) If the dress code is casual, it's Paris casual. Paris casual is chic casual, so you wouldn't be caught dead in tennis shoes at this particular party. No, you've thrown on heels and a pretty scarf or your favorite piece of jewelry. If you've got on jeans, they're the *right* jeans. If boots, the *right* boots. Do you show up with food? Not unless you've been asked to, which would be highly unusual. Do you ask to tour the house? No. Do you go in the kitchen to help? No, a thousand times no.

A Parisian dinner party is a combination of laid-back and formal. The clever French host and hostess have planned it so that all the guest has to do is sit back and enjoy. *Parfait.* That's the laid-back part. On the other hand, the guest needs to be clever. If he's French, he knows the rules governing the Parisian dinner party, which is a species unto itself, many times arranged as long as a month or two in advance.

These long bourgeois affairs with dish succeeding dish first appeared in the court of Louis XIV, where his courtiers gathered to watch him dine. After the Revolution, the aristocratic habits filtered down into the bourgeoisie, as did certain rules and ways of acting at the table. I think that in my first years in France I probably violated every rule in the book and then some.

"I can't figure out why you Anglo-Saxons get up to go to the bathroom when you're already seated at the dinner table," a French friend married to one of those "Anglo-Saxons" told me. "For the French, once you're at the table, you remain there." Having to get up to use the toilet means that you weren't using your brain to go before—and it's seen as slightly graceless.

Another thing the controlled French don't get is why those Anglo-Saxons (and other foreigners) continue to drink so much once they've had their first glass. The French drink, and wine is an integral part of the meal, but they know how to pace themselves. If you look at what most French people, Frenchwomen especially, are imbibing, you'll see that it's in *modération,* a word the French revere and practice. For example, when I told a French friend that some American friends were taking advantage of a trip to France to dine every single night for a week in a different three-star restaurant, he almost choked. "But how can they enjoy the experience?" he asked, truly puzzled. "They'll be too sick." *Logique.*

Modération is not a word I'd apply to myself, so I couldn't help but be fascinated as I watched Frenchwomen *nursing* their glass of wine. Most Frenchwomen, I noticed, have their glass filled and then baby it for the rest of the meal, unlike Barbarian Me, who can't wait for a refill. *So refined,* I would think, eyeing the bottle I wanted to grab—but couldn't. Woe to and shame on the woman (or man) who reaches for the bottle to serve herself or himself. That is on the list of "not done" and one of the major faux pas.

Of course, you may say, if your host isn't serving the booze, then you should. If your host isn't doing it, he's a dolt, but you're an even bigger dolt if you reach for the bottle. Sarah Turnbull, in her book *Almost French,* describes a scene at a party in which there's an open bottle of champagne that all the guests are ogling but no one dares to pick up and pour into the waiting glasses. Finally, she does, but it's obviously a dicey moment: some of the guests take the drink, others hesitate. What she did was so utterly non-French.

So many rules . . . Sometimes I don't know which are "French" and which are "my husband." For example, when it comes to giving a toast, he can't stand it when people clink their glasses together. Maybe it's because the clinking becomes crashing and he fears for the crystal? In any case, if *he* were giving etiquette lessons, he'd say, "Raise the glass, but keep it to yourself."

I decided to offer a class on French table manners to my journalism-school students at Sciences Po, where I was teaching a course called Reporting on France. If they really wanted to know about France, I reasoned, in addition to learning about French politics, education, immigration, and religion, they needed a session on French etiquette, what's polite and not polite, what to do and not to do. After all, the French invented the *art de vivre*. What could be more typically French?

And who could be a more "typically French" purveyor of *politesse* than our guest speaker, Countess Marie de Tilly— the stylishly thin, *très parisienne* daughter of a diplomat— who teaches etiquette to foreigners, French individuals and companies, and young job seekers in what are euphemistically called "the troubled suburbs." For don't think that all French people know their p's and q's. Many do indeed know about "what's done" and "what's not" practically from birth, especially if they were born into a traditional French family in the staid and proper seventh arrondissement. If, on the other hand, they are the children of immigrant parents and grew up outside Paris in Garges-lès-Gonesse, they won't.

So, for my brood who are clueless because they're foreigners, Marie de Tilly is standing in front of a desk on which we've placed a plate, a couple of glasses, some knives, forks, and spoons. If my students learn nothing else about French *savoir-vivre,* I muse, they'll at least be able to Get Through a French Dinner Party Without Making Fools out of Themselves.

Before we even get to the table setting, though, an obviously worried and liberated young woman gets one fear off her mind straightaway. "What if I'm at a French dinner party and some man tries to give me the *baise-main*?" she asks with a tinge of dread in her voice.

"He won't," Madame de Tilly assures her. "The *baise-main* [a slight bow and light kiss of the hand] is only for married women."

Whew.

Marie de Tilly picks up a fork. "Tines up? Tines down?"

A timid voice volunteers, "Down?"

"Yes. But why?"

Here's one that shows my knowledge of the aristocracy is next to zero. Ready? So you can see the family crest—if you have one. Madame de Tilly does, which is why she brought her own *couverts* to the class, but whether you've got engraved silverware or it comes straight from Monoprix, the rule is the same. Tines down!

Next comes a thorny subject: Where are hands to be placed? In France, they are on, not under, the table (to discourage hanky-panky?). Not only that, but ladies can and should put their elbows on the table with the hands crossed up in the air—to better show off their rings.

Ladies may be encouraged to flaunt their *bijoux*, but they are *never* to serve themselves wine, Madame de Tilly tells the astonished assembly, confirming a custom it took me a few years to figure out.

"But what if the man next to you doesn't serve you?" a student quite logically queries. "Toy with your glass a bit until he gets the hint," the countess advises. "If he still doesn't catch on after several tries, you can ask him politely," she says, adding, "If you're really stuck, you can serve yourself water—it's the only drink a woman is allowed to help herself to at the table." (Why do my students look depressed?)

As if things weren't already complicated enough, next comes the salad. Cutting it is an unforgivable sin, a holdover from the days when vinegar rusted the iron knives and forks. The knife should gently be used to help fold really large lettuce leaves so that they can be speared with the fork—with the ever-present risk that one will pop up and unfold before reaching the mouth. A good hostess will cut the leaves into bite-size pieces.

Finally, we reach the *fromage*. The cheese plate only goes around once (no one seems to know why). Take a small portion of each, don't cut the Roquefort so the person after you ends up with all the white, and never spear a piece of cheese on your knife and bring it to your lips—as if anyone civilized would.

What if you don't like the *escargots* or the *blanquette de veau*? *Tant pis.* Leaving food on your plate is a definite no-no. "Finish it, even if it's horrible," de Tilly instructs the students.

Last but not least: if you wished everyone a hearty *bon appétit* at the beginning of the dinner party . . . you were wrong. It is considered *très vulgaire,* the phrase having more to do with simple digestion than a considered appreciation of fine dining. If, when you were introduced to someone, you uttered a simple *"Enchanté,"* it was insufficient. Only a full sentence, *"Je suis enchanté de faire votre connaissance,"* will do. De Tilly then reiterated my French friend's point about getting up from the table. If you did so, it's already strange, but if in addition you *said where you were going,* you committed a major faux pas. If you must leave the table, the rule is to quietly slip away.

My students are looking stunned. Do "the French" really observe these codes? As inquisitive future reporters, they couldn't wait to test the dinner-party tips. The verdict came in a postmortem at the next class, in which one astonished young lady said that she'd dined with a young French friend and "he observed every single rule Madame de Tilly talked about." Another young woman reported almost dying of thirst as she waited and waited for her hosts to serve her wine. A few of their classmates, however, were relieved to relate that they'd met French people who weren't aware of some of the rules.

How could they be? There are so many, mostly unwritten. For example, there's no "rule" for it, but try to share a dish in a restaurant. At best, you'll get raised eyebrows. At worst, a scolding. One evening, I almost crawled under the table from embarrassment when one of our old friends, an American married to a Frenchman, asked for one dessert and four forks. I thought the waiter was going to have an apoplectic fit. Why? I asked my husband afterward. Easy, he said. First of all, if you ask to share food, you look cheap. Second, if you go to a restaurant, you "participate in the ritual"—and order your own dessert. If you're not hungry for an entire dessert, you simply don't order it. There's also an unwritten (and sometimes written) "no change" rule. Waiters in general freeze or frown when people look at the menu, see *steak frites* and ask if they can have zucchini instead of the fries and veal instead of steak. *Et quoi encore?* (And what else while we're at it?)

If the French don't split dishes, they do, however, share the restaurant bill—equally. If you go out with a bunch of French friends (unless they are very very young and very very broke, and even then), when the bill comes, everyone will pay his or her share, not based on what they ate, but on the number of people.

My husband says this perfectly illustrates the French concept of *le repas*. It's a social occasion, it's all about the relationships and the conviviality, and breaking the bill down into who ate and drank what totally ruins the atmosphere and the *joie de vivre*. So if this happens to you, think of it as participating in a ritual—not as an exercise in inequality. I witnessed this intercultural difference one night at a dinner with a group of Frenchmen and their American wives. We each ordered different "real meal" dishes and wine for all— several bottles by the end of the meal. When the time came to pay, everyone agreed to divide equally as usual. There's no real need to ask since this is the custom, but that night one woman piped up with: "I had only a salad and drank one glass of wine, so I don't see why I should pay for the rest of you." In purely factual terms she was right—but she'd broken the tacit agreement that says that when you go out, it's for fun, not to be a bean counter.

I love all these rules, especially because everyone breaks them. Paris resident Ron Fox gave me a good example of getting around the rules. At his favorite restaurant, Joséphine–Chez Dumonet, the (unwritten) rule is that steak doesn't get served well done. When an American friend with whom Ron was dining asked for "well done," the waiter said he couldn't violate house policy. The only thing he could do for him, he suggested, was to take the order and then "if Monsieur found it wasn't cooked enough," take it back to the kitchen. Eventually the steak would be done to his taste.

I'd totally integrated the "don't share" rule into my head when a French girlfriend I was having lunch with one day ordered one salad for two. My husband would never have done that—so I waited anxiously to see what would happen. Nothing happened. The waitperson didn't see anything extraordinary about the request, perhaps because the food in that particular restaurant was so copious. As for unequally splitting the bill, I've even witnessed some French people doing it. (My husband never would! He thinks it lacks class.) And when it comes to clinking glasses, the French (minus my husband) seem to do it more than I would have thought.

At that point I decided that rules are guidelines only. If you can remember the most basic ones, such as not serving yourself wine and not getting up from the table once you're there, you're already almost French. And if you can't, not to worry. You've got a wonderful excuse: you're a foreigner.

Interview with Philippe

HWR: *You took philosophy in high school. Did it have some effect on your life? Do you think the French are different from people whose cultures are more pragmatic and more wrapped up in "doing" than "thinking"?*

PhR: We prefer thinking because it's something you can do anywhere, anytime, including on the terrace of a bistro. When you work, you can't do anything else but work.

HWR: *You have so many rules! It's a miracle you can have any* joie de vivre!

PhR: We don't like things that are black-and-white, we like to live in ambiguous situations. You'll never make a Frenchman happy by saying, "Let's be clear."

HWR: *That's for sure . . . but your rules are black-and-white. How do you live with them?*

(continued)

PHR: When you live in a country with so many rules, you have to get around them to survive. For example the manual of the laws governing work, the Code du Travail, is twenty-seven hundred pages long. Do you think anyone reads the whole thing? *Trop de lois tuent la loi* [too many laws kill the law].

HWR: *So what you're saying is that all these laws and rules encourage people to play with the truth?*

PHR: What truth?

Having Fun While You Disagree

Don't lose your nerve if you meet an argumentative French-
man or a Parisian salesperson who curls his lip. For the Gauls,
a day without a clash is a sad and boring day indeed. Contro-
versy is the French national sport.

The one main thing to know about the French is not that
they disagree, but that they *love* to disagree.

It may sound strange to people of other nationalities who
seek nothing more than agreement and consensus, but I'd
wager that if you took contention and discord out of French
life, you'd remove a huge slice of their *joie de vivre*. Disagreeing is not just a Gallic game, it's part of their lifeblood.

The French are happiest in strife. They embrace provoca-
tion. Looking back on it, I realize that the main reason I
decided to make Herculean efforts to speak good French
was because a conductor in a train from Calais to Paris
spoke to me in a way I didn't like and I couldn't answer
him. I didn't speak French well enough to grasp what he
was saying (maybe he was being funny with a dour face, but

how was I to know?), but the expression on his face spoke volumes. I decided he hated me. And I vowed on that day to get myself up to speed. I did, and thank the Lord, because in the ensuing forty years I've had plenty of occasions to spout off in rapid but accented French. And am *so* happy every time I do! It's a joy, a national sport, and when you get the technique, it is indeed most amusing (I know it sounds insane, but read on).

Some Americans mistakenly think that the French are anti-American because they are aggressive. Think again. The love of being contrary, irritable, easily aroused, and quick to fight goes way back in time and has nothing to do with others' nationality. Ammianus Marcellinus (A.D. 330–400) wrote, "The Gauls are generally tall, with white skin, blond hair, and frightful and ferocious eyes. Their mood is quarrelsome and extremely arrogant. Any of them in a fight will resist several brawlers at a time with no other help than his wife's, an even more dangerous fighter. Whether calm or wrathful, the Gauls always sound threatening or irritable."

Well, there you go. Some people just don't change.

Don't Be Frightened—They're Simply Having Fun

In *C'était de Gaulle,* writer-diplomat Alain Peyrefitte quoted the general as saying that the French "have not changed since Julius Caesar described them. Their strengths are bravery, generosity, unselfishness, impetuosity, curiosity, creativity, the gift they have to adjust to extreme situations. Their weaknesses are a clannic spirit, mutual intolerance, brusque anger, internecine quarrels, the jealousy they feel for the advantages that the others have."

Yes, yes, and yes! Those "internecine quarrels" and "brusque anger" they've been indulging in—and I suspect immensely enjoying—for the past two thousand years are innate to the French national character. What we non-French consider a "disagreement" is for them a mere "conversation," a little promenade in the park. The thing is, they sound as if they are picking a fight even when they aren't.

In the question period after a speech on cultural differences I gave to young Americans in Paris on a university program, a puzzled-looking student asked me about something happening in his host family. "They're always fighting," he confided in a hushed and worried tone. After a few questions to determine the situation, I assured him that what he thought was contentious and threatening was normal, everyday conversation. I advised him to listen carefully to find out the subject of the supposed controversy. "You may be amazed to find that your French 'mother' and 'father' are discussing the brand of mustard or the qualities of the wine," I told him—and I'm convinced they most probably were. In even a mundane conversation, the French turn up the heat. They raise their voices, their eyebrows, and move their hands with energy and passion. Since the tone of French can sound argumentative to non-French ears, it's true that we often think they're going to come to blows.

That fellow was a young man here on a short-term program. An acquaintance who has lived in France for decades got the shock of her life when her daughter married a Frenchman. The man's parents invited her to their home to spend a few days, an eye-opening experience to this American, who speaks excellent French but who had never been exposed to the way French families or friends interact with each other.

The weekend unnerved her. "You can't believe the way this family yells and the way they talk to each other!" she exclaimed. "The father provokes everyone, the son talks back to him, and they go on and on, telling each other they're stupid, don't understand anything, and are wrong." Not only that,

she exclaimed, although she was convinced when she went to
bed at night that none of them would be speaking to each
other the next day, "when I came down for breakfast, they
were all bright and cheery and kissing each other." (She obviously thought she'd find dead bodies on the floor.)

After forty years in my husband's French family, I could
only laugh and give an opinion and some cultural advice based
on long experience: "You didn't get it! Their words may have
seemed harsh to you, but (a) they were most probably putting
on a little extra show for you, and (b) *they* were having fun."
"Fun?" she asked. "Insulting each other is fun?" I repeated
what I now know, that the French have a way of shaking
things up, that words that may sound offensive to foreign ears
may not be at all (how they're given and taken depends on the
tone of voice and context of the conversation), that for them,
a dinner party or family gathering in which there's no banter,
no controversy, no disagreement, is a total bore, and that she
shouldn't take everything literally. "Loosen up!" I advised,
and believe me, I know what I'm talking about.

For years, I thought the house was on fire, so vociferous
and excited did my husband become about . . . almost everything. It could be a glitch with the computer, it could be the
mayonnaise's not taking (especially the mayonnaise's not taking), it could be something on the news that upset him mo-
mentarily, the list is long. In the beginning, I took it personally
and thought he was on my case when he was only talking
normally (normally for him). Caroline Aoustin, a young
American married to a Frenchman, told me she would accuse
her French husband of "arguing" with her until she saw that
everyone else in France was using the same tone of voice. "I'd
see people doing what I thought was 'fighting,' then laugh
and have a glass of wine!" she exclaimed.

As Caroline and I and my recently shocked acquaintance
all discovered, conversations in France encompass strong

emotions and engender vigorous controversies. If a conversation doesn't contain any of these elements, it's considered a dud. We primmer Anglo-Saxon types, who have been brought up not to show emotions and certainly not to voice disagreement or lose our cool, have a hard time figuring out what the French flap is about. They are so . . . combustible! Some American friends of ours, used to the calm of academia and reasonable exchanges (reasonable because they take place among people who all agree), are alternately fascinated and secretly appalled by the way Philippe and I "carry on." One of them asked us a question about French teachers that got the two of us practically frothing at the mouth about teachers' unions, school vacations, and related topics about which we had passionate opinions. Our friend was penned in between us and couldn't get a word in, something unusual and frustrating, surely, for a college professor. True, these animated discussions are daunting to outsiders, but I have a lot more fun now that I'm able to joyfully join in these "impassioned discussions."

Even the Weather Provokes Passion

In England, where it rains all the time, people keep a stiff upper lip and don't make too much of the weather. In France, the weather can provoke all kinds of interjections, exclamations, exasperation, horror, delight, or depression: "Drat this dratted, horrid cold rain." "How long can this hot spell last?" "What a beautiful day—finally—*profites-en*" (take advantage of it). These admittedly banal remarks can lead to considerations on global warming, which can lead to a discussion on ecologists, which can lead to a debate on nuclear power plants, which can lead to politics and why the deuce the president isn't doing anything about the weather. An old joke

in France isn't that far-fetched: *Il pleut. Que fait le gouverne-
ment?* (It's raining. What's the government doing about it?)
That's a reference to the government's involvement in every
part of French life—so why not the weather? If you want to
improve your French, get a Frenchman started on the weather.
It's better than French 101 could ever be.

Disagreeing Without Getting Personal

The French like talk, and they certainly don't mind when
suddenly there's a challenge or disagreement or controversy.
One person challenges what the other says, and off we go.
Someone may "win," but more often than not, no one does,
but that's not important. The opponents will go back to
drinking that nice glass of Menetou-Salon. Actually, they can
pick the Menetou-Salon as another topic of discussion, its
qualities, its drawbacks—that will take at least another hour,
or the whole night.

I cannot even begin to imagine discussions I've had or
heard in France in an American context. By about the second
or third controversial point, both parties would be mortal
enemies. In France, no one's going to change his or her mind,
but the adversaries don't get personal. They may totally disapprove of, disagree with, and reject the other's point of view
but remain friends.

This would hardly seem to be the case in the States. When
President Bush decided to go to war in Iraq and the French
said they wouldn't join (bringing Franco-American relations
to a new low), I was confronted by a friend of a friend who
challenged me about the French stance. I'm not a representative of the French government because I happen to live there,
I wanted to reply, but I was handy, so . . .

He gave me a hard look and asked, "Do you really want to

get into this?" It wasn't exactly the promise of a stimulating intellectual exchange. It was a clear announcement of a bloody battle, an ultimatum. The presupposition was clearly that we would *not* remain friends. Did I take him up on it? You bet I didn't. However, I inwardly chuckled as I thought back to all the raucous dinner parties in France where Philippe's old school friends, some of whom are conservatives and others who are Marxists, almost let the plates fly as they argued. They will never agree, that's for sure, but somehow (maybe it's all that good food and wine) they remain friends. But as I said before, the French love strife, *n'est-ce pas?*

At a family gathering in the north of France, a Francophile American friend who is politically on the right and has French relatives on the left discovered this French talent for disagreeing without breaking off social relationships. He told me he was "amazed" by their acceptance of him, their warmth, and said in wonder, "That kind of mutual tolerance and more could never have happened in the States." That's because, as I said, the French are used to rejecting the arguments and not the person arguing. Another key reason is that criticism is seen as a positive, not a negative, trait in France. When children are little, they are taught what's wrong, not what's right. They are not stroked and praised and made to feel fine when they hand in bad homework. They're told it (the work, and by extension, them, while we're at it) is *nul,* zero. This sounds harsh to American ears, but that's the way it is in France—and perhaps the exacting standards are the reason the country has such great cooks and artisans and creators. Bottom line, people criticize all the time, and criticism is not, repeat, *not,* viewed the way it is in the States. Lastly, many disagreements take place during meals. Since the French like nothing more than to eat and drink and fighting is bad for the digestion, they don't let things go too far so as not to spoil their enjoyment.

Their attitude of "let's not get personal" explains why the French are surprised that Americans can think that the French hate them *personally* each time there's a political controversy between the two countries. For them, it's clear that disagreeing on ideas, concepts, actions, has nothing to do with individuals. (Other major point: it's also clear that they don't care if they're hated, while we Americans like to be liked.) An American reporter friend was asked by a major U.S. publication to ferret out all the instances of anti-American behavior she could find in France during the Iraq controversy. She dutifully interviewed hotel and restaurant managers and came back with a disappointing report. "Nothing anti-American is going on," she told her editor, who could scarcely believe it. On the other side of the Atlantic, the furious anti-French were feverishly dumping bottles of red wine and refusing Roquefort, so it was logical that the American editors expected the French might boycott Coke or attack Americans. Different strokes for different folks, as they say.

Consensus Is Boring

"Perhaps," reflected Luigi Barzini, "France would not have become the great, admirable, and endearing country it was, and still is, in many ways *la lumière du monde,* had it been inhabited by uniform, dull, and docile people."

Dull and docile they are not.

The French pride themselves on their individualism and on their contrasts. They are much more interested in being "against" each other, showing off and taking pride in their differences, not their similarities. As Barzini points out, the country was formed and "molded down" by the antagonisms between tribes and clans, the provinces and Paris, the center and *la banlieue,* the nobility and the bourgeois, farmers and town dwellers, patrons and employees, and the list goes on and on. If you don't know how to "be against," you're not French.

In other countries, people *start* by trying to agree and—perhaps—end up with a clash. In France, people *start* with a clash and a bang and—perhaps—end up agreeing.

A Frenchman feels no compulsion to agree, make nice, find a consensus. Here are the instructions Couve de Murville, the French minister of foreign affairs under de Gaulle, gave to the French ambassadors: "The important thing in a negotiation is to defend one's point of view. An agreement can come as an extra." Would you marry a guy who behaved like that? Imagine trying to do something simple like buying a car. Speaking of cars . . . early on in my marriage, my sister overheard a conversation in which my better half was explaining what kind of wheels "we" were going to buy. She wondered about the "we" part, though, because it sounded as if Philippe had his mind made up. He did, and he hadn't asked me. I did point out that while I didn't give a hoot about the car, it might be nice to ask my opinion from time to time. I do believe he took note—every once in a while. But we're far from the "let's sit down and decide everything together point by point" style, that's for sure. Each to his own, and with a French husband, good luck on getting consensus. Agreements between French partners, or at least between us, seem to come not after a summit meeting but as the result of a clever little game in which subtlety and nuance count. All very complex, this life in France!

Being Right Is So Much Fun

What's this thing about being right? I have often asked myself in France. From the saleslady who sets me straight when

I say an outfit is black (no, it's navy blue—oh, all right, already, I'm color-blind) to the graduate of the French school ENA (the equivalent of Harvard and MIT and the cornerstone of the French Power Elite) who pedantically explains to me the formalities of getting a U.S. passport (as if I didn't know), I've found myself in many situations in which I am being corrected. Are we still in school? Is it necessary to prove you know more than the other guy? Maybe so. Think of it. In French schools, when the teacher hands back homework, she reads the grades out loud for all to hear. The results of the *baccalauréat,* the school-leaving exam, are posted for all to read. A pecking order of who's best and who's worst is established early in life. So if you were at the bottom of the heap, wouldn't you want to be in a position to push other people around a bit? If you go to the prefecture to get your residence or work papers, you'll see a slew of civil servants finally getting their chance to dump on poor dumb foreigners after being dumped on all their lives. They've finally got their day in court! Another twist to this matter is more pernicious because it makes you feel as if you're the one who's crazy. That's when the salesperson looks you straight in the face and tells you that whatever it is you're asking for *"n'existe pas."* Adrian Leeds, French property expert and author of numerous online publications, tells the story of going into a shop to ask for pillowcases for *traversins,* rapidly disappearing but still existing (!) hot-dog-shaped pillows that rest against the headboard of the bed, and being informed that the size she wanted didn't exist. Since Adrian had already bought them in that size, she maintained they did. The salesperson insisted they didn't. In the end, the two came to a compromise with Adrian suggesting that perhaps the person meant they didn't exist in her store. Ah, there we go! The saleslady assented. My personal opinion is that the French tell you something "doesn't exist" (a) when it doesn't exist for *them,* and mostly (b) when they don't want the thing to exist because they're busy or not interested and want to get rid of you. When I was expecting our first child, I suggested that if it was a girl, I'd like to name her Anne-Claire. Philippe smiled and declared almost triumphantly, "It doesn't exist!" What? I couldn't believe it (and anyway our first child was a boy, so no problem). All through the succeeding years, though, I've seen many an Anne-Claire. The name does exist. It just didn't exist for him.

Dissension's in Their DNA

The French could say in a paraphrase of Descartes's famous *I think, therefore I am,* "I quarrel, therefore I am." At least a good quarrel proves you're alive and kicking.

Quarreling is in their gene pools, people. So much so that in Luigi Barzini's book *The Europeans,* the chapter on the French is entitled "The Quarrelsome French." If you've ever picked up an *Astérix* comic book and seen the feisty little Gaul single-handedly fending off the giant Romans, you'll get the picture (literally). When, today, I see the Little Gauls standing up to Big America, whether on Iraq or anything else, I can't help thinking that nothing has changed since the heroic Vercingétorix, the charismatic leader who unified the dispersed Gallic troops, was besieged by Caesar's army at Alésia in 52 B.C. He went down, but he went down fighting. Whenever I think Philippe is getting too hot under the collar, I remember that he was born in a clinic on the rue Vercingétorix in Paris and that he, like the hero of the Gauls, hails from Auvergne—and I immediately forgive him for being so easily excited. It's hereditary!

When a Frenchman is riled, he's got plenty of ways to blow off steam and lots of words for what he's doing. He can *râler, rouspéter, ronchonner,* three words that describe moaning and groaning. The French, especially the Parisians, *râlent, rous-pètent,* and *ronchonnent* a *lot.* Come to think of it, they do it all the time. That's how they get their kicks. Weird, but true.

If you're not happy about the weather, politics, your dinner, or anything else, well, you can *râler* and no one will think anything of it (wonderful country). There are degrees, of course. A polite, civilized, well-brought-up Frenchman will not disagree the same way that someone without that polite veneer will. The latter won't hesitate to give you a *bras d'honneur* (up yours). The genteel one will ever so politely shred you to pieces with words.

They have to cut and leave the person gasping. Here's an example. In a restaurant in Arizona where the service was beyond abominable (I'll be nice and not give the name of the place or the town), as we left, Philippe looked the hostess in the eye and said, "I've never seen a place like this before." Not used to verbal confrontation, the eye contact, or the tone of voice, she was speechless. In the same situation in France, the waitperson would have replied, "You haven't traveled enough, jerk" (and *jerk* is polite). You may find this breathlessly unpleasant, but if you live in France, you get used to exchanges like this. I don't necessarily like them, but (confession) miss these kinds of verbal exchanges when I'm in the States. I can't believe I'm writing this, but it's true. I'm convinced the French keep their blood pressure and their weight down because of their ability to confront each other without killing each other.

If you always agree, you're viewed as a wimp, a blah, a milquetoast. Disagreeing means that you're attentive, alive, on it. That you have opinions. It's all very different for an American brought up to believe that "being polite" means keeping things neutral. Sometimes at French dinner parties I worry about the china as the guests vociferously express their contradictory views on philosophy or politics. (And for heaven's sakes, don't get them started on Freud!)

As usual, though, nothing's black-and-white, so take the above with a big bag of *sel de Guérande*. You can argue, disagree, discuss, make your views known, if you're light about it. The minute things become heavy, the game is over. I have attended many Parisian dinner parties where the host or hostess cleverly deflected conversations that were getting beyond the point of light or funny. The French like controversy, but they don't like leaden conversations. Sparkling, yes. Heavy, *non*. That's the subtlety of being French.

To conclude, I often wonder about all the time spent on outing emotions, but maybe that's how the French get the juice for the *joie de vivre*. Maybe that fighting spirit *is* their *joie de vivre*. . . .

Don't Fall into the Trap

Since the French are so good at impassioned discussion, foreigners who live in France and speak good French as well as foreigners speaking to Frenchmen who speak English are delighted to find they can both dig into fabulous food and wine *and* have a scintillating conversation. In an interview with *Paris-Insider,* Joan Shore, Vassar graduate, former CBS correspondent, and the author of *Red Burgundy,* remarked, "What I still love about the French is their dinner-party dialogue—so different from Americans. Here, it's about politics, literary scandals, and summer vacations. In America, it's about shopping, automobiles, and children."

But sometimes we foreigners get our signals crossed and unwittingly go too far. I have attended dinner parties at which the foreign guests discoursed on almost everything, it seemed, that the French have done wrong: their colonialist past, their collaboration during World War II, their total ignorance of "religious freedom" as shown by laws forbidding the wearing of the burka in public. Why? Because the (French) champagne was flowing, the (French) food was delicious, the (French) hosts were charming, and the guests felt comfortable in the hospitable and elegant (French) environment, thinking that since the French talk freely about everything, so could they. Maybe they even assumed that they were being as French as the French. In the sense of making conversation, they were . . . but on the wrong subject. It's as if French guests were invited into an American home and lectured their hosts on the massacre of the Indians, segregation until 1964, or the existence of the death penalty. I imagine the guests would be out the door in ten minutes. In France, where people are used to discussions and arguments, there's much greater latitude—and a much greater possibility of falling into the trap of biting the hand that feeds you.

It's easy to do. There's a great "freedom of speech" at French dinner parties, in the subjects and the tone and the vocabulary (which is why translating what's going on is so difficult). Sometimes guests ride right up to the brink of what's acceptable; rarely do they actually go beyond boundaries of good taste. Perhaps they remember Patrice Leconte's 1996 movie, *Ridicule,* in which a young noble from the provinces travels to the court of Louis XVI to ask a favor of the king, the drying up of a swamp whose mosquitoes are killing the inhabitants. He enters a cruel, cynical world where everyone is elbowing for favor and survival at court depends on wit. In one famous scene, the Abbé de Vilecourt in a speech before the king and nobility brilliantly proved the existence of God. Then, proud of having pleased his audience, he added that he could also prove the contrary, that God did not exist. He proceeded to do so, incurring the wrath of the king. His words were his downfall. I often have this feeling at sophisticated French dinner parties—you can be clever, but don't be too clever by half.

Public Controversies

French couples do not shy away from disagreeing with each other in public, something that's "not done" in Anglo-Saxon countries. In France it's not exactly high on the scale of polite either, but it's tolerated if done the right way (lightly—there we go with that word again). In this country where *controversy* is not a big bad word, people might even start wondering about a couple that placidly agreed with each other all the time. They'd suspect something was wrong and, worst of all, find them . . . boring.

In public, especially in Paris, people "let go" more than they ever would in the States. One American resident of Paris says she got so used to the "French way" that she applied it on a trip home to New York. "The Parisians are aggressive and in your face. They don't let anything go by," she told me. "So when I went back to the States and opened the door for a lady who went through without saying thank you and who then let the door shut in my face, I went Parisian. I reprimanded her. She simply couldn't believe it. That is not what people do in the States." She remembered another occasion in which she acted the same way when a person jumped her place in line. "I tapped her shoulder and said, 'Did you know you cut in front of me?'" Again, she says, the woman was shocked. Her Parisian behavior probably isn't making her any friends, but did she ever feel liberated.

I did the same thing when in the States also because I was still in my French mode. When an electrical appliance I had purchased didn't work and the salesperson was stonewalling me, I looked him straight in the face and asked him direct questions, fully expecting to get into the kind of exchange I do in France—which can go any way. It can start out antagonistically and end up friendly or start out friendly and end up antagonistically. *On ne sait jamais* (one never knows). Eye contact is essential. Getting your point of view out there, getting an exchange going, a reaction, even if it's negative, is cardinal. When I tried this in the States, I could see that my interlocutor thought I was either ready for the loony bin or the store guards. What in France is par for the course was considered an Act of War in the States.

Why write about this? It's important information. This difference in behavior is one reason Americans and other tourists think the French are snobby, arrogant, aggressive, and hate foreigners.

Well, now you know this isn't true. If a French person is sharp with you, bawls you out, or orders you around, you should feel flattered. You're getting the same treatment the French get. Should we all be so lucky.

How to Be Rude If Someone's Rude to You

First, let me say that most tourists now tell me they are totally amazed by how helpful and polite the French are. They have a hard time fitting the kind behavior to the rude reputation that precedes them.

Steven Gournay, a sixty-three-year-old retired stenographer who lived in Paris for three years, is one of them. "After forty-five years dealing with cantankerous fellow New Yorkers, the 'tough' Parisians seemed like the most affable and easygoing people I had ever met in a large city," he told me. "Rome, on the other hand, was similar to New York in the way that people treated you, brusquely and unapologetically sarcastic." (I admit I almost fell over in a dead faint upon hearing these words.)

How did the French get a reputation for being rude? First of all, they can indeed be rude, and second, when they're rude, it's for real. They are *good* at it.

Another reason is that until recently most French people didn't speak English and felt threatened when English speakers would ask them for directions. Imagine, as an American or an Englishman, being spoken to in Urdu by a Pakistani who assumes you speak Urdu—of course! Now put yourself in the place of a Frenchman who speaks no English and hears it coming at him rapid-fire. If he looks consternated or perplexed or walks away, it isn't rudeness. It is because he can't understand a word. This has changed with a younger generation that on the contrary loves to speak English so much that you can hardly formulate a word of French to them. I guess you just can't win.

Yet another reason for their world reputation for rudeness is that the French on any normal day and for whatever issue is at stake can rev up to foaming at the mouth in a nanosecond. It may just be the way they are, but it assuredly frightens off the tourists.

If perchance in France someone speaks to you in a way you don't like, what to do? First of all, make sure you understand what was said or done. Sometimes French people say perfectly nice things but because of the tone of French it sounds argumentative. Additionally, sometimes they do nice things but without a smile, which causes misunderstanding.

However, if it's not the above, and you're the victim of rudeness, be rude back. How? Be like them. The choices are legion. If your French is excellent, you can have a verbal battle of wits. I say *excellent* French because for this you need to be at the top of your form. Don't do what an American friend did. Thinking she was so clever, she insulted a saleswoman with a choice French phrase, *et ta sœur* (and your sister), which is a sexual joke meaning basically "I screw your sister." Except that she said *et ta cousine* (and your cousin), which had everyone rolling on the floor with laughter. Make sure you've got your gender right. Don't call someone *une salaud* (bastard) or *une escroc* (crook). They're both masculine words—*un salaud, un escroc.* If you mess up the grammar, your opponents will not be offended, they'll be in stitches.

If your French is not up to par, you can do what the French do so well: shrug. It's the sublime expression of indifference, of showing that the other person is so insignificant that it's not even worth bothering with. Glacial stares are also most effective. My husband does this well, but then . . . he's French.

Voilà. It's highly unlikely you'll need any of these techniques. The French treat tourists so much better than they treat each other.

The Customer's Always . . . Wrong

In America, there's the saying "The customer is always right."

In France, there's no saying, but you can bet your bottom dollar that if there were one, it would be "The customer's most always wrong."

Why is this so? Why is customer service in the States so smooth and predictable compared to the bumpy and unpredictable ride you get in France?

Because in France the customer-salesperson relationship is exactly that: a relationship. And relationships aren't always smooth.

Jan Williams, a Canadian who lives in France with her English husband, Nigel, found out that "when you are a loyal customer, you get excellent and outstanding service. You become someone with whom they now have a relationship, albeit one of client and service giver. The person knows you." She laughs as she recalls an unexpected repercussion of that client-server bond. "When I first came to France, I worked in the seventeenth district, where Nigel, then my boyfriend, and I met at the same café after work. The people there got used to seeing us together. We were regulars. Then one day Nigel came early with our friend Liz, and instead of the usual good service, the waiters were rude, almost flinging the menu at him. He couldn't figure it out until I waltzed in, kissed them both, and we saw the waiters visibly sigh a breath of relief. Ah, so my boyfriend hadn't dared to show up at the café with some floozy. We were restored in their good graces." I have had this happen as well—in our local Chinese restaurant, where the Chinese waiters have become decidedly French. If I go in with a male friend, they make a point of saying loudly, "Please greet your *husband* for me."

In America if you're a client, you expect standardized service, politeness, efficiency, and no emotions. An employee can get fired for bad service or bad behavior. In France, you get unstandardized service, which can range from exquisite and efficient to indifferent to downright horrid, but in France no one will fire a salesperson for not being nice to a customer. Bosses can fire employees only for a "grievous fault," and apparently that's not one of them.

Store owners themselves can insult and alienate their customers. My husband, on more than a few occasions, was told by a shopkeeper, "I don't need clients like you." The store owner, like the salesperson, feels no need to kowtow. After all, what was that French revolution all about if you have to cozy up to the people "above" you (in this case, a lowly client)? Mow them down.

As part of her job as an image consultant, Anne-Marie Lecordier knows Paris boutiques like the back of her hand.

She deplores the behavior of salespeople, saying, "We've got a lot to learn from the Americans," in this field. Her remedy for bad service? "I get the attention of the salesperson and say, *'Excusez-moi de vous avoir dérangée'*" (Excuse me for bothering you). The translation doesn't carry the bite, but said in perfect French the message comes across loud and clear: *You are not taking care of me.* She says it at least makes salespeople think about their behavior (for a second or two).

But not to worry. From what most travelers and tourists tell me, customer service is generally helpful and pleasant. The entire "the French are rude" reputation comes from bad experiences tourists have had with unpleasant or harried waiters or salespeople . . . and something else—unpredictability. Since there is no idea of "standard service" in France, you don't always know what you're going to get. However (listen up!), a simple *Bonjour, madame* or *Bonjour, monsieur* and a *Parlez-vous anglais?* (or whatever language you're speaking) will work wonders. Worst-case scenario: you barge into the store without acknowledging the salespeople and don't even bother to greet them or look at them—*not* a good idea. Why? Salespeople, especially in France where no one ever forgets the word *equality* even for five seconds, like to be treated like *people,* not objects.

If you're lucky, you'll have great service everywhere you go. And when the French give good service, it is pitch-perfect, the right combination of the desire to help without being obsequious.

You may, however, get one of these garden varieties of French salespeople. Forewarned is forearmed, so here are a few to watch for.

Preemptive

One of my students told me that she'd been in a shoe store in the Latin Quarter and had tried on several pairs when she was told that if she had no intention of buying, she should leave the premises. "What should I have done?" the shocked student asked me. Put the person down, I replied, applying advice Philippe has often given me. Or, better still, ask for the manager. "But he *was* the manager," she yelped. When I hear stories like this, I remind myself that France is the sixth most productive country on earth and think, not for the first time, that it truly is miraculous.

Passive-Aggressive

In a large butcher shop, a well-dressed and impeccably groomed Frenchwoman in her seventies politely asked one of the white-aproned butchers if he could sell her a half a rabbit. No, he replied, indicating six whole rabbits, head and all, hanging from their paws. "But can't you cut one of them in two?" she inquired with a smile. Since he looked distinctly irritated and she could see she was getting nowhere, she said, "Never mind," and took the matter to his boss, who immediately instructed his employee to give her what she wanted (one would think that would be *normal, non?*). By now, the fellow was furious, but he had to obey and did so with a vengeance. His face crimson, he grasped the knife, raised his arm high in the air, and *whong,* delivered one sharp blow to the poor *lapin.* It was quite clear to all those watching that the object of his revenge wasn't the rabbit. When these things happen, you just shake your head—and change butchers. Otherwise, you live in constant fear that the cleaver will come down on you someday!

Absent

My daughter-in-law and I were at the stand of a well-known perfume and candlemaker at the Printemps department store. The perfumes and soaps were all lined up and there to test, which we did joyfully, spraying them on ourselves liberally because no salesperson was in sight and no sign indicated where she was and when she'd return. Soon a little crowd of waiting customers gathered, so I decided to play salesperson and vaunt the wares. "Try this," I urged, picking up a beautifully decorated perfume bottle. "Floral and wooden tones, you'll love it." Or how about this one, I exclaimed, grabbing another: "Vanilla, with cloves." I went on like this for about *twenty minutes* and had acquired an admiring audience by the time the real salesperson finally showed up. Not one word of apology for her lateness. Not one smile. The smiles were on the faces of her might-have-been customers, now her "opponents." Oh, well, we'd all had a capital time.

Not Interested

On a Saturday afternoon at five-thirty, Philippe called the number of a person who advertised as an art restorer. She answered the phone and said, "Sir, I am now having tea with a girlfriend and you are bothering me." Don't you love it? In a fruit-and-vegetable store where I went to buy sweet potatoes, I saw that the sole salesperson was busy with another customer—busy talking. The two started their chat at the back of the store and moved up to the front, where the client slowly selected various vegetables as they continued their interminable discussion about real estate in La Rochelle (quite expensive, I gathered). The salesperson never once looked at me. I was invisible, a ghost—a ghost who stood patiently for twenty minutes before finally leaving *sans patates douces*. In cases like this, not only is the deal not closed, it's not even opened.

When I say that in France "it's not about money," that's what I mean. And if you're not into capitalism, it's even rather nice. It means that the store owner's relationship with one particular customer is more important than an additional twenty or thirty euros from another. I rest my case.

* * *

Of course, as I mentioned above, you can also find excellent customer service in France, from top hotels to the corner grocery store. My neighborhood newspaper salesman, who has, sadly, retired, not only sold papers and magazines but relayed messages and kept our keys. In the village where we have our second home, I frequent two shops I love, an art gallery and a secondhand shop, and although I've never bought anything in one and not much in the other, the owners are always friendly. The secondhand-shop owner lends me objects I want to try in my home, as does the lady who runs the local decorating store. When we bought our place, we contacted an armada of electricians, painters, and woodworkers for various jobs. Alas, I couldn't write *A Year in Brittany* based on the funny and frivolous workers helping us fix up our place because all were as serious and professional as the Provençals Peter Mayle described in *A Year in Provence* were comical and *pas sérieux*.

So why go on about bad service?

Because when it happens in France it's so egregious, so blown up, and in some instances so breathtakingly rude. Because coming from the United States, I was raised to think that time is money and that the only reason to work is to make money. Hey, don't they want it? *Non? Pardonnez-moi.* There's another reason: good service happens most of the time, but bad service makes for spicy tales to tell. And wait a minute, do you think we're no longer talking about *joie de vivre*? Of course we are. Part of a salesperson's shtick is doing his or her thing. Remember that the next time you start getting miffed. They're having *fun*.

Mickey Mouse Brings the Happy Face to Paris

There *is* a mecca of standardized service in France where people flash smiles like lightbulbs. When Euro Disneyland, now known as Disneyland Paris, opened outside of Paris in 1992, the French were not exactly ecstatic. One prominent artist colorfully dubbed the American theme park "a cultural Chernobyl." French employees were incensed by certain American business practices. Requiring English to be spoken at all meetings was bad enough, but the Disney appearance code for the staff, which listed regulations and limitations for the use of makeup, facial hair, tattoos, jewelry, and more, was the limit. Requiring workers to smile was even worse. Employees argued that no one in France is required to wear a happy face. Disney argued that the world of Disney is *based* on happy faces. French labor unions complained that the appearance code was "an attack on individual liberty."

In the end the controversy died down. The French adjusted to Disney and Disney adjusted to the French. Yes, Disney made a few memorable mistakes in the beginning, such as serving no wine in the restaurant on Main Street. In France that's the equivalent of no Coke at a fast-food joint. But now all has been smoothed out, and if you want a real reverse cultural shock after the often disconcerting sales behavior in Paris, you can head to Disneyland. You'll relax as you are greeted with big smiles by people who actually act as if they want your money (they do).

But something strange might happen. You may find you're soon bored with it. Too slick, too smooth, too orchestrated. You crave something more . . . unforeseeable. You've become French.

Hanging Out Without Feeling Guilty

How the French manage to take so many vacations without feeling guilty and why the sacrosanct vacances *are a French institution. Work and* lunch. *The joys of sidewalk cafés.*

"How are you impressed with Paris, Mr. Edison?"

"Oh, I'm dazed. My head's still in a muddle, and I reckon it will take me at least a year to recover my senses. . . . What struck me so far chiefly is the absolute laziness of everybody over here. When do these people work? What do they work at? People here seem to have established an elaborate system of loafing. I don't understand it at all." —*From an interview with Thomas Edison in 1889*

Thomas Edison may have invented the electric lightbulb, but he was deeply in the dark about the French attitude toward work and play. At the time he observed the "absolute laziness of everybody over here," the French didn't have the paid leave and the perks they have now. But that didn't keep them from enjoying life.

Another American who was thunderstruck by the French penchant for pleasure, writes Harvey Levenstein in his book *Seductive Journey: American Tourists in France from Jefferson to the Jazz Age,* was Abigail Adams, a friend of Thomas Jefferson's and the wife of John Adams. She was, he wrote, "shocked by French disregard for the Sabbath, and was disgusted to see the Bois de Boulogne and other parks full of Sunday pleasure-seekers munching on cakes, drinking wine, and crowding various entertainments."

Oh, those hedonistic, pleasure-mongering French, always out to enjoy themselves!

The French do indeed actively seek delight. But that's only part of the story.

The uniqueness of France is that it's a serious country whose inhabitants work hard *and* live the good life. "All work and no play makes Jacques a dull boy" could be the national motto.

How do the French manage to maintain the balance between work and play? How do they hang out without feeling guilty?

Isn't that the mystery we'd all like to crack?

But First: Are They Lazy?

Only in 1936 under the Socialist government of Léon Blum did French workers obtain two weeks of paid vacation. That was the beginning of what the French proudly call their "social model," which, to sum up a complicated system, is kind of a giant security blanket with guaranteed health care for all and *beaucoup beaucoup de* holidays.

The French now enjoy—and take for granted—retirement at age sixty (which was progressively pushed to sixty-two after months of strikes), a thirty-five-hour workweek, and a *minimum* of five weeks paid vacation a year plus perks most of us would trade our eyeteeth for.

So are the French lazy?

"The French are lazy! That's the stupidest thing I've ever heard!" Joseph Stiglitz, the winner of the Nobel Prize for economics, told readers of *Le Point* magazine in 2011. "Your country is one of the most developed in the world, you have magnificent companies, you create value. . . . It's the fruit of history, of course, but also of the work and the creativity of your nation for generations and generations. . . . Contrary to many developed countries, I sincerely think that you, the French, have succeeded in building a generous social model that leaves hardly anyone by the side of the road."

The French tend to take that "generous social model" for granted and get a shock when they see how the rest of the world lives.

When our son moved to Montreal and found a job at the same French company he worked for in Paris, he was in for a *big* surprise. He lost all the goodies French workers in large companies like his *take for granted*: a paid thirteenth month (a companywide entire month's salary at the end of the year), subsidized lunch vouchers, subsidized transportation, an in-house medical service with an in-house doctor, a share of the profits, a certain number of "rest" days, *chèques vacances* (vouchers for your vacation and travel to use as you wish), and a *comité d'entreprise* (worker's committee) in charge of distributing Christmas gifts and getting the employees good deals on vacations, concerts, and children's camps. He also lost certain worker's rights. For example, should a French employer fire a worker, he is obligated by law to give ample notification. In Canada, my son observed, your phone can ring on Friday at five and you're told not to report for work on Monday.

That simply could not happen in France. The French worker would sue his boss—and win.

Three Reasons for Their Joie de Vivre

Three main powerhouse reasons explain why the French look and act so relaxed about life (especially compared to Americans).

First of all, they benefit from a national health-care system (yes, Virginia, there is a Santa Claus, and they *can* choose their doctors) that ensures them that *if they lose their job, they won't lose their health care*. It's there and no one is going to take it away from them. Simple as that.

Second, a college education is *virtually free* compared to the cost of a U.S. university education, and although the French grumble about increasing costs, they couldn't conceive of a system in which you have to start saving for college the day the kid is born and where many college students remain in debt for years as they reimburse student loans.

Lastly, retirement and pensions are paid by those working and are not linked to the stock market, which means *there's no fluctuation and no uncertainty*.

For all the above reasons, and although French workers may be unhappy about this and that within their system, particularly and legitimately the bugaboo of unemployment, they don't spend their lives being *worried* that the bottom will fall out.

Take it from me, an observer of the French for the past

four decades: the French like their jobs and they like money as much as the next guy. In their minds, though, the job and the money are linked indissolubly to what really counts: family life and personal happiness. An example: When I first met Philippe, he told me that he would never bring home work at night or on the weekend. It was easy to say and do in the beginning but became harder as he climbed up the ladder. He did eventually work from time to time on the weekend, but never without a break to visit a museum or for some other activity with the family. Like the good Frenchman he is, he separated work and "life" and maintained the balance.

The Trade-off

You can't have a system like this without a trade-off. The French pay higher taxes and earn lower wages; they opt for security and solidarity rather than risk. To protect workers, it is difficult to hire and fire. Social charges for employers are high. The French worker doesn't make as much money (you only have to compare French lawyers' or doctors' earnings with those of their American counterparts to see that), but they have more time and more of what they call "quality of life." The average American would love the relaxed style of life in France but chafe at the high taxes, intervention of the state, and other constraints. The average French person would love the buzz of energy in the United States but wouldn't necessarily like the risk and insecurity. To each his own.

Reality Check

"Hanging out" does not apply to every category of worker in France. Farmers don't hang out, the heads of self-owned businesses or start-ups don't hang out, the butcher and baker and hairdresser don't hang out. Many have never seen a thirty-five-hour workweek. They work long, hard hours, don't go on strike (who'd hold down the shop?), and some don't take vacations either because they have no time or because it's too expensive. We foreigners, like Edison, often get a false impression of the French and their work habits because what we see in "gay Paris" is just one part of the picture. Indeed, when you see Paris office workers lunching and strolling and looking so relaxed on their lunch hour, you get the idea that no one is particularly stressed. Maybe that's because in the time they have—and they do indeed have longer lunch hours than in many countries—they're exercising their *joie de vivre.*

Work and Lunch

"I haven't mastered all of this yet," admitted Rachel Kapelke-Dale, as we lunched on the terrace of Le Nemours, a restaurant that has a view of La Comédie-Française and the slightly zany, glass-beaded "kiosk of the night walkers" entrance to the Palais Royal metro stop created by French artist Jean-Michel Othoniel. I love the lightness and joy of the entrance combined with the formality of the adjacent Palais Royal gardens, which makes this one of my favorite places to meet friends and conduct interviews.

As Rachel and I chatted and watched Parisians stream out of their offices on the sunny spring day, the twenty-seven-year-old, who is working and living in France, told me she marvels at her French friends "who work and who have two-hour lunches or *apéros* that seem to go on for four or five hours." She paused as she mused, "I used to take twenty minutes for lunch in New York, and in one of my jobs we weren't allowed to leave the office. It was on Central Park and we'd look wistfully out at the leaves. I can't imagine my French friends in the American work context. It's not that they're not hard workers—I think they're probably even harder workers. They separate things out and they don't talk about work like we Americans do. And with the vacations and long lunches, it's easier to take time for a life of your own."

A Sempé *New Yorker* cartoon of hundreds of office workers lunching on sandwiches outside their office buildings in Manhattan couldn't be transposed to Paris. Not because of the sandwiches, because many French workers eat them as well. In France, the workers would be window-shopping or strolling or sitting together in a restaurant instead of, as in the Sempé cartoon, silently and separately hunched over their computers.

Should the French worker want to lunch at his desk, he might have a problem. French labor laws forbid lunch at the desk in companies with more than fifty employees, which are obliged either to have a restaurant on-site or provide lunch vouchers. A manager might eat a sandwich in his office if he's on an urgent project, but that is to remain an exception. "The idea," said our friend Dr. Jean Salomon, a former head of health services at a major French insurance company, "is that eating at the desk should be something totally exceptional and not a habit, which would put pressure on the worker and contribute to eventual burnout." *Toujours* the balance between work and . . . life.

Speaking of lunch . . . The Anglo-American Press Association, of which I'm a member, organized a "brown bag" get-together one day in the offices of our hosts, *Le Monde*, the French gray-lady equivalent of *The New York Times*. The editors agreed to the idea and had a plate of sandwiches ready, not knowing that the Anglos really would bring their "brown bags," a mysterious and unknown concept. Even the cleaning staff was mystified. When informed that the meeting room would be used for lunch, they wondered why they hadn't been instructed to set the table with plates, knives, forks, and glasses. The idea of guests bringing their own victuals and eating with their hands was totally foreign to them. You may see many French people lined up in front of the *boulangerie* to buy sandwiches at noon, but few are taking them back to eat at the desk.

Unhappy? Strike!

Anytime the French are upset about any reform, be it retirement or education or unemployment, they take to the streets. *First* they raise havoc, *then* they negotiate. (Always good to express yourself, *n'est-ce pas?*) Actually, statistics show the French strike *less* than workers in other European countries (even the sober Danes strike more, but who talks about a Danish uprising?), but their strikes are, well . . . French. They are spectacular, showy, ebullient, and hit where it hurts. French strikers almost always choose holidays for maximum effect. Even if their compatriots suffer from their actions (good-bye, vacation as they fume at the airport during an air controllers' or pilots' strike), you won't get them to say anything bad about the strikers. Some even say, "I can't strike [for such and such a reason] so am glad someone's doing it for me."

How ironic that the day I write this, I can't read my morning paper because the distributors are on strike. Not so ironic when you think about it. After enduring hundreds of strikes in this country—strikes by airplane pilots, flight controllers, teachers, students, farmers, truck drivers, you name it, I've finally accepted them as a fact of life. Oh, it's a strike day. How will I dress? Where will the marchers be? (Don't want to get stuck in a traffic jam or find that my metro line has been closed.) After one particularly memorable strike in Paris in which nothing was moving and people walked miles and hitchhiked to get to their jobs (without complaining!), I bought a pair of special tennis shoes, which I baptized "strike shoes." Be prepared!

I thought I was almost understanding these strikes until the day I saw with my own eyes *high school students* joining their elders to protest against *pension reform*. My American mind couldn't wrap itself around that one. I don't know about you, but when I was fifteen or sixteen, retirement was not even remotely on my radar screen.

Bosses and Workers

One thing is sure: the class war did not end with the French Revolution. A systematic opposition is built in between bosses and workers. For the French, the battle lines are drawn from day one, with management and workers in an atmosphere of mutual suspicion. That can go as far as boss-napping—harassing and locking up bosses on their own premises—which although not a frequent occurrence, happens from time to time. Philippe Poutou, a car worker at Ford and the fringe candidate of the New Anticapitalist party in the 2012 presidential elections, told interviewers in a solo appearance on a national TV political talk show that he wasn't used to being alone. "When we sequester the boss," he disclosed, disarmingly, "we do it in a group. When we occupy, it's as a group. We go on strike as a group." Nice work if you can get it!

As far as a friendly atmosphere among colleagues and team building, the French don't plunge into it with joy; from what I've seen, the French generally make their friends in grade school and keep them the rest of their lives. They may make friends at work, but it's because they want to, not because they have to. I do know cases of people making fast friends at the office—but they were English and American teachers in France. Palling around with officemates seems to be more of an "Anglo-Saxon" thing to do. One good thing about this distance is that everything's clear: in France you don't have to invite your boss to dinner, it's the hierarchical superior who invites, not the reverse. We have indeed dined at the homes of Philippe's bosses, but none of them ever dined *chez nous*. Great system!

I Love Loafing

In case you think I agree with the moralistic tone of Edison's remark or that my Protestant ethic has me wringing my hands in horror over a society of "loafers," think again. *Au contraire*. I admire the distinction the French make between the workplace and home, and their idea that work shouldn't get in the way of life. I am totally amazed by the time the French devote to their vacations, which seem to be for almost everyone in this country, my husband excepted, a fetish, a mania, an obsession, a sacred rite and right. Someone asked me how I adapted to the French conception of leisure . . . the question proved the person didn't know me. I was *made* for this country. Let me see, how long did it take me to adjust? Two seconds? Maybe three?

A French Exception?

Ironically, as much as I love loafing, I married one of the only men in France for whom work is such a value he could be German and for whom the word *vacation* does not, to say the least, evoke a thrill. I exaggerate, but let's say he doesn't fit the French stereotype when it comes to *le travail* or *les vacances*. How did this happen? I would ask myself as I compared him to my friends' French husbands, who seemed much more "French" when it came to kicking back.

When I first met Philippe, he was a researcher in a think tank and had plenty of time for leisurely lunches and a game of tennis before coming back home. When he changed jobs and moved up, his schedule changed as well. Did you know that in French companies important meetings are set at the *end* of the day, around seven p.m., and that in any case, for an executive or manager to leave the office before seven-thirty is a cardinal sin? He was out the door by eight a.m. and returned around nine p.m. He had those five weeks of vacation and even more but didn't take them all and certainly not in one go.

At this, I would shake my head in wonder. How, in a country of 63 million souls, did I get the one person who in no way corresponded to vacation-happy Harry? But before you get out your Kleenex box, I should probably tell you that in spite of his refusal to take off for an entire month at a time, we took many varied trips throughout the year, in France, but also to Egypt, Italy, Spain, Hungary, Malta, Canada, the States. The difference is that, unlike most of Philippe's vacation-obsessed friends, we didn't spend our entire year . . . planning our vacations. My better half finds his pleasures close to home, in food, in wine, in his genealogy research, in his stamp collection, in the many associations he's a part of, in the crazy political column he inflicts on his children who have opposing views. Just because he's not vacation obsessed doesn't mean that he doesn't know about *la joie de vivre*. And while I'm on a riff about my unusual husband, I'm happy to tell you that although he's in the minority, he's not alone.

I laughed out loud when reading an article in *Le Figaro*'s

summer series *Le bonheur d'être français* (The happiness of being French). The reporter, François Hauter, started the article with what, in France, is an almost blasphemous lead: "I'm going to be honest: I detest vacations."

I wonder how many subscriptions the paper lost that day. . . .

He went on to explain that as a reporter he traveled enough not to feel the need to spend holidays in faraway places. However, when by sheer accident he found himself stuck in 750 kilometers of traffic jams along with his compatriots and a horde of northern Europeans traversing France for *les vacances,* he was stunned and depressed. The entire experience was "decadent," he wrote, and the haggard, exhausted vacationers brought to mind "a caricature of Goya."

Sacred Leisure

Vacations can indeed be depressing if you don't like being crowded on highways or beaches listening to other people's loud radios and seeing their fat guts (although one good thing is that you see few fat guts in France). I found I could almost skip vacation because there are so many things to do in Paris—especially in August when all the Parisians have fled to the mountains and the shores. In Paris, I always have the feeling that the French grab occasions to enjoy life whenever they can in any way they can. Take a recent day when I decided to go to a movie in the afternoon, which I rarely do. I was quite sure there would be next to no one. The place was so packed I was lucky to get the one seat that was left. I almost felt like Edison, asking myself, *When do these people work?*

"There's a relaxation to the way people hang out in Paris," American screenwriter and Francophile Diane Lake observed as we took our time over a drink in the Montorgeuil neighborhood, where almost every seat at the Père & Fils café was filled at eight p.m., with people indoors and outdoors enjoying the coolish summer evening and the sky that stays light until ten or eleven p.m. She cast her eye on the scene and remarked, "People meet friends, and it's not necessarily about hooking up. People take their time to live over here."

They certainly do. And here's a paradox: the French have a high standard of living, good roads, good schools, good hospitals, good doctors. They have extensive vacations. They strike. They sleep more hours per day than the Americans, Spanish, Polish, Belgians, and Japanese. Wouldn't you think that if they spend their time striking, sleeping, and vacationing that they'd have a *lesser* standard of living? Or a much lower level of productivity? Get ready for another "French exception": even with all its vacation days, France remains one of the most productive countries in the world. (And if you don't believe it, take a look at the statistics gathered by the Paris-based thirty-four-member Organisation for Economic Co-operation and Development.)

No wonder we foreigners wonder how they do it. Give us the secret so we can do it too. We'd have *joie de vivre* in *buckets* if we had their deal, *non?*

Not only that, but the French are inventive (that's why their business meetings are such a mess—they can't stand being bored, it cramps their creativity). Although the entire world thinks wine, cheese, chocolate, silk scarves, when the word *France* is mentioned, they could also think TGV, Airbus, and the smart card. Invented and patented by Frenchman Roland Moreno in the midseventies, the ingenious chip in the "smart" card established a brilliant system of instant payment. In the States, I'm always disconcerted to see the waiter walk off with my Visa card. In France the waiter comes to the table with a Marvelous Machine into which you insert the card, type your code, and presto—the deed is done right there

on the spot. I have to put this plug in for the French chip.
Now if we could just get it in the States . . .

The French work, but they are convinced, persuaded, sure,
that *work is not all.* They are always thinking of ways to
spice up their lives, have a good time, experience something
different. And when I say "the French," I'm not talking just
about the wealthy French who can hop on a plane to the Sey-
chelles islands. In a hospital bed one day, I started chatting
with one of the young nurses, who glanced at a TV program
about the annual Christmas fairs in Alsace. "We're going to
Colmar this weekend with the children," she told me, and
from the way her eyes lit up, I could tell she was already
thinking of the delight her two-year-old and four-year-old
would feel at seeing Père Noël in that fairy-tale town with its
half-beamed houses painted in yellows and greens and pinks
and reds. And a nurse is on a modest budget. When our children were little, we took them all over France, not only to the
family country home near Chartres, but to Corsica, Brittany,
Provence, Alsace, Auvergne, Ardèche, and the Loire Valley
castles—and those are only the ones I remember.

So there you have it. Leisure is sacred in France, right up
there with foie gras and Sauternes. And isn't it logical? Even
if he never left his own country, the Frenchman could spend
his life exploring its monuments, its castles, its regional food,
its natural wonders. And then there's the rest of the world to
see as well. So many vacations, so little time.

A Movable Feast

One fine day Paris mayor Bertrand Delanoë decided it was
pas possible that so many Parisians were stuck in the capital
in July and August while their more fortunate compatriots
bronzed on beaches or breathed pure mountain air.

Thus was born Paris Plage, an ephemeral beach on the banks of the Seine. No sea, no coast? No problem: take almost two miles of road along the Seine, truck in more than two thousand tons of sand, dump the load, and rake it. Add hundreds of deck chairs and parasols, spruce up the scene with a passel of hammocks and palm trees. Parisians and tourists don't have to head for the "seashore": the seashore comes to them.

Paris Plage is truly a "movable" feast.

Even if Monsieur le Maire hadn't invented a summer playground by the Seine, it wouldn't have been a major problem. Parisians are never bored. How could they be? Lovers meet on the banks of the Seine, friends in their favorite cafés and bars scattered all over the city, families take to the city parks. In summer, professional and wannabe musicians spill into the streets for La Fête de la Musique (Music Festival); in October, before the winter doldrums, La Nuit Blanche (All-Nighter or White Night) provides a good excuse to visit museums until all hours of the night; and in the spring, the Fêtes des Voisins (Neighbors Day) is a coveted moment of conviviality. I never thought the French would go for this Neighbors Day idea, which was instigated by a young French government official in 2000 and which has since spread to countries all over the world. In my experience it seemed that most people in Paris ignore their neighbors or try to, but I was wrong. The first French Neighbors Day in 2000 attracted half a million participants; last year's attendance shot up to a vertiginous ten million. The fête turned out to be immensely popular and a great excuse to pool food, eat, drink, and make merry while exchanging names of babysitters or favorite addresses or philosophizing about life over a glass of wine. This being France, where everything gets mixed up, you might even find yourself smiling (hypocritically) at the neighbor who's threatened to kill your dog if it doesn't stop barking. Well, if you've had enough to drink . . .

If you're a communist or die-hard leftist, you can attend the Fête de l'Huma, organized by the communist newspaper *l'Humanité*. That fête has been going strong since 1930, when it was founded to create "proletarian solidarity." But if you prefer food and wine to politics, there's a *fête des escargots* (snail feast), a *fête des champignons* (mushroom feast), a *fête des crêpes* (pancake feast), and of course *la fête de Beaujolais nouveau* in November. You won't find me at the Fête de l'Huma since I'm not into "proletarian solidarity," and as for the *Beaujolais nouveau,* as long as you know not to expect too much (it started as a commercial gimmick and the wine can range from bad to okay), it's always a good pretext to get together with friends.

Club Med wasn't actually invented by the French (it was started in 1950 by former Belgian water polo champion Gérard Blitz), but the French bought the concept and developed it as only the French, with their appreciation of leisure time, could. In its early days, it was known as a place for singles to meet—and more. My husband dubbed it "affair land." He should know: on one family vacation at the Club Med in Vittel, an attractive woman slipped a piece of paper with her room number into his pocket. I saw her do it! It's not only French men who make the moves.

A Permanent Vacation in Paris

On one sunny June Sunday morning, we parked our car in front of our son's apartment near the Place de Clichy and then walked to Montmartre, a good place to go in the morning when it's not yet too crowded. Transforming ourselves into tourists, we stopped and listened to a group called Les Frères Zitoun, who had transported a piano, bass, and percussion to play outside on a pretty square. Up the rue Ravignan we trekked to our ultimate destination, the Relais de la Butte, founded in 1672, or so the sign says, and a perfect place to sip coffee while getting a stupendous view of Paris. From there we strolled to the Place du Tertre, and into the Église Saint-Pierre, a twelfth-century church filled with locals and tourists, some participating in the service, others visiting.

As we came out of the church, we happened upon one of the ubiquitous street mimes, who was silently entertaining passersby. He was in whiteface with two red spots on his cheeks, a red hat with a black band, a white shirt, red tie, beige suspenders, and black slacks. When a little girl put a coin in the open sack there for the purpose, he leaned over and solemnly gave her a charming *baise-main,* a little kiss on the hand. I instantly thought of Marcel Marceau, France's most well-known mime. With a few precise and elegant movements of his eyes, eyebrows, hands, arms, and torso, *le mime* Marceau conveyed a vast array of emotions: sadness, sorrow, happiness, joy, chagrin.

That was Sunday morning and we'd gone to Montmartre on purpose, but on most any day of the week, as I go around Paris on errands or business, I find unexpected delights: a house with unusual architecture, a historical plaque announcing that some famous person had lived or died in the building, a street name I'd never before seen.

No wonder the French don't feel guilty about hanging out. It's educational.

Proud of Their Playground

The French are rightly proud of living in a land that was made for "hanging out without feeling guilty." I've traveled to almost every corner of France and found that even in the coldest, dankest, darkest unattractive areas, there's something to see that is spectacular. Reims (excuse me, citizens of this august city) is not exactly a place where I'd like to own a second home, but the cathedral built on the basilica where in the year 498 Clovis, the king of the Francs, was baptized into the Catholic religion is a magnet, as are, in the same city, the capacious champagne houses and cellars, repositories of France's famed sparkles and bubbles.

I once covered the entire east of France on assignment for a travel magazine. It wasn't my first choice—I would have preferred Provence or the Riviera—but after hitting the village of Hautvillers, population 850, snuggled in the vineyards outside of Épernay, on the first day of the wine harvest, and admiring its 120 wrought-iron signs signaling the butcher, the baker, even the fireman, I was smitten. That hamlet, by the way, is where the Benedictine monk Dom Pérignon invented the recipe for making wine festively effervescent. On that particular road trip, I also discovered Rodemack, "the little Carcassonne of Lorraine," with its six hundred meters of high walls, before driving on to Alsace, where I wandered through the entrancing gingerbread villages of Obersteinbach and Niedersteinbach. I searched for storks and found them perched on the roofs of houses in lovely little Hunawihr, the stork capital. In Obernai I started wending my way down the Alsatian wine-tasting road. I adore Alsatian wines, their unique flavor as well as their names, ranging from the melodious-sounding Sylvaner and Riesling to the hard-to-pronounce Gewürztraminer.

The real wine-tasting shock happened in the mountainous Franche-Comté region, where I sampled the unusual walnut-and-curry-flavored, amber *vin jaune* in Arbois, the birthplace of Louis Pasteur. It's not univerally known or appreciated, but I loved it, especially when paired with a slice of comté, the cheese made in the same region. My trip ended in Vézelay, the "eternal hill," as the sun slipped down behind the Basilica of

St. Mary Magdalene, which for nine hundred years has welcomed pilgrims on their way to Saint-Jacques-de-Compostelle. And that was the east of France, which isn't that well-known. There's not a region in France that doesn't possess magnificent treasures, some renowned, others well-kept secrets. No wonder the French are attached to and proud of their land. No wonder they're chauvinistic.

Pétanque and Pastis

I did eventually get to the south on one of those trips, where I spent many happy hours "reporting" from my perches on café terraces, where I'd sip a *pastis* and watch the locals play *pétanque*. (Hard life, but remember, we're talking about *joie de vivre*.) *Pétanque*, pronounced PAYT-HONK, is a French game *par excellence*. Any number of men and women (yes, women also play *pétanque*, but it's true that it doesn't seem to be a woman's thing) throw a weighted silver ball in an attempt to get as close as possible to a wee, round object called a *cochonnet* (piglet). It's a stand-up sport. It takes a long time. The players use strategic and varied techniques for throwing, for striking the opponent's *boule* out of the way. *Pétanque* can be played almost anywhere but usually takes place in a village square or a park. Photographers loved to snap pictures of singer Yves Montand in the village of Saint-Paul-de-Vence as he played *pétanque* and then headed off to drink a *pastis*, a licorice-tasting drink composed of one part anise to five parts water. *Pétanque* and *pastis* evoke the South of France, slow, hot days, vacation. Neither is limited to the south, though. You see *pétanque* players in Parisian parks. As for *pastis*, on sizzling summer days at our country place near Paris, my mother-in-law, who loved a glass of the yellow-colored liquid, would position herself on the terrace, then ask me what was

a strictly rhetorical question: *"Un petit pastis, ma petite-fille?"*
She knew I couldn't resist.

Sharing the Good Life

The French share their hexagon, so called because of the
country's six-sided shape, with a bevy of foreigners who, even
if some of them can't stand the French, *love* France. No contradiction there: loving France and not the French, I've noticed, has never stopped anyone from buying a splendid castle,
an old farmhouse, or an elegant apartment in Paris. The sub-
title of one of the best books about cultural differences, *Sixty
Million Frenchmen Can't Be Wrong: Why We Love France
but Not the French,* reflects this sentiment. *The Wall Street
Journal,* not known for rampant Francophilia, opined that
after reading the tome "you may still think the French are arrogant, aloof and high-handed, but you will know why." Nice!
And I'll bet my last euro that some of the *WSJ*'s editors have
homes in France.

Nationalities vary in their predilections. The English, who
do not fear "wet," go absolutely everywhere, including to the
most remote and rainiest areas to buy country homes they fix
up. They either learn the language and blend in—or stick to
English, and themselves. The Americans basically stay with
what they know: Paris (mostly Saint-Germain, the seventh
district near the Eiffel Tower, the Île Saint-Louis, and the sixteenth district), Provence, the Riviera. The Dutch and Germans head for the south to find sun, where the Dutch—some
of whom really, really don't like the French—are reputed to
bring their own food with them. The Germans—well, the
Germans love France so much that after occupying it a couple of times, they came back to invest in real estate. That's

normal: the Germans even have a saying, "Happy as God in France." As for the Italians, they love old monuments and tend to buy expensive properties on the Île Saint-Louis. Eighty thousand apartments in Paris alone belong to foreigners (Russians, Middle Easterners, Italians, Americans) who visit their places a few times a year.

Why do they keep coming, year after year, marveling at the monuments, but also the lifestyle? As Gong Li, the Chinese film star, told *Le Figaro* in an article entitled "Why They Love France," "What the French have that is the most attractive, what they show the entire world, is that work is not the essential thing in life." (I told you!) She explained that in China everyone works too hard and too much—and that she thinks the Chinese should take a tip from the French. Interviewed at the Cannes Film Festival in 2011, Brad Pitt, when asked why he was renting a home in the south of France and why he had said he'd like to stay longer, replied, pointing at the azure skies and Mediterranean, "Just look around you. The joy of life is profound here."

Personally, I think the French are really nice to share their wondrous country and their lifestyle and *joie de vivre*. *Très sympathique.* But I've also got a theory: that Parisian non-smile is part of an elaborate ruse to keep foreigners from wanting to stay and find out just how good life in France is. That didn't discourage me and shouldn't discourage you!

Résidences Secondaires—A World Record

Foreigners visit or buy in France, but where do the French go on vacation? To foreign climes, to the beaches and mountains and the French countryside, and many, to their *résidence secondaire* or second home. *Second* home? Isn't one enough? I was introduced to this concept early on when my future husband invited me to his parents' place outside Paris near the town of Chartres, famous for its majestic Gothic cathedral. Like many Parisians, they had both an apartment in Paris and a country house. Two places, two lives. In the country, my in-laws knew all the neighbors, my father-in-law was a member of the city council; in short, the village wasn't some anonymous place they went to unwind. It was truly, and still is, especially for my sister-in-law, who is herself now a member of the city council, a profound part of their lives.

In this, they are very French. And the French—as usual—are an exception. With three million "second homes," they have twelve times as many as the Germans, and more than anyone else in the world. Their love of a second place dates back to the ancien régime, when nobles had a private home (*hôtel particulier*) in Paris in addition to their property in their native province.

The phenomenon became democratized in the seventies, and now, with the fast train and the euro and the thirty-five-hour workweek, the field is wide-open not only for the French but for their European neighbors as well. When you consider that the happy owners of second homes spend an average of only forty nights a year in them and a good amount of time and money on plumbing and other repairs, you might wonder why they do it. I remember my in-laws taking off each weekend. Like lambs going to slaughter, they'd get on the Paris ring road Saturday, in the worst of the traffic jams, when they could have left a day or two earlier. "Why on earth do they do that?" I asked Philippe. "Keeps them young," he replied. I rolled my eyes. But it was their life. They drove eighty kilometers to the second home, opened it up, did the grocery shopping, readied the house for the onslaught of family and friends, spent the entire weekend making and unmaking beds, graciously feeding a minimum of eight. Then on Monday after everyone left, they cleaned the house, closed it up again, and headed back to Paris. And that for fifty years. But, as my mother-in-law told me, "I would never want to live full-time in the country. Too boring."

I agree with her. But the French, especially the Parisians, like the idea of having a totally other life outside the city in a place where the kids can run around outside, take their bikes, be in a house rather than an apartment. They love those long meals with family and friends where everyone has more time and more space than in their Parisian apartments. They love the mixing of the generations with the grandparents and the grandchildren, uncles and aunts and cousins, all together. They love the way time takes on a different dimension, where everyone slows down, if only for a weekend.

When we'd go to the country with our children, we'd drop them off with their grandparents and then go shopping in the nearby village or take a walk or see friends, knowing the little ones were in good hands and had already forgotten our existence. My mother-in-law would offer to mend all the clothes that we'd managed to tear during the week, cook up delicious food, tell interminable stories that had a beginning but no end (no middle either as far as I could tell). On cold winter nights after dinner—a long dinner, I might add—we'd sit in front of the fireplace and perform a ritual: one of us would go to the cupboard to fetch thimble-size glasses into which my father-in-law would pour the pear alcohol that *we* had made. Yes! Every year in the fall we'd all get in the kitchen and cut up a thousand pounds of purchased Williams pears (no fruit trees on the property) in four, then put them one by one into two wooden barrels until spring, when the distiller would come along, all red-nosed because he'd been inhaling (or drinking) too much strong alcohol. With his copper still, he'd transform the pear juice into alcohol that would take every hair off the chest of even the hairiest man. But we love it and it's good. We either drink it straight or do what the French call a *canard* (a duck)—that's to say, take a sugar cube and dip it into the glass. Every time I uncork a bottle (by the way, a thousand pounds of pears only yields about thirty bottles), the smell of the wood in the fireplace and the country air and the happy faces of the friends and family in the room pop out and float in the air. Nostalgia's one benefit and there's another: our minimum-80-proof pear alcohol will kill any germ that comes near it. When we have colds, we don't go to the pharmacy. We heat milk, then pour it into a mug with some *poire* and sugar, and rush to the bed, where we swig the foolproof combination under the blankets (it can't work unless you are totally covered). It's the ultimate cure.

When I think back on our weekends at the country house, I wonder how my mother-in-law did it all, and with a smile. I remember us going off to bed while she'd be up watching TV or playing cards with one or more of the grandchildren. She did get a rest from her incessant activity of cooking and gardening and mending. On Sunday morning, my father-in-law, who adored her, got into the kitchen (he helped a lot, but cooking was not his thing), where he made the coffee and buttered slices of spice bread. He then arranged it all on a big platter and took her breakfast in bed. The thing is, she wasn't alone in that bed. Generally, from one to four grandchildren had jumped in with her, eagerly awaiting *their* breakfast in bed. Is there a medal for *joie de vivre*? I definitely think my in-laws deserved one.

I could write pages and pages of my memories of the parties and the dinners and the gatherings that took place in that house—and so could, I would imagine, any French person who has one. Those French second homes are often first in the heart.

Organizing Vacations—A Full-time Job

Other than the French educational system, which would require another book, the one most important cultural difference that struck me after moving to France was vacation time. Growing up in a normal American family where the outings we took were so few and far between that I still remember almost every detail of them today (the Rocky Mountains! Mount Vernon!), I could not conceive of what it is like to live in a country where *les vacances* return with almost frightening regularity. If you have children, you are faced with the dilemma of what to do with them not only for the long summer break but all during the school year—as there's a two-week vacation every eight weeks.

When our children were young, I discovered that French parents have this all worked out. If they have considerable means, the family flies off to some exotic location (the Bahamas, South Africa). If they don't, the children are sent to a *colonie de vacances* (vacation camp) or to the grandparents'. They rarely do what I did sometimes with our children, which was . . . have them stay at home with me. My French friends looked at me as if I were certifiably insane while I babbled on about "downtime" and "good for children to have nothing to do but dream." Right. Sure. Get organized, lady. Get them signed up for tennis camp, send them off to ski! Once I figured this out, I did from time to time try to fill their schedules, but I never rose to the heights of what the French manage to do, filling every single vacation with things to do and people to see.

Nothing's changed since my time, Allison Lightwine, the mother of two young daughters in French schools, told me. "Every year at the *crèche* [day care], they ask for summer holiday plans sometime in January or February so they can sort out staff holidays. I am always amazed that anyone would have their plans made so far in advance. I asked the *directrice* about this one year and she replied, '*Mais bien sûr, madame, c'est normal.*' So I am always the *pas normal* mom in the group as I give them our holiday dates sometime in May, if I'm lucky."

Indeed, vacation planning is such a full-time job that every agenda "made in France" features the official French school breaks in its front pages. My husband, who, as I said above, is not a typical Frenchman, came home one day grousing that every time he's trying to set a date for a business meeting, his staff members check their calendars for the school vacations.

The school vacations?

"But these are adults and they're talking about business!" I exclaimed.

"Sure, they're adults," he said, "but everything that happens in this country is conditioned by school vacations—after all, when your kids knock off, you might too."

The French may be disorganized during business meetings, but when it comes to organizing vacations, they're positively Prussian. And if you think that the economic crisis means "no vacations," just turn on the TV and listen to the traffic reports. Highways all across the nation are clogged with eager vacation-goers.

How do they manage? Search me!

Tykes and Tots Crisscrossing France in Silver Bullets

Orly Airport, a hot day in July. Philippe and I were there to pick up our five-year-old granddaughter, Judith, who was flying alone from Marseille to Paris on her first solo trip. I feel I should underscore what to me is so radical about the previous statement. For an American, or at least this American, it is unfathomable that a *five*-year-old would travel *alone*. At age five, I was still hiding in my mother's skirts, sitting on my dad's lap, and hoping I'd never ever have to leave the safety of home. But we're in France, and French kids "leave home" for day care as babies and never look back. (And everyone is happy!) But I digress. We waited anxiously as all the adult passengers filed out, then waited some more. Just when our anxiety level got so high we thought we'd call the police, we spied in the distance a group of tiny tots walking sedately and quietly, two by two, behind an adult leader. After we showed our identity papers and Judith had been released and handed over, I asked her how she felt about her adventure. Did she like the plane? Did she like the journey? Her answer came out fast and sincere: *"J'adore."* Once again, I had this feeling the French were onto something (that *joie de vivre*) no other country knows about so well.

When she was six, Judith's parents put her on the bullet train in Marseille to come to visit us once again. When she arrived in Paris, we met her at the designated car. This time she didn't need to tell me that she *adored* traveling alone—she was already an old hand.

French youngsters are used to these trips. Many divorced parents living on opposite sides of the country use the Unaccompanied Minor services. Sometimes you see sad scenes, such as the one I witnessed the day we took Judith to the station for her return trip. A father and uncle (I presumed) had bid good-bye to their son and nephew; all three were doing their best not to let their tears show. Finally the little boy got in the train, and then there was the interminable wait until the "All aboard." During it, the father would go off and cry while the uncle would tap on the window and smile at the boy, then the father would come back and the uncle would go somewhere and cry. I kept hoping that Judith wouldn't witness the scene so that she too wouldn't be upset. Fortunately she was busy being entertained by one of the young leaders hired by the train company to amuse and keep tabs on the traveling children (generally, no more than ten for each adult).

When July and August roll around and I see a plane in the sky or watch a train pull into the station, I think of all the thousands of little French children in those silver bullets criss-crossing France, singing songs, playing games, striking up con-versations with new friends, digging into their lunch bags, eyes bright with expectation at what's to come, whether it's the departure or the return.

August

August is a lovely month. All of France, it would seem, is *en vacances*. The national news opens with stories of happy va-cationers lounging on the sand, in their deck chairs, romping in the ocean, climbing mountains, visiting castles. No, what am I saying? It doesn't *open* with them. The stories of peo-ple's vacation joys and sorrows (basically traffic jams) oc-cupy 80 percent of the entire newscast.

Foreigners flock to Paris in August to visit the Louvre, the Eiffel Tower, Montmartre. The only thing missing? The Pari-sians, who have graciously left their city to the tourists. I told you, those French are nice.

There's one important thing to know about August. It is *the* month of the year not to be old, get sick, have a baby, or need a haircut. In August, many doctors and nurses are on vacation, and you can end up getting the replacement of the replacement of the replacement. Philippe's doctor, who is head of a cardiac prevention unit in a huge Paris hospital, told him he was simply closing it down for the month of August. It was, he affirmed, too complicated trying to figure out the vacation dates of the personnel.

Having a baby? Why not, if you don't mind the absence of your regular physician or midwife, both of whom are most surely tanning themselves on the beach. As for the hairdresser, one August I decided my hair was too long and needed a cut immediately. Fueled with purpose, I walked into a place I'd never been. Not a good idea in general, and especially not in August. (There's a reason to stick with the devil you know.) I got a beginner, a real dud who took me for a sheep. My hair was shorn. Fortunately, none of my Parisian friends saw me—they were all on vacation.

August is a lovely month. Just make sure you've made all your backup plans for food, hairdressers, and hospital care.

And now for an epilogue in which I cheerfully eat my own words. Shortly after writing about not being sick in August, I ended up in the emergency room of a Paris hospital. I was amazed at how quickly and efficiently I was taken in hand. After a night of observation and a battery of tests, I was sent home with the necessary medicine and a date for a checkup. When I arrived at the hospital, I was asked for my *carte vitale,* which shows I'm with French social security, and given forms for the reimbursement of ambulance and cab transport. The hospital bill (*very* low compared to one for similar services in the States) would come later. The focus was on my health, not on how I'd pay. That alone made me jump up and down with *joie de vivre.* (I did finally get the bill a few months later. It was for the astronomical sum of 14 euros. I don't even want to think what I would have paid for the hospital stay and treatment in the States. And you wonder why I sing the praises of the French health system?)

A French Paradox

As we near the end of these remarks on the unique world of work and play in France, I'll leave you with a mystery, a French paradox. Wouldn't you think that the French would be the happiest people in the world? All those paid vacations, in a country where the wining and dining and the scenery are superb, where "quality of life" comes first?

According to the annual BVA-Gallup poll, in 2010 France was the most pessimistic country in the world, or as Bruce Crumley wrote in *Time*, the French were "the sourpusses of the planet," with extremely low expectations of the economic year ahead.

Here's my entirely nonacademic theory on that. Anyone listening to the French news with its continual *misérabilisme* and doomsday reports would be depressed as well. I've often wondered how the editors and journalists who crank out the news, and who most undoubtedly lead good and satisfying lives, manage to focus on absolutely everything that is wretched and depressing. I tell you, after watching the nightly eight o'clock news on France's Channel 2, I want to immerse my head in a bucket of Bordeaux.

But on second thought, I think all that pessimism is a good sign. It's very Cartesian, in fact. The French know they've got it good—good roads, good schools, good health care. And so, logically, as they look around at the rest of the world, they begin to have doubts as to how long it can last.

They know that their Gallic fortress is besieged by the outside world, that what makes them French is threatened, that to join the world they'll have to give up a little, or a lot, of what makes them unique. Maybe, they think, they'll have to forgo those long vacations, those long meals, maybe they'll

Some Hanging Out Homework

As a practical exercise in hanging out without guilt, go to any café, inside or outside, depending on the weather. Choose it carefully for the view, the ambience, the music, who's there. This alone will take time. Order an espresso, which you can keep next to you for hours as you do whatever you're there to do: meet friends, write your novel, dream, watch people.

When you leave the café, stroll down the street. Check out the stores, but not necessarily to buy. Looking is important while hanging out. Throw away your to-do list. Wander. You'll find surprises. That's what hanging out without feeling guilty is all about. Serendipity.

If by chance you are in France on business, you can do the same thing, although you will have to show up at the office. Still, in a country where lunch at the desk is not the custom, you can take advantage of your break to forget about work. Just look at all those Frenchmen and Frenchwomen lunching at noon. It's as if during their time away from the office they magically shed every concern they had. Believe me—I speak French and can eavesdrop—their animated conversations are on just about every topic *but* work.

Now if you'll please excuse me, I've got some serious hanging out to do.

no longer be able to live in a society where the words of philosophers are listened to and respected, where attention to food and drink is of the utmost importance, where hanging out is an art form. No wonder they're popping pills. It's all too horrible to contemplate.

Not to worry, there's a long way to go before any of that happens.

Writing in *Le Figaro,* François Hauter, the same reporter who couldn't bear the sight of the summer hordes clogging up the highways, described the delectation of a train ride through the magnificent scenery of France. Watching the little villages spread out around their churches, each one more charming than the next, the reapers in the fields, the soft light streaming across the "vast sofa" of gentle hills, and even the faces of his fellow travelers, whose expressions softened as they contemplated the *beau paysage,* he is won over by the beauty of his own country. He concluded, "France is savored slowly, like a glass of very good wine. . . . She whispers to you: don't hope for the impossible, the only thing that counts is *joie de vivre.*"

Interview with Philippe

HWR: *So, when do you guys work?*

PHR: What a question. When we're not on vacation, of course.

HWR: *In your opinion, is the thirty-five-hour work-week a success?*

PHR: [Expletive deleted.]

HWR: *Is it true that in France you don't have to invite your boss to dinner and that it could even be seen as a faux pas? Why is that?*

PhR: Seeing each other in the office is highly sufficient for us both.

HWR: *How is it possible that the French can work less than anyone else, have so many strikes, as well as so many enviable vacations, and come out sixth in terms of world productivity?*

PhR: I told you, you have to be smart when you're small. You also have to be smart when you're lazy.

HWR: *You're French, but the least one can say is that you're not into vacations. How can you explain that?*

PhR: I can hardly believe you're asking me this question while we're on vacation.

HWR: *But you're retired. . . .*

PhR: Just because we're retired doesn't mean we should be deprived of vacation.

Dressing, Acting, and Pouting
Like a *Parisienne*

It's a fine day in Paris, and as I get ready to cross a busy street, a cyclist pulls up to the red light and stops. She wears no helmet—perhaps to reveal her stylish, well-cut, shiny auburn hair. She's wearing a waist-length, white jacket over a perfectly fitting T-shirt, a short pencil skirt, and spikes. (No, I am not hallucinating.) I don't know about you, but when I hop on a bike for a long ride in the city, I wouldn't wear white, I wouldn't wear a skirt, and I certainly wouldn't wear heels. Not our Parisienne. Sacrifice chic for comfort? Never! For her, elegance is innate, something she practices as an art form, every day, everywhere, whether it's going to the opéra or taking out the garbage. Her motto: "You never know whom you'll meet, so why not look spiffy?"

La Parisienne—Why So Special?

In my early days in France, I went on vacation to what was then Yugoslavia with a French-university student group based in Paris. It was an almost foolproof way to learn French by total immersion and an even better way to observe my French sisters. And how curious I was about those young *Parisiennes*. I couldn't figure out why we both had on tennis shoes but their footwear was fashionable and mine simply functional. I couldn't figure out how our group leader magically produced the most adorable little bikinis from her dusty backpack. I especially couldn't imagine how she could skip the nightly spaghetti dinner. We were all young and starving and ravenous. How could she forgo food? But she seemed to have low-cal substitutes (also magically produced) and announced that for nothing in the world would she sit down and get *fat* on her vacation. *What?* For me, *la petite Américaine,* absolutely everything she did and said was a revelation, a world apart. Unlike yours truly, who was starting to feel like Jabba the Hutt, she was watching what she wore and watching what she put in her mouth. And although I didn't notice it at the time, I'm quite sure she was watching people watching her. Otherwise, why go to all the bother? I'd like to say that she was also a barrel of laughs, but I won't go that far. I guess you can't have it all. (I distinctly remember hoping she'd get her wallet stolen or fall on her poker face. *Excusez-moi.* Just a bit of cattiness in the face of such perfection, and, hey, it's not my fault *les Parisiennes* inspire strong reactions.)

Because, trust me, even at her fair age, even as a student, even broke, she was a real *Parisienne.*

For most people, the *Parisienne* represents the quintessential Frenchwoman, willowy, feminine, self-confident, and sophisticated, with a *je ne sais quoi* that's indefinable. "The Parisian isn't just anyone. She's a certain kind of riffraff aristocrat, an ennobled—commoner," wrote Alain Schifres in *Les Parisiens. Parisiennes* have a way of inspiring such tributes, which they regally accept as their due.

This mystery is what makes her so special, so unique, so

aggravating. Even if you try to deconstruct the *Parisienne,* analyze her makeup or her hairdo or her outfit, you won't be able to take it all, apply it to yourself, and become a *Parisienne.* For the *Parisienne* is a combination of everything she puts together—in her own personal way. Unfortunately for all of us Americans who want guidelines and recipes and how-tos (if only I could dress the way she does, put makeup on the way she does, walk the way she does, pout the way she does, I could attain that look!), there's no rule book for how to become a *Parisienne.* And if there were, wouldn't that be too bad? We'd all look alike and there'd be no magic. I'm not saying you can't get the look. But unless you get the mind-set (*good luck!*), there will always be something missing. An American woman might, for example, get the dress, makeup, and hairstyle right, but she can't change her wide-open, trusting, smiling, innocent American face. I would have to undergo plastic surgery to get that closed, reserved Parisian look!

Our *Parisienne* is, of course, part myth. You only have to ride the metro or take the bus in Paris to conclude that she is not to be found everywhere. You can find *Parisiennes* in the metro, but the metro is definitely not filled with *Parisiennes.*

Color Me a Parisienne

So what is it that makes *une Parisienne*? What are her secrets?

We foreigners would love to find out—and this isn't recent. In the mid-nineteenth century, English writer and people observer Fanny Trollope wrote in *Paris and the Parisians,* "That manner, gait, and carriage—that expression of movement, and, if I may say so of limb . . . at once so remarkable and so impossible to imitate, is very singular. . . . It is in vain that all the women of the earth come crowding to this mart of elegance."

"I really wanted to be a *Parisienne,*" Franco-American, Barnard-educated singer Kay Bourgine told me. Kay, a statuesque, five-foot-eight-inch former house model for Patou, was raised in Boston but as a child often visited France, where, she recalls, she was "totally fascinated" by her maternal grandmother. "She was an elegant Parisian" who, Kay remembers, "dressed incredibly well"—in spite or because of a few eccentric or flamboyant outfits (a leopard-print jumpsuit, and what Kay called her "astronaut suit," a short jacket, narrow pants, pointy boots with black laces, and a wide-brimmed hat, all made of silver leather). "She never allowed her husband to see her not entirely 'put together' and told my sister she'd never get married if she kept wearing flannel pajamas," Kay recalled.

For Kay, the superiority of the Frenchwoman is that she knows how to make herself attractive even if she's not pretty. In the States, says Kay, if you're not good-looking, it's all over. In France, women don't necessarily have the raw material. "They may have mousy hair and bad teeth or skin that isn't clear, but they know what to do with what they have." She pauses. "There are a lot of very attractive American women—perhaps even more—but they don't know how to show themselves to their best advantage, and comfort is more important to them."

Not to mention that the American woman doesn't see it as her sacred mission to look smart in public. The *Parisienne,* never forget, has the most beautiful city in the world as the stage on which she struts. It's almost a duty to look good. Dressed in a leopard-spotted jacket, perfect-fitting gray pants, and stylish flats, one sophisticated Frenchwoman of a "certain age" noted, "I feel like a woman the minute I am in Paris. Being in a city with such beautiful architecture and surroundings makes one want to be beautiful, to shine, to please at any age. Paris creates an osmosis between itself and us."

A longtime American resident of Paris, the perfect portrait of the independent, liberated woman, told me almost the same thing in different words: "Living in Paris is like being in a room of wonderful furniture. You want to dress up and look good to fit in with the surroundings."

That's surely the reason that Parisian ladies on motorcycles or bikes look like no other cyclists you've ever seen on wheels. No "comfortable" attire for our *Parisienne,* and if you don't believe me, take a good look around you. Even with unflattering headgear, which they often don't bother to wear, the *Parisiennes* are smashing in their skirts and open-toe sandals or high heels.

At work Parisian women look like . . . women. One day I attended a late-afternoon inauguration of the new bathrooms, of all things, in a Paris shopping mall in the upscale sixteenth district. The architect and the marketing director could only have been *Parisiennes.* Here we were in an ugly basement listening to a presentation of the new *toilettes* by the architect, who was young and slim, outfitted in a well-cut black dress with a deep neckline, black heels, and one piece of jewelry, a big, black ring that sparkled as she moved her hands. Her attractive features were set off by her simply cut, shining, brown, shoulder-length hair and carefully applied, minimal makeup. The mall's young director of marketing, also slender (natch), wore a sleeveless green dress and beige heels. Both were professionals but neither felt a need to don a tailored suit. I would have worn the clothes they had on to a party, but this is Paris, and they feel free to wear whatever they want, as long as it's terribly chic. Which it most undeniably was.

The *Parisienne* isn't a personality-less clotheshorse, though.

On the contrary, her personality is what makes her a *Parisienne*. She's lively and cultured and critical—especially of other women—and frankly, says Hélène Lurçat, author of *Comment devenir une vraie Parisienne* (How to become a real Parisian), she also "cultivates a bitchy side in a way that's almost comical." I don't know about the comical, but bitchy, yes. In addition, she's a complainer, a moaner and groaner, opine two French journalists, Layla Demay and Laure Watrin, in their book, *Une vie de Pintade à Paris*.

The writers depict the *Parisienne* as she is, with her good sides and her bad (weak points: she bites her nails, loves to eat, but has an inordinate distaste for exercise, and she loves to criticize). Among the *Parisienne*'s good points: her understated elegance. *Understated* is the word. The Frenchwoman's credo seems to be "never overdo it." In Italy, wrote Richard Gianorio in *Le Figaro,* "women are afraid of not doing enough, where in France women are afraid of doing too much." Italian women love red lips, sunglasses from sunrise, hair done even on windy days . . . and "being negligent remains a crime of *lèse-séduction*."

If you ever watch French TV, check out the anchorwomen, and you'll see that Frenchwomen, even those most in view, have no problem not being perfectly coiffed or *sans* lipstick. Yet, as French designer Vanessa Bruno, whose mother is Danish and father is Italian, told *Grazia* magazine, "The Parisian, even in her negligence, will retain a certain chic. . . . The Parisian is sophisticated but relaxed. She has a good base of clothes, a pretty jacket, dresses, and perfect blouses."

If one thing reveals a real *Parisienne,* it's her way of describing herself. Vanessa Bruno, says, for example, that the *Parisienne* doesn't "wear" a dress. She "incarnates" it. A tad over-the-top? That's what happens when a *Parisienne* drops her guard and pays homage to another *Parisienne*.

What Is It About Black?

If a little green man from Mars descended on Paris at any time of the year, he might think he'd landed in a giant cemetery.

New Yorkers tell me they think black is much more prevalent in their city. One even told me she thought that by comparison, Parisians dress brightly. Maybe my New York friends weren't here in the winter, when everything looks black as night—black, rain-spattered pavement, stark, black trees, and Parisians in black boots and black coats.

Many years ago my mother came to stay in Paris for a few months. An elegant woman who dressed with care, she excitedly packed her bags with some recent purchases for her trip, including a bright red coat that turned out to be her cross to bear in the city of supposed light. "Why did I let myself get talked into this?" she would wonder aloud, as she glanced around to see that she was absolutely the only person within five kilometers wearing anything other than *noir*. (She really did get talked into it, something unusual for her, as in addition she never wore red. Apparently the Minneapolis salesperson's idea of Paris was brighter than the reality.)

What is it that the *Parisiennes* have about black? In winter, the black coat, the black skirt or slacks, the black shoes or boots. In spring, summer, and fall, they don black as well. It's true that even when the sun deigns to shine in this northern climate, there's something about Paris (maybe the grime in the metro?) that doesn't click with white.

Even when designers from Marc Jacobs to Prada to Jil Sander come out with flashy colors, real people know it's nothing to get excited about. A *Parisienne* might buy herself a scarf or sweater or jacket in the color of the season to accentuate the black, but that's about as far as it will go. Paris swims in a sea of black.

Commenting on the colorful 2011 spring collections that flaunted "leaf green" and "banana yellow" among others, Suzy Menkes, the longtime fashion writer for the *International Herald Tribune,* wryly asked two questions: "Why orange? Why now?" She seemed skeptical that these happy hues would hit the streets, concluding that fashion-conscious Parisians would adopt them solely for their handbags or other accessories. "It is wise to remember," she wrote, "that, like fireworks against a night sky, bright shades look great against black."

Black would indeed seem to be the best bet. American fashion writer and Paris resident Tina Isaac ticked off a list of logical reasons for the enduring popularity of black in the following long, breathless sentence: "Black is timeless, a no-brainer, works in all situations, day to night, never appears overdressed or out of place or in bad taste, does not need (much) accessorizing, does not need to be expensive (or rather, if inexpensive does not look cheap), is slimming, lends an air of sophistication and intelligence (thank you Chanel and Audrey), regardless of whether it's deserved, and for all those reasons I would say it's kind of the spirit of Paris, sartorialized."

If you want to gaze at the little black dress in a magical setting, walk through the arcades of the Jardins du Palais-Royal and check out the Little Black Dress shop owned by Didier Ludot, a vintage-clothes expert. Didier was in Moscow the day I showed up, so I sat down in the red-carpeted boutique and talked to his knowledgeable assistant Dominique Fallecker, who—dressed in black—reminded me, "Before Chanel no one but widows and maids wore black dresses. Chanel succeeded in doing something revolutionary. Black and the black dress became the emblem of the Parisian." For Dominique, black has many advantages, one of which is that the color varies according to the fabric. And black is versatile. "Parisians love the little black dress because they can dress it up or dress it down, wear it with flats in the morning and heels in the evening." And for *la Parisienne,* says Fallecker, black is ideal, as she has her own personality and is able to "do something wonderful with nothing." A real *Parisienne,* she says, "will buy an inexpensive but well-cut dress with horrible buttons—and change the buttons."

Advice from Two Parisiennes

Former model, fashion designer, and *Parisienne extraordinaire* Inès de la Fressange is typical of many *Parisiennes* in that she wasn't born in Paris and isn't even wholly French. Inès, who is the new face of L'Oréal and the ambassadress of the Roger Vivier haute-couture shoe brand, was born in Saint-Tropez to a South American mother. In her bestselling guide, *La Parisienne* (translated into English), you'll quickly catch on that being a *Parisienne* is not as easy as it looks—and that most of being a *Parisienne* requires less, not more.

In particular, I loved her advice on looking younger: don't wear neon colors or real fur, which, she says, make you look ten years older. Since I own no real fur and don't like flashy colors, I guess I'm okay on those points. However, there's one item Inès says never never never never to wear because you'll look old and unstylish, and that's a shawl. I *love* shawls, stoles, wraps. Well, the French are all for differing, so on that one we diverge. Sorry, Inès.

I also differed—initially—with a Parisian makeover expert I interviewed. I didn't realize that while I sat there, conscientiously taking notes, she was sizing me up. "You know, you really shouldn't wear dangling earrings like that," she said, looking me in the eye. "They're not your style." I started to protest but thought it might be more interesting to see what else she had to say. I had the feeling I was to become her personal project. "What movies have you seen lately?" she asked, and was disappointed I hadn't seen much of anything recent. "You've got to be on top of what's new!" she exclaimed. By the time I left, she'd made a list of all the films and theater performances I should see plus all the new books I should read. But her parting words of advice weren't about activities but a personal goal I and all *Parisiennes* worth their Louboutins should have when getting dressed to go out. "Make them jealous," she exclaimed, "them" clearly being "other women." I admit I was horrified, but the comment has remained with me to this day. "Make them jealous"? It sounded so petty, so trifling, so little-girl competitive. I imagined myself in front of my mirror changing outfits to see which one would succeed in making "them" envious.

And you know what? Even though I didn't appreciate the way she phrased it, I discovered that if I simply asked myself if the way I looked would make anyone jealous and the answer was yes, I'd be well dressed. (Ordinary does not inspire envy.) I also discovered that most Frenchwomen *do* have that goal: look better than every other woman in the room.

The Parisienne Dragon

To say that *les Parisiennes* do not always have the best interest of their "sisters" at heart is an understatement. These tough cookies could gobble you up for breakfast, lunch, and dinner, plus the afternoon *goûter*. Unlike with their New York counterparts, though, the steel is concealed underneath layers of femininity and softness. But watch out. If they show their claws, you're in for it. They're examining your every move, how you talk, how you walk, how you eat, how you dress. And will comment on it the minute you leave the room. As the authors of *Une vie de Pintade à Paris* point out, *Parisiennes* love to find fault with everything and everyone, starting with each other.

One of the reasons they look so good is that they spend so much time analyzing women who don't. But says savvy fashion coach Susan Sommers, "There's no appreciation of someone else's looking fabulous." She told me about walking down a Paris street one day. Crossing her path was a *Parisienne* who gave her a look of "pure unadulterated hatred," she said. "That's when I knew I looked great and had been accepted." Sommers continued, "Another French secret is that Frenchwomen view every woman as their competitor. You don't get this in the States, mainly because the competition among American women takes place in the world of work."

Sommers's comment shed new light on what to me has always been a mystery, the rarity of woman-to-woman compliments in France. For years I'd felt I was doing something wrong, but in fact I was probably doing things too right. "Frenchwomen," says Sommers, "are very grudging in their compliments unless they know you well." Like about two hundred years of well? In the interim, I'll rely on my American friends for compliments. That's what I was doing anyway, but at least now I know why. (Still, sometimes with some particularly buttoned-up Frenchwomen, I want to shout, "It won't kill you to give a compliment!" (Of course, maybe it will. . . .) But I shouldn't complain. Philippe gives me compliments all the time, and one Frenchwoman, my mother-in-law, never failed to admire either my haircut or the brooch I had chosen or the color of my lipstick. *Merci, ma belle-mère!*

Too High Maintenance?

During an interview, I asked a young Parisian what he thought about *les Parisiennes*—and almost wished I hadn't. We were on high barstools and I thought he was going to fall off his as he passionately listed all the reasons that neither he nor his friends take out Parisian women. They are obsessed with thin-ness, for starters, he told me, specifying, "They have skinny bodies with the appearance of a soul inside" (ouch). Empty? I repeated. Really? Backing down, he qualified his comments: "They're no fun. Other girls are more open-minded, up for new things. None of my friends is in a relationship with a Pa-risian girl. It's normal. Anyone who's been lucky enough to travel realizes how boring Parisian women are—they're prob-ably the dullest women in the world." I got the impression the fellow may have been emerging from a bad love affair with one of the thin, tedious *Parisiennes* he was describing.

Another young Parisian, though less emphatic and accu-satory, gave me basically the same story: "I tend to run away from *Parisiennes*. They are too perfect. It's fishy." He laughed. "They're smart, well dressed, lovely to look at, they exercise [he was referring to the ones he saw running around the Parc Monceau in the upscale seventeenth arrondissement], they're doing well professionally. It's intimidating." He hesitated, searching for a flaw. Finally he found it: "They look very self-assured but I think it's a façade." But, he reflected, "Even if it's a façade, it remains intimidating." The final blow, he con-cluded, is that "in any case they're always taken."

Sounds high maintenance to me. I would imagine that even getting a *Parisienne* to smile, let alone laugh, might take years. Wanting to get to the bottom of why *Parisiennes* don't laugh, crack up, split their guts, hee-haw, or even make a stab at the *Mona Lisa* look, I popped the question over coffee to *Parisienne* expert Hélène Lurçat. Her answer came in a split second: "They don't smile because they're not natural. They have to be in control. If they smiled, it would take away the mystery." (When I don't smile, I don't look mysterious; I just look glum—how do they do it?)

Hélène fears for young *Parisiennes,* who, she says, spend more time thinking about their clothes and how they look and wondering why they can't find a boyfriend than learning fundamentals such as ... how to cook. "I may be old-fashioned," muses this divorced Parisian mother of three daughters, "but if these girls would learn how to make a steak and french fries for their guy, they'd keep him. It's a gift that you make to a man." She confesses that she's with an Italian who claims he never thought he'd go out with a *Parisienne.* He ended up doing so, but, she said straightforwardly, it's because "he loves to eat and I know how to cook." In fact, she remarked, looking at her watch, "I'd better go get dinner on the table."

Some men feel they understand the *Parisiennes.* Not only do the *Parisiennes* not threaten or exasperate them, they find that underneath their distant exterior they are "touching" or "fun." One of them is Laurent Fléchaire, a filmmaker and self-described "provincial" who came from Orléans to live in Paris at the age of twenty-nine and has never regretted it. For Laurent, who made an incisive and entertaining film on *les Parisiennes* for French TV, Parisian women are anything but static, intimidating, or dull. They're "always moving, always trying to be something."

But are they all that different from women in the provinces? I asked. He laughed out loud. "And how. Time stops in the provinces. Women get married, settle down. No one's going anywhere."

For Laurent, *les Parisiennes* are playing a game because they are fragile. And they never stop trying: "The lady who runs the newspaper kiosk near my apartment could be my mother or even my grandmother, but she is always elegant. Given our difference in age, I'm not interested, but I like the fact that she makes this effort."

They do make the effort, but there's a price to pay. One Frenchman ventured to say that if so many *Parisiennes* are single, it's because although they're well dressed, they're "never natural." They're elegant, for sure, he says, but complicated and "hard to live with." Some men like that. One Frenchman, an ardent *Parisienne* admirer, observed, "The American woman finds you wonderful right away, whereas it's harder with *la Parisienne*"—and clearly he preferred the difficulty.

He did—but not all do. Many Frenchmen are attracted to American women because they *aren't* difficult or complicated. I belong to an association of American women founded in 1961 by an American woman who saw the need for Americans to get together to work on common concerns about voting, U.S. taxes, maintaining U.S. citizenship, and bilingual education. These six hundred women are the divorced or still-married wives or partners of Frenchmen, which goes to prove that at least six hundred Frenchmen opted for an American wife rather than a French one. Whoever would have thought . . .

Author Sanche de Gramont, who took the American name Ted Morgan and is a naturalized American, was one of those Frenchmen who married an American. Perhaps because he observed that "while admiring the genius of the Frenchwoman in her various mutations . . . I find that the common denominator of all these ladies is that they ask a great deal, and that other women are more gracious and natural because they are less demanding." Thanks, Sanche/Ted, for helping me cast away my inferiority complex (you know, the bull in the china shop, the lady who can never be thin enough or pout enough). The next time I stand next to one of those perfectly slender and perfectly garbed *Parisiennes*, I'll keep those complimentary comments in mind. There's hope for all of us American women in Paris!

Different Types of Parisiennes

Though *les Parisiennes* may all look the same to you, universally weedy and well put together, the universal Parisian type has many subgroups, easily recognizable when you get the hang of it. Many have attempted to typecast *les Parisiennes,* either by neighborhood or by social class. Laurent Fléchaire did a geographical tour of Paris, classifying his *Parisiennes* into the mythical *Parisiennes* of the Latin Quarter; the unselfconscious and fun, drink-beer-in-a-plastic-cup *Parisiennes* found in the northeast of Paris; the inaccessible *Parisiennes* in *les beaux quartiers;* and finally, the wives and mothers pushing prams in the south of the capital in what he's baptized the "Maclaren belt," referring to the name of the baby buggy. Of course there's no one criterion, and, as he says, if you're in the first, second, and third arrondissements, you'll probably see all these types because those are places everyone passes through.

I made my own list, a combination of my own observations and the various descriptions I've read—and there are tons of books because Parisians love nothing better than to read about other Parisians. Of course this is just for fun. It would be folly to think you'll find carbon copies of these types in their assigned neighborhoods, although you're more likely to find a BCBG in Passy than at the Bastille, for sure.

One thing the *Parisiennes* have in common is that it's hard to drag them away from their *quartier.* My Left Bank *Parisienne* friends break out in hives at the thought of crossing the Seine to the Right Bank, and my Right Bank friends are aghast at the idea of traveling to the Left Bank. And let's not even talk about a trek to the suburbs. One Parisian friend, whose offices moved to Neuilly, a wealthy western suburb, described the new location and the arduous (to her) trip to it (even though it's on the number one metro line) with more than a tinge of Parisian condescension. "So far away, so utterly dull," she complained. You'd never guess she was referring to a beautiful, upscale, sought-after residential haven surrounded by the verdant Bois de Boulogne. But that's highly Parisian—people tend to stick to their own neighborhoods, bars, and boutiques. *C'est comme ça.*

Following are a few categories of *Parisiennes*.

BCBG (Bon Chic Bon Genre)

This *Parisienne* lives in the upscale neighborhoods of the sixteenth and parts of the seventh and fifteenth. So many of them are found in the tony western enclaves of Neuilly, Auteuil, and Passy that they have been dubbed "NAPs." A BCBG will wear her Hermès scarf with a pearl necklace. Conservative and proper, the BCBG would rather die than wear clinging clothes or flashy colors. Vulgar!

The Intellectual

In Saint-Germain-des-Prés, you'll find the Left Bank type, generally a university professor or journalist or someone working in publishing. Her look is chic casual, but she's more original than the BCBG. She's not eccentric, though, because she never goes too far. "There's no greater sin in Saint-Germain-des-Prés than overdressing," comments a writer friend who's a longtime resident of the neighborhood.

"L'artiste"

Her territory? The artsy east end of Paris, the place where new things are happening. The *"artiste"* loves an original look and mixes and matches pieces she picks up from secondhand stores or the latest designers. One thing is sure: this spontaneous, loosened-up Parisian wouldn't be caught dead in a BCBG suit—or in the stuffy sixteenth arrondissement.

Showbiz, Jet Set, Nouveau Riche

Lives in Neuilly or the eighth or sixteenth, but unlike the proper BCBG adores flashy, pricey clothing and sporting handbags and T-shirts with the designer's name splashed all over them. Spends holidays in Deauville with all the other *nouveaux riches.* Does her errands and trucks her kids around in one of those outrageously huge SUVs—for a safari *en ville?* Bawls *you* out if she's double-parked and has penned you in. Hair is dyed blond. I am well acquainted with this type of *Parisienne,* as when living in the sixteenth and Neuilly I have many a time been imprisoned in my humble *automobile* while they ran their errands. Fascinating, but definitely not endearing.

An American friend who's a fashion journalist in Paris told me she attended a children's party organized at the Hôtel Meurice and "felt like a fish out of water" next to the Parisian mothers with their Hermès bags, skinny jeans, faux-rhinestone appliqués, and expensive V-neck, cashmere sweaters. They wore their hair in ponytails and sported no makeup. "The look was sloppy chic," she said. "If I dressed that way, I'd just look sloppy."

The combination of the expensive bags along with hair up in a ponytail and no makeup is "so French," she finds. "In France they don't pull out the big artillery because they have such a problem with money and showing off wealth. Even wearing a huge diamond solitaire here is *nouveau riche*—the exception is when it's an heirloom piece."

The Concierge and the Aristocrat

On opposite sides of the social scale, the concierge and the aristocrat are real *Parisiennes.* The concierge is no fashion plate but there's nothing more *parisienne* than a *gardienne* with her trademark cheekiness and impertinence. Unfortunately this species is being fast replaced by entry phones or door codes. Too bad. She, like the aristocrat, is a real character with a strong personality. The aristocrat may be "on top" with riches, the concierge "on the bottom" with next to none, but they're similar in that each does and says exactly what she likes in a refreshing, unpolitically correct, unconventional way.

If you live in an affluent neighborhood, you may meet an artistocrat, a *baronne* or *comtesse* or *marquise.* My downstairs neighbor in Neuilly was a *marquise,* a fact I discovered by accident. My preconception of the "aristos" as snobs was turned on its head by this simple, elegant, reserved, but kind lady in her nineties. She always inquired politely after my children and never complained about their noise, even when one or the other would fall out of bed, making a loud thump on his floor, which was the ceiling of her bedroom. This *Parisienne* was a model of impeccable manners, good humor, *savoir-vivre,* and *savoir-faire.* She was the only *Parisienne* I have ever met whom everyone, from the concierge to the pharmacist to all the neighbors, universally admired. This simply doesn't happen in Paris.

A Few Things Parisiennes Know About Dressing

In terms of your "look," which the French pronounce *loooook,* here are a few things to consider should you wish to pass for a *Parisienne*—or at least not look too much like the foreigner you are.

The French Foot Fetish

La Parisienne spends inordinate time finding exactly the right footwear. Shoes and the handbag (but not matching) are probably the two most essential elements in her wardrobe. My friend and yoga teacher, Madeleine Volpelier, a stylish *Parisienne,* affirms that for her "a beautiful pair of shoes is the proof of elegance." It's good to know about this French foot fetish. A newly arrived American friend who was planning a party in Paris on a Japanese theme told me that when her guests arrived, she intended to have them take off their shoes at the door. "Did you tell them?" I asked. When she told me she hadn't, I suggested she do—pronto. I didn't even want to think about a bunch of fashionable *Parisiennes* and *Parisiens* being asked to decompose their carefully put-together outfits, of which the shoes play an essential role. And I certainly couldn't imagine them walking around barefoot. She followed my advice and told me she was glad she did. They all came in their fancy footwear, which they shed at the door. They then put on the equally fancy slippers they had brought with them to wear inside. They had saved "face" (or would that be "foot"?).

The Comfort-Versus-Glamour Issue

For *Parisiennes,* there *is* no issue. They simply never let comfort get in the way of glamour. Their Louboutin spikes may be killing their feet, they may be freezing in their low-cut top, their earrings may be pinching their lobes, but they never show their pain. (French secret: I always wondered about how these Frenchwomen wore such thin tops in winter until a French friend one day told me she had on *très sexy* warm-but-lightweight silk underwear.) Comfort versus glamour is not restricted to young, tall, anorexic models. More years ago than I'd like to tell, I had an operation at a French hospital. I was a young thing then, in a room with two women who were the age I am now (let's not be coy—I was in my twenties and they were in their early sixties). And who looked better than whom? My sexagenarian French roommates had on dainty, sleeveless nightgowns as opposed to my long-sleeved, grandmotherly flannel pajamas. I was unnerved and appalled. It had never occurred to me that one didn't dress for *comfort,* especially in a hospital. Oh, I looked sooooo bad. That, I believe, was my first glimpse into the ways of French-women. Look your best, even when "a certain age," even when lying on a hospital bed.

The Art of Accessorizing

The little, basic black dress or pants suit needs accessories the way plants need water. But how do those Parisians do it? Is accessorizing an art? Is there a secret? "From my French boyfriends, I learned how to unaccessorize," American fashion designer Joyce Kraus told me. "From their critical assessment—'This looks good, but let's take this other thing off'—I learned how to wear one or two great pieces, the great shoes *or* the brooch *or* the terrific watch but not all of them together. Frenchwomen know how not to look like a Christmas tree," she said. They favor one remarkable piece over a variety of cheap trinkets and have firmly in mind Coco Chanel's stunningly sound advice on accessories: always take one thing off before leaving the house. Less is more!

Dressing Well All the Time

This one is capital. The *Parisienne* dresses well *all the time.* In the States, we are much dressier when we get decked out for a formal occasion, but when we're at home, we're casual—very casual. The Parisian woman might not get as dressed up for the dinner party (because she already looks great); on the other hand, even if she's going to the market to shop, she'll still put on a pair of pretty earrings or a special scarf. In all situations, she'll make an effort to look as good as she can (following the axiom "you never know whom you'll meet"). I once knew a much older woman in the country (as in *the middle of nowhere*) who would not go out of her house without makeup and spike heels. Sometimes it seemed a bit much, but she explained that making that effort made her feel good. Once, when going out to a dinner party, I'd thrown on a baggy sweater, old slacks, and well-worn flats because I wasn't inspired. I didn't get far because my ever-vigilant better half nixed my plans. On another occasion, I started to go to a museum in tennis shoes and gym pants. No *way*. For my French husband, not making the extra effort is a lack of consideration for other people. His motto is "The worse you feel, the better you should look," an idea I find *pas mal* (the French equivalent of "great"). It follows that one reason Frenchwomen are so chic is because Frenchmen are watching. They care! Helena Petaisto, the permanent correspondent for a Finnish TV station in Paris, wrote that she often wondered what the motivation for the Frenchwoman's elegance was and came up with her own explanation: "More than anywhere else, [French] men compensate women's efforts to be elegant." Maybe that's why a *Parisienne* is so upset when no one's looking. If no one's looking, it means no one cares.

Mixing It Up

Forget the "total look." Frenchwomen love to mix and match. Pascale Camart, womenswear buying manager for the Galeries Lafayette, told me that having designer labels next to ordinary ones on the same floor was "on purpose. The Frenchwoman likes to put different things together." The *Parisienne,* she says, doesn't buy evening dresses. She sticks with basics and then finds the one distinctive jacket or scarf or top that will make the ensemble a knockout. For Inès de la Fressange, one of the cardinal rules of dressing is knowing how to combine the expensive and the inexpensive, the old and the new, the Monoprix T-shirt and the bracelet from a jeweler. The *Parisienne,* she declares, eschews "the outfit." *Parisienne* image consultant Anne-Marie Lecordier lauds her fellow *Parisiennes* for their ability to make original combinations, "mixing and appropriating a style," instead of blindly following fashion. "The *Parisienne*," she says, "has a sense of elegance that is very special." For Anne-Marie, if the elegantly offbeat Sandro and the feminine, urban, and creative Maje stores are so popular with her clients, it's because they reflect what's current, as does Zara, whose inexpensive prices and fast turnaround allow her clients to come up with a Céline, Prada, or Chloé look that's affordable.

All of the above sounds rather formidable, *n'est-ce pas?* Do all the women in Paris spend their time shopping, dress up before buying their baguette, and possess self-confidence in spades? It can't be true. You're right. It can't. In Paris you'll find plenty of women who are far from fashion plates. You'll find women who have no sense of style at all and who rely on magazines to tell them how to dress. You can find frumpy. But only in Paris can you also find that unique creature, the *Parisienne*, who stands out in the crowd with her inimitable self-created, self-possessed look.

It's a hard act to follow, and some foreign women don't want to be a *Parisienne*. Many live in Paris for years but never acquire that *je ne sais quoi* because they don't have it and never will or they don't want to work at it or they find it futile. One gaspingly beautiful, statuesque, and graceful American woman told me that it was "really painful" for her to try to fit into an environment where seduction is life-or-death. Her advice: "You can emulate being a *Parisienne*, but I would suggest simply remaining who you are."

Sound counsel, but is there any hope for all of us non-Frenchwomen and non-*Parisiennes* who would like to become *Parisiennes* if only *un tout petit peu?* Sure, there is. All we've got to do is observe and imitate them (for about a hundred years). We'll know we've succeeded when we walk

into a room full of *Parisiennes* and become the focus of attention and envy. Remember the advice of my Parisian makeover lady: make them jealous!

If you succeed, you're on your way.

La Parisienne: *What Makes Her Special?*
She's :

Slender: Every foreigner who travels to Paris asks the
same question: How do the *Parisiennes* get and stay so
slim? For one thing, the *Parisiennes* could have invented
Weight Watchers if only in the sense of "watching." *Vigi-
lant* would describe their behavior. They may enjoy a
wonderful meal (or two or three) on the weekend, but for
lunch during the week they order big salads, skip the
bread, and even ask for the dressing on the side. They refuse dessert and opt for a tiny but strong espresso. They
think the gym is depressing but walk miles in the metro
to get to work (does wonders for the figure), and they
drive like maniacs. All that adrenaline burns calories.

Sensual: Perfume, bubble-bath oils, fine-smelling soaps,
facials, massages, charming lingerie—no matter whether
the *Parisienne*'s budget is Monoprix or the rue Fau-
bourg Saint-Honoré, all *Parisiennes* are vitally interested
in whatever makes them look and smell and feel good.
Would a *Parisienne* reject a pair of heels as high as stilts
simply because she risks permanent sciatica? *Mais non.*
Does she treasure alluring bras and silk nighties? You
bet. What's unseen is as important as what's seen (and

of course our *Parisienne* hopes her carefully chosen lingerie *will* get seen).

Subtle (Cattiness Elevated to an Art Form): You may manage to look like a perfect *Parisienne (formidable!)*, but to be a real *Parisienne,* you'll still have to learn *Parisienne*-speak. A *Parisienne* can insult you without your ever knowing it. Two weeks later you suddenly understand what the comment was all about and where the arrow was pointed; three weeks later you figure out your response. Too late. You have to be on the ball to deal with a *Parisienne.* Here's an example of an exchange at my local *boulangerie*:

Very stylish lady talking to herself: "Now, what was it I wanted?"

Salesgirl (a tad cheeky): "If you don't know, I can't tell you."

Very stylish lady in a condescending tone with a glacial stare: "You'd better believe you can't."

The subtlety in that exchange came from the *change of tone of voice.* This is why *Parisienne*-speak is hard to imitate. But not to fret. Even if your French isn't up to snuff, you can practice the scowl of displeasure, yes, of haughtiness, in the mirror and come off looking, if not sounding, like a real *Parisienne.* And when in doubt, pout.

Self-Confident: The *Parisienne* has perfected the art of taking disparate items and creating harmony—which takes bags and buckets of self-confidence as the result can be a huge success or a total disaster. Writes fashion

(continued)

editor/journalist Susan Sommers in her book *French Chic: How to Dress Like a Frenchwoman,* "Frenchwomen have something special. They're feminine, sure of themselves, and seem to delight in breaking all the fashion rules, yet making it all work."

At one afternoon tea party in Paris, I focused my attention on a lively Frenchwoman of an indeterminate age. She was dressed in a mixture of classic and off-the-wall: high-heeled, black-and-white tennis shoes, short, white socks with ruffled tops, classic black pants topped by a well-cut, short, cream-colored vest with black-lined pockets trimmed with gold and pearl buttons. On it she wore a big gold brooch studded with black pearls. It was obviously an outfit she had taken great care to assemble, but she wore it as if it were a second skin. After my initial inspection, I forgot about her getup. But first impressions count, and she'd certainly made hers.

That Parisian "look" and personal style is a result of our *Parisienne*'s self-scrutiny. In the words of one *Parisienne* admirer, "The Parisian woman is conformist but likes to have that little something that makes her stand out from everyone else." She's in the habit of frank self-appraisal. What can I emphasize and what can I hide? Many years ago a French colleague asked me if I thought she looked better in pants or skirts. I had given no thought to the matter—but she obviously had. I wasn't much help to her then, but I certainly would be now—continued exposure to this kind of no-holds-barred self-evaluation has rubbed off.

Why is the *Parisienne* so interested in looking at herself? To see how she looks to others! Paris is a one huge scope-out scene. The street, the office, the bakery, is theater, a permanent festival, and if she's out in the world and no one looks *her* way, it's a bad day indeed. One Parisian plastic surgeon, whose life is devoted to beauty, told me that he admires *la Parisienne* and the complicated games she plays. "The Parisian woman needs to check out men, hoping they're checking her out at the same time—without either of them being too obvious." (Never forget that Parisian women are checking out their fellow *parisienne* rivals as well. Beware!)

What is the *Parisienne*'s secret? For one adept *Parisienne* watcher and amateur, it's simple: "She is convinced that she is the most elegant woman around—even if she clearly isn't. You can see she thinks she's special in the way she moves and walks and dresses." In other words, other women may have prettier hair or skin, a better figure, more expensive and better clothes, but the *Parisienne* will beat her every time solely because *in her head* she's the best. She thinks she is, and therefore she is. Kind of a "I think, therefore I am." Very French, *n'est-ce pas?*

Le Parisien

I can't write about *la Parisienne* without writing about Parisians in general. They truly are a separate species. The thing Parisians most love to do is make fun of themselves, criticize themselves, recount how horrible and how special they are. (They're quite taken with themselves, those

(continued)

Parisians.) There's a cottage industry of books doing this, but two I particularly like are Olivier Magny's *Dessine-moi un Parisien* (Stuff Parisians like) and Jean-Laurent Cassely's *Paris: Manuel de survie* (Paris survivor's manual). Both are light and humorous, both scrutinize our Parisian, observing and explaining various Parisian mysteries such as why they wear black, why they love sushi, why they want to be buried in the Père Lachaise Cemetery, why they not only don't smile but sulk (*faire la gueule*).

In Magny's chapter "The Americans" he explains that the inability to smile is one of the prime components of the Parisian's personality. Another facet of the Parisian's personality is that he loves to talk about *les Américains*. The Parisian is fascinated by *l'Américain* and especially his or her aptitude to be "immediately cordial and enthusiastic," which makes our Parisian go around the bend. "Cordiality, enthusiasm, are very American qualities," writes Magny. "In Paris," he continues, his tongue firmly in his cheek, "these character traits are discreet symptoms of a form of intellectual degeneration, the proof of an acute absence of refinement. A capital sin!" (That's why every time I smile in Paris, Parisians look at me with wonder or pity. At least you can tell I'm not a *Parisienne*.) A *Parisienne* can *not* smile spontaneously. It is not written into the script. Writes Cassely in his send-up of Parisians, if the Parisian simply doesn't smile, *la Parisienne* goes even further. She pouts. On purpose. That's *definitely* in the script. "She excels," he declares, "in the art of the nonchalant pout showing her supreme indifference."

Now, if you're feeling that the Parisian scowl is directed against you, the foreigner, think again. It is directed against *all humanity*. The French provincial who gets off the train at the Gare Montparnasse, the Japanese businessman landing in Roissy, even groups of schoolchildren visiting museums—no one will get a smile out of the Parisian, affirms Cassely. Why? The Parisian, he informs us, is "entirely preoccupied by himself" so a smile coming his way is tantamount to an insult. "He feels only disdain for your *joie de vivre*. . . . Never forget that the smile is a vulgar, almost obscene intrusion, into the intimate sphere of the Parisian."

Other than not smile, what do Parisians do? For one thing, they'd probably laugh at my description of the traditional French dinner party. A *branché* (trendy) Parisian would probably find it boring, preferring tapas or brunch or hamburgers, which are thought to be "cool" these days, although the Parisian will attend any function where there are what he or she calls "a people."

Those last two words are, of course, a mistake in English. One of the distinguishing marks of the Parisian, although he may look askance at the American smile, is that he positively worships English words, sprinkling them into almost every phrase and generally misusing or mispronouncing them. The result? Hilarious or weird combinations such as *a people* for "celebrities," *sweetshirt* for "sweatshirt," and the irritating *girlie,* as in "le sweetshirt est très girlie." A Parisian doesn't go out to a café or bar *après le travail* (after work): he goes to an *after,* pronounced *aft air.* When someone's acting strangely, he's not *fou,* "il est borderline." A low-cost flight is not,

(continued)

as you learned in French 101, *pas cher* but *low cost,* pronounced low *coast*. Reading a women's magazine one Sunday, I had to stop after the fifteenth ridiculous word in English. For some reason this infuriates me. I came to France to speak and hear good French, not bastardized English. Sometimes you start wondering if there are any French people who still speak and write the Real Thing. (Yes, thank *Dieu,* there are: the white-haired guys at the Académie française.)

But I'm unkind. In the same way that we love French expressions such as *je ne sais quoi,* the French (mainly the Parisians) find that English (excuse me, American) words are the ne plus ultra (now what language is that?).

Having It All: The Pleasure of Being a Frenchwoman

I'm seated in a café lunching alone watching the couple at the next table. Although they are speaking in low voices, parts of their conversation float my way. I surmise that the woman is a reporter and the man, perhaps, her editor. I'm guessing she is in her late thirties, but it's hard to tell. She has on little makeup and her brown hair is pulled back in a casual chignon. She's wearing a well-tailored pink-and-white-checkered shirt, perfectly fitting jeans, and high heels. The label on her coat says Zara woman. She talks animatedly but with gestures that fit her space. She has ordered a salad of cold green beans—and that is all she eats. Need I say she is slender?

I've been in France for years and years, right? Yet I find myself trying not to stare at this woman. I want to take her apart, analyze that class emanating from her—but it's impossible. Foiled again.

The Frenchwoman fascinates. But why? What is that *je ne sais quoi?*

Asked to describe *la femme française,* most foreigners would immediately volunteer "chic," followed by "svelte." Those who know her better might add "complicated" and even "intimidating." And all would add, "Plus something else I can't quite put my finger on."

The aura projected by the Frenchwoman, the air of self-confidence, the way she has everything right even if "everything" is mussed-up hair and blue jeans, is a source of endless fascination to her non-French sisters, who would kill to find out precisely what it is she does and how she does it. In her simple (but oh-so-well-cut) black dress with hardly any makeup and only one piece of jewelry, she's not only elegant but intriguing and even mysterious.

Before going any further, a caveat. The Frenchwoman I described in the above paragraph is the one of myth, the image evoked when we hear *Frenchwoman.* What I didn't describe are all the other Frenchwomen who make up France, women who in no way, shape, or form correspond to the mythical vision. They may be short or tall, slightly overweight or immensely overweight, not particularly fashionable or even dowdy, they may emanate anything *but* chic and style. To say that all Frenchwomen are slender and chic and know how to dress is like saying all American women are overweight, loud, and wear the pants in their households (French stereotypical version).

This being said, it's safe to say that in general no Frenchwoman could be like an American woman or an American woman like a Frenchwoman simply because of our different histories and the different ways we relate to the world around us. Edith Wharton, a great admirer of the Frenchwoman, wrote in 1919, "She is, in nearly all respects, as different as possible from the average American woman." How true that was, and still is.

Frenchwomen in History

When I think of American women in early times, I immediately think *pioneer*, with all that entails: bravery, working alongside the men, setting out to discover a new life together.

When I think of a Frenchwoman's past . . . first of all, her past is much, much longer. As French history rolled on from monarchy to revolution to republic, women were saints, heroines, mistresses, the power behind the throne—and with the exception of Catherine de Médicis—never on it. Frenchwomen may only have obtained the vote in 1945, but they've been exercising power for centuries. In a man's world, the women learned how to speak and act and look and seduce, manipulate and manage, with style and *savoir-faire*. For Sanche de Gramont, the author of *The French*, the Frenchwoman is made of "iron and velvet."

There's more, though, to the Frenchwoman and our fascination with her than her style. As Henry James, that astute observer of women, pointed out in *A Little Tour of France*, written in 1864: "There is, in fact, no branch of human activity in which one is not liable, in France, to find a woman engaged. . . . They are very formidable."

Far from taking a backseat, Frenchwomen have always occupied a vital place in society, and the self-confidence that emanates from them is due to their engagement with it. Modern Frenchwomen seem to be able to do it all—hold down a full-time job, take care of husband and children, whip up elegant meals, all the while remaining infuriating cool, composed, and feminine. Could this be because Frenchwomen put men first? This doesn't mean they don't love their children—they adore them—but the society is generally less child-oriented and child-fascinated than ours.

What it may boil down to is that Frenchwomen are purely and simply very much at ease with their femininity. Marie-Laure Sauty de Chalon, the chief executive of the successful auFeminin website (37 million followers), told the *International Herald Tribune* that she thinks that young Frenchwomen are done with feminism. "We want to be treated fairly, equally. What we defend is femininity. That, I think, is a French speciality."

They are so at ease with their femininity that appearances can be deceiving. I will *never* forget a blunder I made many years ago when seated next to an attractive, well-dressed, stylish blonde at a concert. I hadn't been introduced but hastened, like the Midwestern-born-and-bred American that I am, to make some conversation. "Do you work?" I naïvely asked in a vain attempt to say something (and remember thinking at the same instant that maybe the French are right to be so reserved—it keeps them out of verbal hot water). I asked because I imagined this soft-looking woman picking up her children after school or—why not?—baking cookies . . . or waiting for her husband to come home from the office. I didn't imagine her toting a gun—but I guess I should have. At the time she simply answered, "Yes," to my question and smiled. I later found out that she was the highly respected first woman in France to head the entire French police force. Good thing she didn't arrest me for the faux pas.

Famous and Not-So-Famous Frenchwomen

Let's face it: when we think about our mythical Frenchwoman, we don't think about the lady behind the cash register at the Monoprix. No, we think about Coco Chanel, Edith

Piaf, Simone de Beauvoir, Frenchwomen who are known the world over, women whose lives were played out on the public stage: Chanel, the orphan from the mountains of the Auvergne who created an empire of fashion and a perfume that's a household name; Piaf, whose tragic love affairs were belted out in songs the whole world knows; Simone de Beauvoir, the feminist intellectual who influenced a generation of women . . . the list is long.

But we don't need to look back to the past to see influential Frenchwomen. One of the most admired women in France is Simone Veil, who, in 1974 as minister of health under President Giscard d'Estaing, stood in front of the National Assembly and defended a law that would legalize abortion. "I say this with all my conviction: abortion must remain the exception, the ultimate recourse for situations with no way out." But, she asserted, "We can no longer close our eyes to the three hundred thousand abortions that, each year, mutilate the women of this country, flout our laws, and humiliate or traumatize those who resort to them." Her carefully constructed speech won the day, and the law was officially adopted in 1975. Veil served in other cabinets, continued her career as a successful lawyer, and was elected the first president of the European Parliament. The sixth woman to be admitted to the prestigious Académie française (in 2010), her sword bears the number 78651, the number inscribed on her arm at Auschwitz, as well as the mottos of the French republic, "Liberty, equality, and fraternity," and of the European Union, "Unified in diversity." Each year a list of the top fifty most popular Frenchmen and Frenchwomen is published. Perhaps as a realization of the work she has done and her quiet dignity, Simone Veil in 2011 rose from thirty-fourth on the list to fourth. Now retired from public life, Madame Veil doesn't need a stamp of popularity, but it was gratifying to see that the French paid this tribute to her remarkable career.

Although women are underrepresented (19 percent) in the National Assembly, they have been and are at the head of important political parties. Today, women lead parties on both ends of the political spectrum: on one end, the extreme right-wing National Front, and on the other, the Socialist Party.

For years, the National Front was run by the xenophobic Jean-Marie Le Pen, an easy figure to hate given the anti-immigrant and anti-Semitic phrases that more than a few times landed him in court. When he finally stepped down, his daughter Marine took the reins with a radical change of scenery. She's a slim, blond mother, and if you didn't listen to her message, you might be fooled into thinking she's not her father's daughter. But she is—with a soft touch. She's more accessible, more popular, and because of her feminine look, more insidious.

With a totally different style and discourse, Martine Aubry, a former government minister and the head of the Socialist Party, is Marine's polar opposite. Aubry also had a famous political father, Socialist Jacques Delors, and like Marine took up the challenge and went her own way. Whereas Marine—who lost about fifteen pounds to achieve an attractive silhouette—projects a modern image, Martine Aubry alternates between "ordinary" and styleless, certainly not your idea of the ultrachic Frenchwoman. Her fellow Socialist Ségolène Royal corresponds much more to the prevalent image of the Frenchwoman: beautiful, daring, obstinate. And for the French twist: Ségolène had four children with her partner, Socialist François Hollande, with whom she has since split. This being France, no one really cared about their not being married. They were much more interested in the rather zany things Ségolène was saying and the way she was acting (kind of like Joan of Arc on a mission to save France), which cumulatively turned out to be so absurd that her political star fell as fast as it rose.

In her mid-fifties, former French finance minister Christine Lagarde is striking, with an athlete's grace (no surprise: she was a member of the French national woman's synchronized swimming team). Unlike Marine Le Pen and Martine Aubry, Christine Lagarde has lived and worked abroad, notably in Chicago, where she was CEO of the Baker & McKenzie law firm. She possesses a natural elegance and is one of those few-and-far-between women who look terrific with natural silver hair. Lagarde, who succeeded Dominique Strauss-Kahn at the head of the International Monetary Fund, is admired for her sangfroid, her straightforward way of talking, her wit, and her excellent English.

Making the Best of What They Have . . . in Every Way

The genius of the Frenchwoman, all agree, is that even if nature has dealt her imperfections—a big nose or fine hair—she turns them into assets or accentuates the rest so much that attention is paid to the whole, and not the parts.

For Franco-American singer Kay Bourgine, "Frenchwomen are the most elegant in the world, the ones who know how to make the best of what they have. Italian women are drop-dead sensational until they get older. Englishwomen are more creative and wacky. Frenchwomen know how to do makeup, get the best haircut for their face, wear clothes that fit their type."

Susan Sommers theorizes, "The French are very comfortable with their bodies because they're not puritanical. That whole suggestiveness that exists is their way of life. We have very big rules about what's right to wear to work. They always have their bras showing and will wear white blouses and black bras. In the U.S. you wouldn't wear anything sleeveless over the age of sixty, but Frenchwomen will. Here it's not all about being young. They have the confidence of people whose families pass along things to them." Those "things" can range from the mother's Hermès scarf to a piece of heirloom jewelry from the favorite aunt to antiques that have been in the family for years. Frenchwomen learn to respect the past and live in a continuum.

Self-Confidence and Sensuality

"I always wanted to marry a Frenchwoman," says Kris Mackay. Over a cup of coffee near his office at the Madeleine, the thirty-five-year-old Scotsman who is director of Made to Order Europe for a fashion company in Paris, told me why he's happy he did. "I think it's because of the way they're women. They take ownership of their femininity. They use it as they wish and know what they're doing."

And *voilà la différence*. Because of their different traditions, French and American women are confident about different aspects of life. "Parisians," observes Sommers, "are surer about their sexuality and the way they dress. New Yorkers are never sure they look good. Parisians always are or seem to be. They think they're fine even if they're not." That's because, she theorizes, Frenchwomen can fall back on the "cushion" of their heritage.

"American women are confident about their intelligence and their jobs," she surmises, "while Frenchwomen are confident about the way they are in the world." This may explain the comments of an American writer friend who lives in France with a Frenchwoman: "It's as if women in the U.S. are ashamed to be feminine, like they're going to get walked on if they are. I had a hard time distinguishing the men from the women." That hurts—but I guess after living with a Frenchwoman, he felt the contrast strongly.

One thing is sure: no one would mistake a Frenchwoman for a man. Even women in high-powered positions—yes, they exist—don't aim for a mannish look. Several attractive French female ministers adopted classic and well-cut pants suits to wear to work but, this being France, added a scarf or pin or a distinctive piece of jewelry for a feminine look.

But being feminine is more than clothes. After viewing Woody Allen's charming movie *Midnight in Paris*, a French friend commented that Inez, the fiancée of the American writer Gil, reminded him of American women in general (oh, thanks!). "What do you mean?" I asked warily. "All she cared about was what she was doing, about her shopping, and her own agenda. Totally cold and brittle, off-putting—there's no way a man could think of her sexually or sensually." "All business?" I volunteered. "Worse than that," he grumbled. As a contrast, he said, Adriana, the character played by French actress Marion Cotillard, "sparkled, her eyes and mouth were so expressive, she was sensual, you wanted to take her in your arms." Did Woody Allen do it on purpose, or did his two actresses reflect a real difference in the way American women and Frenchwomen go about things? Let's get over it: not all Frenchwomen are sensual and sexy. But when they are, they give it free rein.

"The messed-up-hair look, the 'I just got out of bed' look is so French," commented fashion designer Joyce Kraus. "I think part of what makes the Frenchwoman sexy is her sensuality. When American women go for sexy, it's overt. In any case, in the U.S. it's either the chastity belt or tight clothes and boobs hanging out, whereas in France it's seduction and flirtatiousness. One of the major things in France is that men really appreciate you. You can tell by the way they look at you. It's in the air—you can be vampish. Frenchwomen feel more sensual and start with the underwear."

She mused, "If I had a tip to give to any woman wanting

to become French, I'd tell her to have a great sexual experience. It's great for that 'morning after' look you see a lot of here. Plus, Frenchwomen never feel they have to be perfect, perfectly coiffed, perfectly groomed." *Au contraire.* Joyce Kraus laughed as she recalled, "When I first came here, I felt like I couldn't go out of the house if my hair was greasy, but now I rearrange it or put it in a ponytail."

Look at Me

After writing the above about going out with greasy hair, it may seem strange to posit that Frenchwomen want to be looked at. Yet they can and do live with not having the perfect manicure or hairdo. There's always something awry, but that's part and parcel of the sensual "connected with the body" look. They don't *want* to look too perfect. They want men to see them first and foremost as women, not Barbie dolls.

The first thing you learn in France, especially in Paris, is that everyone's looking at everyone else. The café terrace is the ideal perch for people-watching. Unlike at U.S. cafés, where people face in and look at each other, French cafés face the street, which becomes the show. Two months into living in France with her French husband, thirty-seven-year-old Caroline Aoustin, with an American friend, spent a happy moment doing what all French people do: checking out the street. She marveled that she and her friend always pointed out the same kind of women. And what was it about them? I asked. Even in casual garb, she noted, Frenchwomen still look dressy. "The word my friend and I kept using was *effortless*. There's such an ease about the way they dress and walk and present themselves. And there are a lot of heels here—I saw a woman wearing teeny designer jeans and major spike heels to go shopping." How did they know which women weren't French? Simple, she answered. "They didn't look as put together."

Abroad, a Frenchwoman stands out in a crowd, not because of her makeup or hairstyle or dress, but because of that (once again, infuriatingly inimitable) self-possessed and self-confident "way" she has about her. During the Dominique Strauss-Kahn affair, in which the head of the International Monetary Fund was accused of sexual assault and attempted rape, squads of French reporters were sent to the Big Apple on short notice to cover the event. In an article called "For French Media, Story of a Lifetime—and Culture Shock—in New York," which focused on the French reporters covering the event, Sarah Maslin Nir, writing in the *International Herald Tribune,* observed four things that made the French reporters different from the American ones. They smoked (a dead giveaway in nonsmoking America), they greeted each other with the double kisses, one on each cheek, and "despite their fatigue, they were, well, better looking than many of their American counterparts." In addition, they also did something very French—they zipped down to the hotel bar for a drink in spite of their stressful schedule and the need to be "on" every minute. "So it feels like we are living," Anne Lamotte, a reporter for Radio France, explained. That struck me as a valuable lesson and one of the reasons Frenchwomen always look so good—even when working, even when stressed, even when conditions aren't perfect, they are totally engaged in living. You can't get that French look if you are a robot.

Going back to "look at me," Frenchwomen are used to dressing not for one person (themselves, or a man) but for the entire world. When you know that the street is a place you get looked at, you dress for the street and get into the "looking" game. Foreign women like it as well. Author Doris Lessing, who was born in Rhodesia (now Zimbabwe) and came to London in 1949, wrote in her autobiography that after the dreary, claustrophobic war years, the British, especially the women, dreamed of Paris because "French men loved women and showed it." Lessing says that when she went to Paris, although her toilette "was hardly of the level to attract French compliments, it was true that every man gave you a quick, expert once-over—hair, face, what you were wearing . . . a dispassionate, disinterested summing-up, not necessarily leading to invitations." Her father's girlfriend, she noted, had purchased a smart new outfit and went to Paris to have it judged—on the street. "She came back restored," wrote Lessing. "Quite a few women I knew said that for the sake of one's self-respect one had to visit Paris from time to time."

A French friend in her early forties told me that during the year she lived in the States "I felt like a dead body with no boobs. There was no eye contact because of fear of sexual harassment." She found this most strange because to her it's obvious that "men and women are different and like to flirt." When she returned to Paris, she experienced a sea change. As she walked down the boulevard Saint-Germain in the month of June, "I literally had the feeling I was naked." She laughed. "I had lost the feeling of being watched by men. Especially in Paris, and especially in May and June at the end of winter, when everyone's putting on lighter clothes, everyone's looking. In the U.S., whether it's summer, winter, spring, or fall, no one looks at you." This friend is a highly intelligent world traveler at the head of a successful business with no hang-ups about being a woman. And she likes men to look at her.

A French lawyer working in the United States told me she was astonished *not* to be looked at one day when she wore an adorable little Cacharel skirt she had picked up on her last visit to Paris. "It wasn't even all that short," she exclaimed, "but the men turned their heads away whenever I came within their range." For this Frenchwoman who was used to Frenchmen, their reaction was shocking. Don't they know a pretty skirt—and nice legs—when they see them? And if so, why didn't they compliment her? In addition to feeling sexless, she missed the banter in French offices, lighthearted teasing that might touch on the sexual without anyone's going to court.

It's inconceivable to imagine an American woman lawyer saying she wished the men in the office would perk up, notice what she wears, and indulge in some light conversation with sexual overtones. *Quelle horreur.* Our Frenchwoman, though, truly felt she had tumbled into a grim world where both sexes are aligned against each other rather than being in tune. She certainly wouldn't consider a compliment sexual harassment. France, of course, has laws forbidding both sexual and moral harassment. The difference between the United States and France is that Frenchwomen don't consider a compliment or a slightly off-color joke a motive for charges of sexual harassment. They deflect silly or inappropriate behavior with a flip comment or a shrug or a put-down. After all, they're grown-ups, *non*? The sexual harassment cases brought to French court are of a much more serious nature. The failure of Frenchwomen to get riled by comments or looks that would have an American woman calling her lawyer may be because the "special relationship" between Frenchmen and Frenchwomen is based on the premise that women will never get too upset by men being men. As a young Frenchwoman told me, "It's not because a guy is looking at your derrière that it's harassment. It's each person's own business to put him in his place." She compared it to having neighbors who put their sacks of garbage in front of their door. "It's unpleasant, but you don't call the police." (I don't know—I think I'd call the police!) On the other hand, if a guy puts his hands on your bottom, she qualified, "It's the equivalent of the neighbor

who drills a hole through the wall—which is another story."
She's in her thirties and told me the young men in her office
are *always* saying stupid things and making sexual allusions.
Her take on that is that she can't change them so she simply
ignores what she calls their silliness as long as nothing gets
personal. I admire her. I worked in a French office when I was
young and couldn't get over the way the men talked, the sexual allusions, and the posters of naked women. (I saw one just
the other day in a factory I was visiting!) One day I decided
to even things up and brought in a poster of naked men. My
male colleagues didn't like it. Hmmm. Doing that was *so*
American. . . .

Underneath It All

It's a stereotype—but it's true. Frenchwomen love lingerie. I
discovered this while shopping at Monoprix, a chain of city
stores that for reasonable prices sells everything from food
and kitchen utensils to baby clothes and men's and women's
undergarments. I never imagined I'd stop to admire panties
and bras in between buying a steak and inspecting outfits for
the grandchildren, but they're so stylish you want to pick up
a few to throw in your basket along with your cabbages. If
Monoprix features good-looking underwear, it means that all
women, not only the well-heeled and the young, are paying as
much attention to the unseen as the seen. And if it gets seen,
tant mieux (so much the better).

On a cruise organized by my college roommate, I stood in
the pocket-size cabin I shared with a friend of my friend's
and, while changing clothes, commented on the lingerie I'd
bought before the trip. It wasn't even for my husband, who
wasn't on this girls-only expedition. It was because I'd become used to wearing pretty things under my outfits. I got the

feeling, though, that references to my undergarments embarrassed my cabinmate. *I guess I have been living in France too long,* I thought.

But I was proud of myself because when I first came to France, my underwear was disastrous, beyond horrible, old lady (and I was young). A physical therapist friend of my husband's and mine, whom I went to see for a massage, still remembers the day I entered his office in my underwear (standard procedure: in France whether at the doctor's or at the physical therapist's, you strip right down to your undies and no nurse is present). He was therefore used to seeing women's bodies in all shapes and sizes as well as all kinds of undergarments, but never, he told my husband, had he seen anyone my age in a white bra and white panties that weren't even bikinis. "He couldn't get over it," my husband says, teasing me. "He was used to the fetching, pretty underwear of Frenchwomen, and your grandmother getup gave him a shock."

Cultural difference. For the Frenchwoman, sexy or delightful lingerie is not something to reserve for sex. Yet it wasn't always easy to find undergarments that "went everywhere," designer Chantal Thomass told *Madame Figaro.* "When I started, the choice was limited: either the underwear was very 'ladylike' or you had to buy in Pigalle." Today, said Thomass, whose favorite color is black, "Women wear beautiful lingerie first of all for themselves, for their own pleasure and to feel beautiful. . . . Women no longer make the distinction between the underwear they wear every day and the underwear they wear to seduce."

For Fifi Chachnil, the creator of the Mademoiselle Fifi lingerie, women's lingerie should first of all be for them. Fifi, whose real name is Delphine Veron, and who comes from a family of silk merchants in Lyons, says she considers lingerie like poetry, both necessary and totally useless. Chachnil says she grew up in a family where the women had big busts but

were condemned to wearing unattractive and "mortally boring" bras (mystery: in France, until recently, all the pretty
underwear was reserved for small busts). Since those days,
she says, she has tried to slip in a dose of fantasy and humor
in her creations. Fifi's not afraid of pink or sensual or feminine frills. At the same time, she says men prefer "culottes" to
strings to keep a certain mystery. She thinks modesty is important. "If a woman tries to be too sexy, she risks being
vulgar." Her atelier in the first arrondissement of Paris is in
the courtyard of an eighteenth-century building that cushions
the noise of the street. Inside the quiet boutique, the spring
collection of panties and bras and flimsy garments to wear
over them is lined up on either side of the room. On one side,
black and red and the classic colors; on the other, gorgeous
silks in pastel blues and pinks. I was ready to hear that the
creations were for twenty-year-olds but was instead told that
they're for anyone from fifteen to seventy-five.

One of those "oh so French" moments came when I attended the Fifi Chachnil showing of the spring/summer collection at the Crazy Horse Saloon on avenue Georges V. Since
fashion's not my beat, I had never attended a fashion show and
could hardly believe that my first one would be for *lingerie*.

That particular day was so . . . Parisian. I'd taken a train
from Redon in the west of France in the late morning to get
to the show in the early afternoon. Arriving in Paris is always
a shock. In the provinces, you've been with normal people
who actually smile at you and don't make you feel like a
leper when you take your time. Then, *wham*—there you are
at the Gare Montparnasse with a gazillion people crowding
you as you push your way through them to the metro. The
metro . . . after the sweet air of the country, oh, well, I'm sure
you get an idea of the olfactory contrast.

I rushed home to check my snail mail and e-mail, then,
seeing it was late, hailed a taxi to get to the Crazy Horse in

time for the show. I rarely take either buses or taxis in Paris; buses are too slow, and my theory about Parisian taxi drivers is that they actually slow down when the light is green. Usually I say nothing, but that day I transformed myself into a real *Parisienne* and griped about the traffic. The driver said nothing for five minutes, then looked at me in the rearview mirror and asked, "Why didn't you start out earlier?" Then, as if talking to himself, he mused cruelly, "There's something I have never understood, and that is how all these old, retired people with nothing to do manage to be late. I tell them that if they don't like the way I drive and find it too slow, they can take another taxi." Uh, did I get the message? On a rainy day this kind of encounter can be fun, a battle of wits and wills. On a bright sunny day, though, you simply want to throttle the guy who is *ruining* your contemplation of the majestic Seine flowing under the marvelous Pont de l'Alma, with its famous Zouave (a member of the colonial troops, whose statue is a traditional standard for measuring the water level). Drat him, I thought, in a pique of Parisian rage. It's a fantastic day, I'm going to my first fashion show ever, and not only do I have to listen to this creep, I have to pay him. (The *joie de vivre* point here is that it's good to get your adrenaline up, your heart racing, plus you've got a story to tell your husband that night.)

Once I extricated myself from his clutches, I saw that the show wasn't on time and I needn't have rushed or hassled the driver. That's all right: the goal of any self-respecting Parisian is to mess up the day of any Parisian who's messed with his. That too is *joie de vivre*!

On the pavement, a group of men and women of all ages and garbs chatted and gossiped animatedly. I always wondered how people dressed for these occasions and concluded that in this case, anything went as long as you didn't look boring. Forget Parisian black—a lady with auburn hair in a pageboy was wearing an emerald-green dress with a bright yellow purse and fuchsia heels. Not far from her stood a woman of a certain age dressed in not particularly fashionable jeans, shoes with a zebra motif and wedge heels, and a miltary jacket, her motorcycle helmet firmly in hand. How she managed to look so sharp in that getup is beyond me—but she did.

Another detail that made the day so Parisian: the lack of instructions, which I've mentioned before (if you write out a program, it means you think people are idiots). The proceedings were quite well organized actually, with two of Fifi's press attachés posted at the door, informing the impatient that the show would be starting a bit late. I wondered how we would know when it would start, as there were no announcements, no megaphones, no one telling people to form lines to pass through in an orderly fashion. Bah—that would be too simple. This being France, what happened was a subtle, almost imperceptible change in the air. You first feel, and then see, the crowd turning and moving toward the entrance. Suddenly there's a crush of bodies all trying to pass through one tiny door at the same time. You wonder if you'll get trampled in the ensuing stampede. That's the disorganized part.

Now for the organized. Once inside, names were efficiently checked off, and polite, uniformed personnel led us to our assigned places. Close to the seats were buckets of champagne on ice, which I hadn't even noticed until a uniformed usher showed up with a glass. So, a glass of champagne it was: rosé demoiselle brut—Vranken, I read on the label (not polite but no one was watching). Pink champagne, plush red banquette, a silver curtain that finally opened for the show. I couldn't tell you much about the lingerie being modeled because the spectacle was all about the music and the dance and how good those models looked wearing Fifi's creations, but I can assure you that the dancers were drop-dead sculptural and the program sexy in the French way, i.e., humorous, well thought out, and playful, with good-natured clapping and some whistling. There'd been a rush to get in, but there was no rush to leave.

Frenchwomen Don't Talk About Diets

If you asked me to list a few of the things I appreciate about Frenchwomen, way up at the top I'd put "They don't stand around helping themselves to foie gras or *petits fours* while saying, 'Oh, this is ruining my diet.'"

I swear to you, dear reader, that in the forty years I've lived here, I've never heard such a thing. You may say, "So what?" but to me it's important. It's so French. It means many things: it means "I'm living in the moment, so why spoil the pleasure I'm having now with a guilt trip?" It means "This food is good" and "I'm not into denial (certainly not while I'm eating) and I know that I'm not going to indulge every day." You can be 100 percent sure that the day after the foie gras or *petits fours* those lithe ladies will be sipping bouillon, but they would never say that. Now, take a closer look. Even while treating herself, the Frenchwoman may not eat all that much of the foie gras, but she'll have a nice taste, that's for sure.

Sometimes when you live in a place long enough, you start wondering if perhaps you're imagining things, that maybe only the Frenchwomen you saw are like this, that maybe there are Frenchwomen like the American women you grew up with who, while helping themselves to chocolate sundaes, discuss the next week's diet. So depressing! That's why Mireille Guiliano's comments in her bestselling *French*

Women Don't Get Fat reassured me. She writes, and I can affirm, "Frenchwomen simply do not suffer the terror of kilos that afflicts so many of their sisters in other developed countries. All the chatter about diets I hear at cocktail parties in America would make any Frenchwoman cringe." Frenchwomen, she notes, talk about "what we enjoy: feelings, family, hobbies, philosophy, politics, culture, and, yes, food, especially food (but never diets)."

Frenchwomen don't talk about diets, but they *go* on diets. Come spring, the cover of every single woman's magazine touts the latest *régime* (this year it's Dr. Dukan, but by the time this book comes out, there will surely be a new one). So don't think that because Frenchwomen don't talk about diets that they are not obsessed with their weight or remain slender with no effort. They watch their weight like a mother watches her child on the playground—constantly. If they see they've gained a few grams or a pound or two, they do whatever they need to to get it off—*vite*. One French nutritionist said that whenever she puts on two kilos, she gets them off in two days by having a slice of toast and low-fat cheese for breakfast, as much steamed fish and homemade vegetable soup as she wants for both lunch and dinner, and a dessert of zero-percent *fromage blanc* (a white cheese similar to Greek yoghurt) and a teaspoon of jam—I tried it and it works!

That's what I love so much about France, the French, and Frenchwomen. They separate their concern and their responsibility (I've put on a few pounds, got to get them off) from their joy (I'm at this party with champagne and lovely things to eat—I'll have some and I certainly won't spoil my or anyone else's good time with running comments about why I shouldn't). They've got it right. They love food, they love a good party, they love meals, but they put food in its proper place: one joy among many others. On this score as on many others, *vive la joie de vivre*.

And They Do Take the Time to Lunch

Here's another revolutionary thing Frenchwomen do. They cultivate every part of their life, giving importance to each. They don't get so booked and busy they can't find time for lunch with friends. Susan Sommers, who has lived in France and has many French friends, confirmed Edith Wharton's observation about Frenchwomen tending to all the various parts of their lives.

"Frenchwomen," Sommers is convinced, "understand about the value of life. Life isn't all about scheduling gym, treadmill, work, work, work. Here, even my best friends who are physicians work long hours but find time to meet their friends, take vacations, and indulge in the life part of life, which is as important or perhaps more important to them than work."

I did an informal survey, asking my American friends how often they had lunch with a friend for no reason at all, but only to enjoy a moment together. They each thought long and hard and all came up with the same answer: "Next to never. There's no time." Many told me they had no time to have dinner parties either. After all, they work! Frenchwomen work too and get home late, but that doesn't stop them from inviting people to dinner or going out on a weeknight. Even if they don't have time, Frenchwomen make time. It's part of their investment . . . in life.

The Secret of the "Older Woman"—Sex and Smarts

Do you know many women who like the idea of sagging body parts, wrinkles, and all the attendant mostly negative changes in their looks and status as youth fades away?

I don't.

This being said, if you're a woman and going to grow old (which we all are—*bonjour*, reality), it's probably best to be French or to live in France.

One reason is that French society accepts older women and they accept themselves. Another is that in a country where women are regarded as sexual beings far longer than they are elsewhere, "old" doesn't mean "dead."

An attractive, slim, silver-haired, blue-eyed sixty-four-year-old British friend told me she was delighted and amused when a young man (young to her—he was about forty-five) tried to pick her up one morning as she was walking her dog. "I'd thrown on my trousers, hadn't had my shower, and had on no makeup. You can imagine my astonishment when this guy, who was delivering leaflets, asked me for coffee. He told me he loved my English accent and that he was looking for a long-term relationship. He was disappointed when I told him I was married. At my age this doesn't happen that much, and very frankly it felt good when he told me that I was 'young and beautiful.'" The end of the story: they bade each other *"Au revoir,"* she walked her dog back home, and for a brief moment she did indeed feel "young and beautiful."

Old doesn't mean "young" either, and aside from pathological cases, most Frenchwomen who get plastic surgery for the face and/or the body carry no illusions that the repairs are a fountain of youth that will gush forever. They simply want to look as good as they can for as long as they can. Plastic surgeon Henry Delmar noted in an interview in *Le Figaro* that his patients all say the same thing—they don't want any noticeable changes, they don't want people to know, and they're doing it for themselves. "In France," he said, "never has one of my patients asked me to make her look like someone else or to look like she did when she was twenty."

The "French" thing about Frenchwomen is their lucidity as

they age. As Debra Ollivier, the author of the savvy *What French Women Know,* writes, "We Americans are frequently in awe of how older Frenchwomen cultivate themselves as sensual feminine creatures while they age. But these women . . . [are] realistic about age and view it for what it is: an inescapable part of nature's grand plan, a personal destiny to which we're all tethered. . . . This goes a long way in explaining why you'll never see a Frenchwoman wearing a T-shirt that says LIFE BEGINS AT 70. Because it doesn't."

That knowledge could, of course, give our Frenchwoman a ticket to carelessness and negligence, but it doesn't. In France, rare is the woman who voluntarily "lets herself go," the way the famous and formerly beautiful actress Simone Signoret did when she got older. Another exception, Brigitte Bardot, decided she preferred the company of animals to humans and became a virtual recluse, only emerging from time to time to defend the rights of baby seals or other endangered species.

Most Frenchwomen, on the contrary, keep themselves up. Maybe because of their being French, the words of Coco Chanel ring in their heads: "No one is young after the age of forty-five but one is irresistible at any age."

Perhaps that cultivation of the quality of "irresistibility" is why Frenchmen admire and appreciate the older woman instead of dismissing her. French filmmakers have bravely celebrated the sexuality of the over-fifties with Charlotte Rampling in *Under the Sand* and Nathalie Baye in *An Intimate Affair,* a film portraying a woman in her fifties who meets a younger man. Catherine Deneuve was forty-nine—and gorgeous—when she starred in the film *Indochine* in 1992 and still, as she approaches seventy, remains an icon of French glamour in spite of what appears to be one too many face-lifts. In the 2010 film *Potiche,* by François Ozon, she plays the role of Suzanne Pujol, the submissive wife of a macho industrialist, a despot both at home and work. When his employees go on strike and lock up their boss in the factory (only a Frenchman could have written this script), Suzanne springs to life, taking charge and running the show. The film perfectly illustrates how Frenchwomen take command the French way, with guts and grace. One of the "most French" moments of the film is when the perfectly dressed and made-up Suzanne tells a former lover, a union organizer played by Gérard Depardieu, that he's not, as he hopes, the father of her son. But who is? he asks, perplexed. "I can't remember," she replies serenely, thinking back to her various love affairs.

At age ninety-three, Danielle Darrieux was still starring in films for TV after a successful career in movies with directors such as Billy Wilder and Claude Autant-Lara. An obviously springy Darrieux told *Le Figaro* that she likes nothing more than to walk around in blue jeans and worn-out shoes, that fashion is fun, but that she loves to buy her clothes at outdoor markets.

How many over-fifty women do you know who are praised for their "femininity" and their "flirtatiousness"? Those were the accolades actor Gérard Depardieu gave actress Gisèle Casadesus, who made a film with him at age . . . ninety-seven. In an interview with *The Wall Street Journal*, Casadesus may have given the secret of her longevity. For her, "*retirement* is a banned word."

Whether older Frenchwomen have the don't-give-up attitude because men appreciate them or whether men appreciate them because they have this attitude is moot. When actress Marie-France Pisier was found dead in the swimming pool of her house in the South of France in the spring of 2011, the TV anchor described her as "only sixty-six." I wanted to spring through the screen and kiss him.

Older Frenchwomen don't need to be movie stars to be appreciated: I've seen many strikingly attractive "ordinary" women in France who are no longer in their twenties or even thirties or forties. Designer Joyce Kraus, who lived and worked in France for many years, remarked that in France you can see a sixty-year-old Frenchwoman not wearing pantyhose and she still looks good. "My clients would look at these older women and exclaim 'They're beautiful. They turn me on.'"

Frenchwomen as they age try to keep their bodies healthy, make sure their wardrobes aren't too dated, and in general don't give up trying to look as good as they can. As one older Frenchwoman confided, "I've stopped trying to keep up with the latest fashions. Fashion is good—but elegance is better."

"Senior" Models Are All the Rage

On a nostalgic autumn day as the last rays of light from the west were fast fading over the Pei Pyramid, Françoise de Stael and I chose two seats on the terrace of the Café Marly for a late-afternoon drink.

"What will it be?" the young waiter asked.

I opted for a Perrier, Françoise for a whiskey. She then pulled out a pack of cigarettes, Fine 120, and asked me if I'd mind her smoking.

Well, not at all. Oh, I suppose I'd fear for her lungs if she were thirty. But, *pardonnez-moi*, I love the idea of a woman having a whiskey and a cigarette . . . when she's eighty. "At my age, it doesn't make any difference," she said as she inhaled with enjoyment.

Françoise is, first of all, French, so she can get away with things like this with *classe,* and second, she is not your usual eighty-year-old. A top model who worked for Givenchy and Patou until she was forty, she left the business to follow her husband, then restarted her career at age sixty-seven. With her high cheekbones, natural white hair, perfect skin, and light brown eyes, she's got that *je ne sais quoi* of professional models plus that alluring French reserve and restraint (she remarked that she's a model both because she wants to and needs to work, before we lightly passed on to other topics). As we spoke, I realized I had seen her before—of course. Her face was plastered all over Paris in a series of ads for Hépar mineral water; recently she's modeled for Galliano and Hermès.

Françoise is only one of the senior models in the Boomers and Seniors department of the Masters agency in Paris, which is headed by Sylvie Fabregon, who recruits hundreds of men and women "boomers," either professionals or people who've never modeled before in their lives. On the wall next to her desk in a top-floor, light-filled, eighteenth-century Paris office building on the rue Sainte-Anne are head shots of the seniors who work for the agency Sylvie founded at age fifty-three, when she decided that "getting old wasn't that bad" and saw "a definite need" for older models.

Sylvie, the epitome of Parisian casual chic, who wears black-rimmed glasses and is dressed in boots and jeans and a T-shirt, with bracelets jangling on her wrists, knows exactly what she wants and has no lack of candidates. "They have to radiate something special," she told me. "Sometimes people send me great-looking pictures, but I always want to see them in person, and every now and then I see that they don't look as good because they'd touched up the photos."

She doesn't ask her models to get face-lifts. "They do it themselves if they want," she commented laconically. She says she has nothing against plastic surgery—as long as it doesn't show. While we were talking, she picked up the constantly ringing phone. One of the calls was from Lancôme, checking to be sure that the model she was sending over had *not* had Botox or plastic surgery. I couldn't believe my ears.

I couldn't, however, resist asking Françoise if she'd been tempted by face-lifts or Botox. She promptly replied, "I'm against it. My wrinkles reflect who I am." And, she admitted, she had good-looking parents and has good genes.

Like many Frenchwomen, Françoise is a minimalist when it comes to makeup, dress, and even food. Skin care? She puts face cream on her skin—and that's it. Makeup? "When I go out, I put on just a little." Is she on a constant diet? Not really, she replies. "I eat well at lunch and not much at dinner." I pressed her to uncover her secret for staying slim. "What do you eat?" She reflected a moment. "For lunch, generally a starter, meat and vegetables, a piece of cheese, fruit, and a glass of sauvignon. For dinner, a small whiskey and a cracker, a soft-boiled egg, and yogurt." Not exactly nutritionally correct, but whatever works. . . . Oh, and she loves chocolate. As far as dressing goes: "I have one pair of well-cut slacks made of beautiful material, and an elegant, classic green silk jacket. I love black and always wear a colored scarf." Perfume? Opium for thirty years, Angel for the past fifteen years. *Et voilà!*

At age sixty-three, Eva Colange is another one of the Masters agency's senior models. The mother of five grown children and a baby grandson who lives in Tahiti, Eva is a familiar face in France even though hardly anyone knows her name. She's the beautiful older woman smiling at you in the pharmacy as you shop for Avène beauty products for the "mature skin." She's the lady in tennis shorts modeling for EDF, the largest French electricity company. Recently she hopped on a plane to Malaysia to do a modeling job for Fixodent, a product for dentures. "Not very glamorous," she cheerfully admitted. Like Françoise, Eva was a model early on and put her professional life on hold from age thirty-five to fifty to raise her family. Her new career started one day when she accompanied her sixteen-year-old daughter to a casting—and she herself was hired. Like Françoise, she says she doesn't do anything special to maintain her beauty. She tried Botox when she was fifty but didn't like it because it froze her expression.

"I accept my wrinkles," she says. She thinks the way people look at older women in France and the way they look at themselves has changed since her mother's era. "Now we're in jeans. We're cool."

Sylvie Fabregon's new agency, Silver, hires former models from all over the world. Other than being a professional model, there's an age requirement: forty and up.

It looks as if seventy is the new fifty—and gray is here to stay.

Frenchwomen, American Women: A Story of Polar Opposites

When I was living with my future husband, a French friend of his stopped by in my absence. As they chatted, she spied a pair of huge, comfortable, furry, pandalike bedroom slippers near the bed. She laughed and immediately remarked, "Ah, so you've got yourself a foreign girlfriend." I was totally astonished when I heard this story. First of all, what was wrong with my bedroom slippers? And second, how do you tell someone's nationality from her *chaussons*?

Simple.

My bedroom slippers were totally and completely unsexy. No Frenchwoman under the age of eighty—if even then—would possess footwear like that, especially if she was in a Budding Relationship with a Handsome Young Frenchman. Only a foreigner, perhaps from the north where it's freezing cold, would don such turnoff gear. This was my rather strange and embarrassing introduction into the cultural *différences* between Frenchwomen and American women. Style, my friend, style.

Are Frenchwomen really all that different? And radically different from American women? I would of course say yes—

and so would most French and American women. One young Frenchwoman who lived in the States for a time told me that she had had "some incredible conversations with American women which showed me that we have nothing in common."

I sensed what I began to call "the gap" every time my husband's friends would tease him about marrying an American. For them, an American woman was somewhere between Lucrezia Borgia and Annie Oakley. I rapidly got the impression that he had done something absolutely incredible, something none of them would ever have ventured. Not that they didn't marry foreigners, but their foreign wives were Spanish or Polish or, well, anything but an American. Are we threatening? Too squeaky-clean to be sexy? Do we talk too much and too loudly? Yes, yes, and yes.

It's hard enough adjusting to a foreign culture if you're single or in a couple where neither of you is French. But it's nothing compared to attempting it when you're the American wife of a French husband—unless it's being the French wife of an American husband. One Frenchwoman married to an American told me that when she went to the States, she was fascinated by the "spontaneity, the generosity, and the independence of American women and their bright-colored clothes." Meanwhile, her American in-laws were fascinated by her French ways, notably her ability to eat a chicken without ever using her fingers, mend socks, and "probably a lot of other things, which is why I still seem so French to most Americans." So, yes, we're different.

The Frenchman marrying an American is in for a change. He's delighted by her independence, her free spirit, her big smile offered to all. She drinks a lot more booze than a Frenchwoman ever would, and she's got a lot to learn when it comes to dressing like the Frenchwoman, but that can be handled. As for the Frenchwoman, she might find her American "sister" unsophisticated or naïve or refreshingly spontaneous (a

Frenchwoman doesn't show her deck of cards) and not a threat . . . although, on second thought, those perfect white teeth, those long legs, and that carefree air might make her a menace. That ingénue might just appeal to her French husband. . . . I can attest to this. In my younger days, I generally got the cold shoulder from Frenchwomen and ended up talking to the men—which was fine by me. Now that I'm older, threat time has passed, and I can hang out with the Frenchwomen with none of that former undercurrent swirling by (too bad!).

Many, many American women marry Frenchmen and live in France. Their tales are different but they'd all agree on one thing: Frenchmen are used to Frenchwomen and, although delighted with their American wives, can also be surprised and shocked. In her last book, *Love à la Française,* my late friend Polly Platt took on the thorny subject of Franco-American marriages. She got an earful from some of her interviewees, among them Pascal Baudry, a cross-cultural expert and psychoanalyst who was at one time married to an American. The author of *French and Americans: The Other Shore,* Baudry, who is now married to a Frenchwoman, told Polly, somewhat tongue-in-cheek, that "a Frenchman and an American wife are totally incompatible." He observed that an American marriage is a "partnership" with a cross-ownership, and that a French marriage has fuzzier boundaries. "In marriage as well as in the rest of French life, there is no horizontal equality, but verticality. The husband is on top [author's comment: was that a Freudian slip?] with the power. The French wife plays this game, knowing that, really, subtly, she is superior."

I'd be bowled over with feminist outrage if I hadn't lived here for so long and seen how it works. It's true—every word of it. The man-woman relationship within a French marriage is a reflection of French culture, in which, as Baudry points out, "who dominates whom, who will have the advantage" is key.

With the burden of the not always flattering reputation of the American woman firmly in mind, I realized early on that I could either try to become like a Frenchwoman (I discarded that idea immediately—*impossible!*) or observe her and at least know what kind of paragon I was up against. I concluded that the Frenchwoman (here I must specify the *Parisian* woman, who is the one I ran into the most) is totally opposite from the American woman. She is secretive, where we are open. She is reserved, even cold, where we are spontaneous. She doesn't talk about her husband to other women, whereas (confession) we have a slight tendency to do so. She learned how to cook with her mother or grandmother and turns out scrumptious dinners with no effort, and even if she didn't learn how to cook, she knows how to serve a meal and entertain; whereas for the American woman, the French dinner party, in the beginning at least, is akin to a prolonged torture session. The Frenchwoman has her own mind and basically does what she wants but doesn't seek consensus (but what French person, man or woman, seeks consensus?). She can gauge social situations like a hound dog and knows when to talk and when to keep quiet, a talent for which I greatly admire her.

Another sterling (and amazing) quality? The Frenchwoman—don't ask me how she does it—talks and laughs without making a lot of noise.

I had a long way to go if I planned to get any of these attributes. I totally failed on the talking and laughing quietly. (I'd *love* to be a Frenchwoman on this score, but it seems there's nothing to be done.) I can keep a secret but am not secretive. My face is so open that every stranger in the street asks me for directions, and I tend to talk when I should keep my mouth shut. (Frenchwomen are maddeningly skilled at keeping their lips locked, leaving things unsaid.)

The only tip I took from Frenchwomen was with food and entertaining. I haven't reached the heights of certain Frenchwomen I know (my sister-in-law, for example), but you can't live in France as long as I have and like food and drink and company as much as I do without a wee bit rubbing off.

How do French attitudes and French realities affect the American or other non-Frenchwoman married to a Frenchman? Does she become French? Some American women do become French by taking French nationality, but I can safely say that even with that piece of official documentation, I have never seen an American woman transformed into a Frenchwoman. No matter how slender, how alluring, how feminine, how graceful, she still remains an American woman (with that beautiful big smile and open American face).

Only once did I ever hear of an American woman becoming like a Frenchwoman—and it wasn't a compliment. This American, who had lived in France for many years, was in a Paris taxi with a friend from the States. When they arrived at their destination, the visiting American continued to smile and chat with the cabby, while the resident American coldly and brusquely paid the bill. As he counted the change, the cabby looked her in the eye and said, referring to her congenial compatriot, "*Votre amie* is nice, but you—you have become French." For him, this was the ultimate insult.

That of course was a negative way of describing becoming a Frenchwoman. I got some unexpected praise one day from a French friend who checked out my black pants and black sweater and apparently well-tied scarf. (As I have noted elsewhere, Frenchwomen are *always* checking out other women.) "You've become so Parisian," she exclaimed, giving me a big smile. The highest accolade coming from another Frenchwoman is a compliment on one's appearance, but these—and this might get back to rivalry?—are few and far between. Frenchwomen don't seem to compliment each other all that much, and when they do, there's often a hidden message that needs to be decoded. Beware of the backhanded compliment: "Your hair looks so much better with that cut." Which is why I so desperately wished I could have taped my friend's NUM (no ulterior motives) kudos.

French Mothers, American Mothers, and Mothers-in-Law (les Belles-Mères)

We American mothers have got a bad rap in France. We've been accused either of being too permissive or being too much at our children's beck and call. American mothers may give their children a lot of liberty, but French mothers are ever present long after the children have grown.

The only one thing you can say with certainty about French mothers and American ones is that they are different.

Raised in America, where we go off to college at eighteen and start our adult lives, we become autonomous, or almost, early on. I was amazed to see how long French young people remain at home, mainly for economic reasons, and how even when they finally move to their own apartment or get married, how close "the tie that binds" remains. For example, one young lady I know decided to share an apartment with her friends only a few blocks away from her parents' place. The decision was met with incredulity (why would she leave home when all is well here?) but finally accepted. She moved into a spacious apartment, with a big room where she could set up her desk and her affairs, and all was well. A few days later I learned that her mother was regularly cooking and bringing food to her. The girl was twenty-five.

But this is nothing compared to the next tale. A married

couple in their thirties have a baby; they both work. The woman's mother regularly deposits, in Tupperware containers, meals she has cooked for them. When I expressed my utter surprise, the mother was surprised at me. "But Delphine gets home so late," she said, "and neither she nor her husband have time to take care of meals." In the United States, I explained, her kind gesture would be interpreted as "interfering," with the implication that the young person is incapable of getting her act together. I personally would have been insulted had my mother brought me food once I'd moved out!

"My first mother-in-law," an American friend married to a Frenchman told me, "used to send me—on the train, for heaven's sakes—at least one roasted chicken, a million tangerines, various vegetables. Drove me absolutely bonkers. My husband was genetically incapable of going out to buy a box of Pampers. So when I was laid up, he would call his parents to do it. And they found that perfectly normal."

Early on in my married days, my mother-in-law came to see us in Nantes and brought with her a roast chicken. For her, it was to "help" me. For me, it was an insult, meaning that I wasn't capable of roasting a chicken. Looking back on it, I think that rather than be offended, I should have wised up and encouraged her to make all the meals during her stay. How dumb can you be? But I was young and trying to prove that I could be as skilled in the kitchen as she was.

When I tell my Frenchwomen friends that once the children become adults, they should be fully responsible for making their own food, washing and ironing their own clothes, cleaning their own apartment, and leading their own lives, they nod politely, but I can see they're either thinking I'm crazy or a terrible, hard, unloving mother. I'm starting to feel positively monstrous.

A huge cultural difference is at play here. Explaining it,

Raymonde Carroll in her landmark book, *Cultural Misunderstandings: The French-American Experience,* writes that "American parents worry if their children hesitate to 'stand on their own two feet.'" French parents, I'd say especially French mothers, certainly don't have that problem.

Other than your own mother, whom do you know better than your mother-in-law? Many times this turns out to be unfortunate, with daughter-in-law and mother-in-law either indifferent to each other, at war, or estranged. I'd be an arch-hypocrite if I said that I'd never had a day's difference with my husband's mother, but those differences were minor and she was unfailingly supportive and kind. As the years passed, I came to appreciate her more and more. I grew to admire her immensely, especially when I think back to certain stupid remarks I made when younger, which must have required tremendous willpower on her part not to answer. In my defense, I felt I had to affirm my personality (my husband will tell you there's no problem with that).

My mother-in-law taught me how to cook French food, how to set a (French) table, the importance of discretion— she would wait for me to call her rather than call me for fear of interfering. This is not your usual mother-in-law behavior if I can judge from that of my friends' mother-in-laws. Whenever she wanted to impart advice to me, she would preface it by saying, "And it's free!" She wisely taught me that if you're going to do two sit-down meals a day, you make the major one at lunch, so you can use it as a basis for the meal at night (smart!). She taught me that sometimes, so as not to hurt people, you don't tell the truth. Once, after a ring her sister had given me had been stolen and the sister asked me why I wasn't wearing it, I started to confess. My mother-in-law changed the subject so fast I didn't know what was happening and saved the day. She told me later that her sister had been so happy to give the ring; learning it was stolen would have made her too sad. I must have shocked her terribly: this American daughter-in-law who wasn't overly concerned about making meals, who let her children run around without the constant supervision French mothers and grandmothers subject them to, and who didn't call her on the phone as did her daughter every day (I did, eventually, call her with pleasure almost once a week, which was some kind of world record for me). But—and this is where I think I got an exceptional mother-in-law—she bent over backward to keep peace in the family.

The word in French for "mother-in-law" is *belle-mère* (beautiful mother), rather ironic when you see how the *belle-mère* is mostly portrayed as a harpy or a shrew and how many wives either cut off ties or spend their lives fighting her off. I've seen many cases in France where the daughter-in-law decided that her husband's mother was Enemy Number One. It may have been deserved (French mothers can be overbearing), but *quel dommage.* I guess I got lucky.

Having It All—Children and Work

A front-page article in the *International Herald Tribune* on October 12, 2010, gave a good sum-up of what French-women have—and they've got a lot. For starters, they've got a state-funded course of postpartum physical therapy, which is "as ubiquitous in France as free nursery schools, generous family allowances, tax deductions for each child, discounts for large families on high-speed trains, and the expectation that after a paid, four-month maternity leave mothers are back in shape and back at work. Courtesy of the state, French-women seem to have it all: multiple children, a job, and often, a figure to die for," the reporter concludes.

Having had my children in France, I can confirm that all

of the above is true. The minute I found out I was pregnant with my first child, I was taken in hand by a midwife, who dispensed useful advice, as well as lessons on painless childbirth. (For some reason I didn't buy the "painless" in *painless childbirth* and got an epidural, which wasn't easy to do in 1976.) After the birth at the university hospital in Nantes, I did indeed have several sessions of perineal therapy, we did indeed get the family allowance, tax deductions, and the whole works. I spent an entire *week* in the hospital in a spacious, spanking-clean single room getting used to my new baby and my role as a new mother. This being France, do you know what I had with my first meal only minutes after delivering (I was ravenous)? A glass of red wine.

When I had my second child in 1980, it was in Paris and the scene was different. I opted once again for a hospital, but the one I gave birth in, the Pitié-Salpêtrière Hospital, while safer than a clinic, was no one's dream of a perfect hotel setting. To this day, I can still see the institutional green of the walls and remember thinking to myself that the coddling I got in Nantes was a thing of the past. "Get out of bed and take care of your baby" was the message. But still in those days the stay was long, so long I actually began to wonder if they'd ever let me out. Now France has "modernized" to the point where women are lucky if they can stay three days.

More than 80 percent of the French female population between the ages of twenty-five and fifty-four work. Frenchwomen continue working full-time when they have a child, and why wouldn't they? "They have it made," marvels Joyce Kraus. "Do they have any idea how lucky they are to be able to have children and have their jobs saved for them, day-care centers that are safe and good?" And, adds the slim, creatively dressed American, "They get to go out to lunch."

I soon learned that in France you don't have to put yourself on hold because you've given birth. Children occupy an important place, but not the only place. Although French-women say they have problems with child care, they have no *idea* what that means. They benefit from a social system that provides day-care centers and preschool programs we Americans can only envy. French working mothers put their babies in day care as early as they can (my granddaughter was barely seven months old when a place became available at the day-care center, and that was already late by French standards). I'll concede that Swedish or Danish women may have it better, but for an American, the deal in France looks pretty sweet.

Unlike Germans or Americans, Frenchwomen successfully—and guiltlessly—combine work and children. It's not an either/or choice. You do your thing. In a column written before leaving Paris after a decade of reporting for the *International Herald Tribune*, Katrin Bennhold noted that of the many things she would miss about France, none could beat the privileges that mothers hold. "For my French girlfriends," she writes, "having children is just another thing you do in life. You fit them in—one, two, and often three of them—with your career, your relationships, your other projects." She contrasts that with her native Germany, where "it's your life that has to fit in with the child. Having a baby . . . is still a profoundly disruptive event for women, one that tends to curtail career ambition and earning potential in keeping with a stubbornly traditional vision of motherhood."

In France, the ingrained idea that women can have it all conditions the prevalent mind-set. No one in France was upset or shocked when former President Sarkozy's unmarried justice minister, the controversial and attractive Rachida Dati, the daughter of a Moroccan father and Algerian mother, announced she was having a baby but refused to reveal the identity of the father. No, what upset Frenchwomen was that three days after the birth, she returned to work. That, in a country where women have a maternity leave of sixteen weeks before the birth and ten weeks after, was barely conceivable. What a bad example. What a disastrous precedent. The thinking was "She's got help, so can afford to do that, but we can't. We don't want someone like that setting the clock back." Going back to work early is unheard of; not going back to work at all is strange and unusual. A young journalist who works for a major Parisian daily told me about a Japanese woman she knew who decided not to work after she'd had a child. Her French female colleagues were dismayed, upset, and incredulous. They implored her to return!

So with all the deductions on transport and taxes, the generous maternity leave, the available child care, and their job waiting for them, what don't Frenchwomen have?

They Have It All, Except Equality

The headline on that front-page article in the *International Herald Tribune* touting the advantages of the Frenchwoman was "They Have It All, Except Equality." In spite of the aforementioned privileges that make it so easy for Frenchwomen to work and have children, one thing is missing.

"What they don't have," wrote reporter Katrin Bennhold, "is equality. France ranks 46th in the World Economic Forum's 2010 gender equality report, trailing the United States, most of Europe, but also Kazakhstan and Jamaica."

The statistics are abominable—but do they tell the whole story?

A separate article in the same day's paper reported that the French fall from eighteenth place in 2009, when it was ahead of the United States, to forty-sixth place a year later was due to continuing gender wage gaps, few women in management positions, and the departure of several high-ranking women leaders in President Sarkozy's government. Does the appointment of a few women to top government positions really mean a significant leap in equality? And do the women in Kazakhstan and Jamaica have the lifestyle and quality of life Frenchwomen have? It's true that the salary gap (women in France make about 27 percent less than men) has got to close, and it's the next battle. But even with this scandalous difference, why do I think I'd rather be a woman in France than in those two countries that have a higher rating? And why do I not hear my Frenchwomen friends grumbling about inequality?

Maybe because they started with so little and have come such a long way in a relatively short time? Maybe because they know that Rome wasn't built in a day? However that may be, think of where they were and where they are now. Frenchwomen didn't get the right to vote until 1945, and married women only got the right to take a salaried job, open a bank account, and cash a check without the husband's permission in 1965. Before that, Frenchwomen were held to the Napoleonic code, which considered women "minors" and proclaimed, "The husband owes protection to the wife, and the wife obedience to the husband." Not until 1985 was the notion of *chef de famille* or "head of the family" abolished and replaced by "joint parental authority."

I distinctly remember my mother-in-law telling me that she never had a bank account, never learned to drive, and never took a train by herself in her entire life. I simply couldn't believe it. She loved and was fascinated by my American mother, a widow who was her age. She admired how she lived alone and managed her affairs, drove and flew everywhere, and, unlike her, was totally independent.

The difference between my mother-in-law and her daughter shows the change in French society: my sister-in-law works, has her own bank account, drives, travels, and does everything modern women do. All that in only one generation.

Their Way

Shortly after a stint as a special correspondent for *Newsweek* in Paris from 1995 to 2000, Judith Warner shared her revised thoughts about Frenchwomen, observing, "During the nearly six years I just spent in France, I was convinced Frenchwomen were on the Wrong Track—obsessed with their looks, preoccupied by their men, locked in a perpetual game of kittenish femininity. It seemed that they were willing participants in a culture that made a fetish of sexual difference. . . . I truly believed that American women, on the other hand, had secured a gender-free public space in which they could operate as people first and women second."

Not until she moved back to the States and saw how her American counterparts were living did she change her negative perception of Frenchwomen. "If anything, American women, caught in sex roles more traditional than those I'd seen in France, really did seem to be leading dogs' lives. . . . The French have wedded their belief in difference to a realistic and humane view of modern women's lives. Americans have wedded an abstract belief in equality to punitive notions of women's 'compromises.' "

She concluded, "If things are better for Frenchwomen, it is because of an enduring consensus that life should be made livable based on who they are, not on an abstract moralistic notion of how they ought to be."

In a recent conversation, Judith maintained, "French men and women have a better quality of life than we do . . . the health system, the fact that education is not horribly expensive, and, of course, the family-friendly policies make an enormous difference." Yet, she says, for her "the problem of pervasive sexism is a real one" and "deeply poisonous." She wonders "if a younger generation of men will conduct themselves differently."

Maybe, maybe not. It's up to Frenchwomen to deal with their men. Many Frenchwomen I've talked to want more equality with men but reject American-style feminisim with the us-versus-them mentality and strict rules. One friend, a high-ranking civil servant, told me that during a business trip to the States she behaved the way Frenchmen and Frenchwomen do and gave a playful tap to the man sitting next to her. He froze, she said, astonished. That's when she realized that spontaneous touching between sexes is no laughing matter in the States—and that she would not want to live in that kind of environment.

It makes sense that Frenchwomen, who've grown up in a Latin culture where people are used to dealing with gray areas and nuances, wouldn't want to ape the black-and-white "Anglo-Saxon" way. They prefer the not-so-easy job of negotiating the fine line between what's correct and respectful behavior and what's not. Chantal Jouanno, the former minister of sports, said that one day she realized that she was not wearing skirts to the National Assembly because of the reaction the men deputies would have. She also realized that wasn't healthy—and started wearing skirts again.

The frontal approach isn't the French style. Frenchwomen don't think that they are being treated as inferiors if a man opens a door for them or helps them off with their coat or performs any number of other gallant gestures. As we were eating breakfast in a hotel with an American couple on vacation, the woman noted she didn't have jam. Being French, my husband immediately jumped up from the table and went to get it. When he returned, she looked at him and said, "I could have done that myself." No Frenchwoman would ever have said that. She knows that she could have done it herself. That's not the point. She would have said, *"Merci."*

Besides their history and their culture, Frenchwomen have another thing in common. They make the most of what they have and have succeeded at creating a quality of life many would envy.

To be sure, there's progress to be made on gender equality, mutual respect, the glass ceiling. But I have no doubt that will happen. Never forget: Frenchwomen are one part silk, one part steel. When they want something badly enough, they'll get it.

Their way.

A "Real" Frenchwoman

I started this chapter with the description of the Frenchwoman most of us envisage when we think *Frenchwoman.*

And I'll end it with one we might not.

Florence Le Mat is the total opposite of that stereotypical image of the slim, reserved, mysterious Frenchwoman. She is attractive but not pencil thin like a *Parisienne* (I suspect that for this self-described epicurean, lunch is not a salad without dressing). Her brown eyes sparkle behind a pair of glasses that seem to be made for her face. She's open, spontaneous, and not intimidating the way certain Frenchwomen, especially *Parisiennes,* can be.

I met Florence when visiting her art gallery in the prettily named town of Missillac in the Brière on the edge of Brittany, where we have a vacation place. Within five minutes, we were laughing and chatting as she told

(continued)

me about the gallery and commented on the work of the artists she was exhibiting. "Mostly Bretons?" I asked, looking at a well-executed seascape.

"Mostly *coup de cœur* [love at first sight]," she replied, pointing out the other paintings and sculptures (half and half) of the talented artists she spots and works with.

Ten years ago Florence, now forty-eight, was living in Paris and looking for a job. On a website she met François, a Breton who makes wood furnishings for boats, pulled up stakes, moved to the west of France, and married him.

She says she never regretted her haste. "You must reflect on decisions, of course, but then act quickly. You must seize the moment."

After settling down with her husband and their three daughters, Florence, who says she would have loved to be an archaeologist, found a job in an art gallery in the nearby seaside resort of La Baule. Four years ago she opened her own gallery opposite the neo-Gothic church in Missillac. She spends her days either meeting local artists or trawling the Internet and specialized art magazines looking for artists whose work she'd like to display. She's proud that two of her artists' works are hanging on the walls of a private home in San Francisco, the result of an American tourist's *coup de foudre*.

When I asked her if she'd ever encountered sexism in her professional life, or if she had ever felt unequal to the men she worked with, she didn't hesitate a second. "No." However, she allowed that women in corporations certainly might and affirmed, "It's true that women still do most of the housework." Her father, for example, was served at the table by the women in the house.

Things are changing, though, with the new generation. "My husband takes care of his daughters the way a woman would," she says proudly.

While on the subject of men/women relationships, I asked her if she was bothered if and when a man looked at her or gave her a compliment. "*Mais pas du tout,*" she exclaimed. "It's agreeable to have a compliment. It's like a perfume or an accessory. It's nice."

As we said good-bye, Florence asked me if I liked to *pêcher à pied,* which means going to the seaside when the tide is out and picking up shellfish. Her eyes lit up as she described the vast expanse of beach, walking barefoot in the sand, bringing back a bucket of *palourdes* (cherrystone clams) to clean and eat for dinner. I envisaged her on the weekend or during lunch or after work in pedal pushers on the beach. She may not be our image of that cool cucumber, the perfectly coiffed and dressed *Parisienne* who roams the Latin Quarter in her spike heels and short skirts and pretty pout, but she's got gallons of something that's very French—*la joie de vivre.*

Wining and Dining *à la Française*

The French dinner party—sophistication and simplicity, an improvised lobster feast, the love story the French have with their food, body parts, making a four-course French meal in the blink of an eye (well, almost), the joie de vivre *of eating in France.*

Anyone having traveled to France has dined in a French café, bistro, brasserie, or gastronomic restaurant, but the lucky few have been invited to a meal in a French home. There they can get a feel for the Real Deal, not only how and what the French eat, but how they entertain. My first lessons in the art of wining and dining *à la française* came from observing "how they did it"—and what I discovered was sparkling and stupendous and life changing. I had no idea that so much love and care and detail could go into even the simplest of meals. I had no idea that a French meal is composed not only of savory food served in courses, but of another absolutely essential ingredient that isn't food. The French call that ingredient *convivialité* (conviviality). Following are

a few descriptions of dining experiences I've had in France . . .
to whet your appetite!

Chez des Amis—*A Dinner Party for Six*

It's eight-thirty and we are late to a dinner party at the home
of friends who live in a faraway Paris suburb. "Confounded
Friday-night traffic," Philippe mumbles with resignation as we
are halted in one of those epic Parisian traffic jams. (Moment
of truth: he didn't say "confounded" . . .) Finally there's a re-
prieve, and we speed to our destination, relying heavily on our
trusty GPS since *les banlieues* are an everlasting mystery to
my very Parisian husband. When we finally show up an embarrassing forty-five minutes late, we see to our horror that
all the other guests are well into the *apéritif*—and logically
must be dying to eat. (Word to the wise: if you're at a dinner
like this and impolite people like us show up late, start drinking water while you wait or you'll be sloshed by the time you
get to the table.) Yet in spite of our tardy arrival, Monique, our
hostess, doesn't rush us. That is *so* French—even if her soufflé
risks falling, a French hostess acts as if all is well. (I'd have a
nervous breakdown.)

For another good half hour, we drink our *apéritifs* and
chat, then at the signal rise and proceed to the table, which is
only a few steps away in the minuscule living room. It's a get-
together of old friends, but as usual the utmost care has been
taken. We collectively ooh and aah over the exquisite glass-
ware, the colorful Gien plates that harmonize perfectly with
the tablecloth, and the first course Monique has artfully presented in transparent glass bowls to display the layers of
hues: the green of the avocado, the pink of the smoked salmon,
the white of the goat cheese. After we've finished, she changes
our plates and brings in the main course, a big platter of

couscous, a North African dish and French favorite, made with lamb and succulent fresh vegetables served with semolina. She places the serving dish in the middle of the table so she can ladle out steaming-hot helpings to each guest. The next course is cheese, a tempting Roquefort, a sweet-smelling Saint-Nectaire, an aged comté. Who could resist? The end nears. Since it's the Feast of the Epiphany, Monique has chosen a *galette du roi,* a traditional cake made of a light, puffy dough with a favor baked inside. Tonight's galette is filled with frangipane, my favorite. The person who gets the slice with the charm is king or queen—tonight it's Monique who dons the golden cardboard paper crown. By midnight we are sated, both by the food and drink (red wine, white wine, mineral water, no Coke or soft drinks, *naturellement*) and the animated conversation, but it's too early to go. We're offered after-dinner drinks and herb tea and coffee. Then, finally, when the ritual is complete and after we've spent fifteen minutes chatting as we stand in the vestibule and say good-bye, we're on our way home.

Chez Nous—An Improvised Lobster Feast

One lovely spring evening, we invited some new American neighbors in our building over for drinks. In so doing, we broke one of our household rules: never ask people "just" for an *apéritif.* Since they're coming from afar (for Parisian Philippe, any place more than a metro stop away is "afar"), you mustn't make them come all the way to you unless you're offering a real meal. If we'd followed that Cartesian logic, the neighbors would have had a drink and trekked back up the stairs to their apartment.

But logic has nothing to do with hospitality and generosity, and right in the middle of our *apéritif,* my husband, who is ingrained with great quantities of both, couldn't resist inviting the charming couple to partake of our meal.

Very nice—but there *was* no meal. Earlier that day we'd consumed one of the two lobsters Philippe had been given at the fish store by a fellow named André, a local who was "in his cups." He started chatting with Philippe, thought he looked like a deserving recipient of his alcohol-propelled generosity, and insisted he accept his *homards*. (People either really really like my dear husband on first sight or really really don't. When they don't, it may be because they think he looks like a tax inspector or former president Jacques Chirac. When they do, the sky's the limit, hence *les homards*.) The one lobster left was definitely not enough for four.

Knowing that my husband is a loaves-to-fishes man when it comes to multiplying small quantities, I got out of his way, and our trio beat a retreat to the terrace to continue our drinks. By the time Philippe summoned us, he'd worked his magic. The table was beautifully laid with silver and candles, and the lobster meat was cut up in bite-size pieces on an elegant-looking plate surrounded by hard-boiled eggs, tomatoes, and a homemade mayonnaise dotted with fresh parsley. Our miracle man had reached into the fridge and found a few other things—herring, pâté—to serve as a first course. We had cheese in the house, and he had rushed out to the pastry shop to buy fresh baguettes and a dessert. Fortunately the pastry shop is only a two-minute walk.

Our American guests were astonished, especially the wife, who said she'd never have imagined you could do what he did on such short notice. "French blood," I gaily responded. I supposed I should feel guilty because he's doing the cooking and serving, but I don't. He's so good at it! Beyond the delightful meal Philippe had produced in a snap, it was the natural way he did it with such good cheer. No fuss, no bother, no asking for help. (Oh, he can't stand having someone else in his kitchen.) Maybe he's an exception even for France, but in my mind only a Frenchman could have pulled off that particular improvisation with such grace, such aplomb, such panache.

Panache . . . One Sunday we had my friend Elaine Sciolino, the author of *La Séduction,* and her husband, Andy Plump, over for a simple lunch. For it, Philippe prepared the Rochefort-family potato omelet. When the potatoes are perfectly sautéed in goose grease, he adds the eggs and watches over them until all is perfectly cooked. Then he takes the skillet, puts a plate on top, and flips the concoction onto the serving dish. This time, though, for some reason he chose a plate that was exactly the size of the skillet and decided to perform his act in the living room. Arriving near the table where we were seated, he triumphantly did what he usually does exceedingly well—and missed. Omelet flew everywhere, including on a white chair . . . and I can't remember a single other thing about that meal other than rushing to clean the upholstery before it turned yellow, laughing a lot, and drinking a lot more wine than usual.

Panache is a wonderful French trait—but it's risky. The consolation prize for being that daring is that if you flub it and egg does indeed end up on a white chair instead of a plate, you've injected a mega-mass of *joie de vivre* into what would otherwise have been a conventional meal. I even began to wonder if he'd done it on purpose. . . .

Chez Ma Belle-Mère at the Country House

In marrying a Frenchman and thereby becoming part of his family, I soon found out that the thinking about, buying of, and consumption of food (at least in this particular French family) is a daily occurrence, and a meal is not some happenstance matter that occurs whenever someone's "hungry." A French secret, and the reason the French don't get fat: for Philippe, and the vast majority of his compatriots, *you don't eat when hunger strikes*. You eat at regular times and the hunger will come—no worry about that! As the French saying goes, *l'appétit vient en mangeant* (the appetite comes as you eat).

When my French family repaired to the country house, the entire weekend revolved around food. When we weren't eating, we were talking or thinking about eating, and when we were eating, we'd often discuss . . . eating (meals we had had in the past, meals we would have in the future). Breakfast is the least of anyone's worries, consisting of tea and coffee, grilled toast, and homemade jam. (Rarely croissants, they are too heavy.) That's basically it. Compare that to an English or American breakfast and you might feel cheated. But you have to look at what's to follow.

On a typical Saturday or Sunday morning, while we were sipping our coffee, my mother-in-law would start peppering us with questions. Shall we have lamb for lunch and an omelet for dinner? A *rôti* for all those people coming to Sunday lunch? I'm sitting there blurry-eyed and half-asleep. The first time she did this, I do believe my mouth was hanging open in astonishment. "But it's only nine o'clock in the morning!" I wailed.

That didn't matter. The market was going full tilt in the nearby village and we needed to get there to check out all the food possibilities. I was overruled. (And with a mother-in-law making the delicious food and doing the brunt of the work, who was I to impede progress?)

The big oak table on which we ate our breakfast looked out over a lovely brick terrace and yard, at the end of which was a river trickling by under a tiny bridge the children were thrilled to skip over to "the other side," where land perfect for games of *boules* and touch football stretched out. I can't count how many hours we spent at that table eating and drinking, talking and telling stories, and gazing at that well-landscaped yard, but I reckon it would be in the thousands. The kitchen window also overlooked the yard, providing a pleasant view for my mother-in-law, who spent a good deal of time in there. The kitchen was small and lacked modern conveniences. The refrigerator, especially compared to American ones, was tiny, as was the stove. My mother-in-law possessed worn strainers and only one or two paring knives. Her pots and pans and casseroles had seen better days. But, oh, the marvelous meals that came out of that *cuisine*. My mother-in-law, as well as my sister-in-law, made all the traditional French dishes from *pot-au-feu* to *boeuf bourguignon* to *poulet basquaise* to *pommes de terres boulangères*, plus a variety of always fresh, always well-presented starters at every meal.

Our meals were informal, but every one was a ceremony following inevitable rules and rites. The first rule was that you showed up. I don't remember anyone's ever opting out of a meal unless seriously ill. In addition, you didn't say you didn't like what was served or that you had allergies (more on that later). If that was the case, you smiled, passed the plate, and waited for the next dish. Anyway, plenty was going on besides eating. My sister-in-law would invariably start spouting off about politics and immediately get into a mega but amicable disagreement with my husband. My brother-in-law and I let them go at it while reserving ourselves portions of the succulent fare my mother-in-law urged upon us. The children, thank God, were actually seen but not heard (French children early on learn that monopolizing the conversation is *not* seen as "cute"). And my father-in-law, simply by his presence, brought dignity to the proceedings.

Sometimes I thought this family was Italian, not French,

so Fellini-like were their repasts. But they were typical French meals, in which the wine and food fuel the conversation. The only unwritten rule was not to be too serious about any given topic. People interrupted each other so often and changed the subject so rapidly, I told Philippe I thought they weren't being polite. "Being boring is worse," he told me. "A meal is a meal, not a university seminar."

In the beginning, I was restless. For an American, the Sunday French meal, especially, can be exhilarating or excruciating. Initially, for me, it was the latter. *How can they possibly sit for so long?* I'd ask myself. *I mean, couldn't we consume all that food and wine in about twenty minutes and take a walk? Read a book? Play a game?*

One weekend I calculated that in two days we had dined for a total of at least fifteen hours. That may sound long to you, but for the French it's *joie de vivre!*

How Do They Eat All Those Meals, Spend All That Time at the Table, and Not Get Fat?

As time went on, I became a huge fan of these dinners where everyone, young and old, talked and laughed and got up to help. When our children were growing up, we did the two-meal-a-day thing every day. Not only did they not get fat, but we gained valuable hours of family time around the table. For me, that's an absolutely winning combination.

And here's the kicker: I've always kept my weight down in France. It's in the States where I pack on the pounds. It isn't because I'm eating hamburgers or hot dogs. It's because I'm eating them on the run. I find myself hungry at odd times, have to keep filling up, and am no longer used to huge quantities. In France, despite a lot of food at meals, the portions are smaller. Also, since you know you'll be sitting there once again in the evening for another big meal, you tend to take less. (Like many foreigners, initially I thought that the first course was the meal, devoured everything, and was astonished to see more coming.) Also, the French have a system of checks and balances. They may enjoy a weekend of fabulous food, but come Monday, it's back to lighter fare. Even then, though, they don't separate food into "good" and "bad" or sneak away to eat the "bad" food alone because it's . . . evil. Children are taught that they can eat everything. They also learn to wait. I will never forget going to the babysitter's place and seeing my eight-month-old in a high chair crying for his food. "I think he's hungry," I said to the *nourrice,* who loved him like her own children. "Of course he is," she replied serenely. But—she indicated the five other children— "he's going to have to wait." The first time I heard this, I was astonished, but I have since seen how important the capacity to wait can be. French children and adults simply don't feel they have to stuff food in their mouths every time they're hungry. Chocolate or cookies are reserved for the *goûter* (afternoon snack), and there's no question of downing the box. Our grandchildren are served wonderful homemade puréed vegetables that they most always eat. If they refuse, their moms or dads don't make a federal case out of it. But they'll introduce the vegetable again, either at the same meal or another time. And here's what I love most about France: no child is allowed to whine or dictate what he wants to eat. From a young age, children get a clear cultural signal: eating is a convivial and joyful experience and the parents decide on the menus. Period. Pamela Druckerman, the author of *Bringing Up Bébé,* based her book on her discovery of the unique way the French approach many aspects of children's upbringing, including food, comparing it to the United States and Britain. Unlike Pamela, I brought my children up in a French family where the French way she so well describes was natural. I champion it and hope French parents will never change.

My motto after all these years echoes that Nike slogan, "Just do it."

"Just eat it!"

Eat the French Way and Don't Get Fat

People always wonder how the French can eat all that food and not get fat.

Here's one answer. A recent study by a French think tank, the CREDOC, showed that in spite of the constraints of modern life, the French have maintained their traditional way of eating—three main sit-down meals at regular mealtimes at which all participants eat the same food. The French love variety in their meals, and it's unusual to eat the same thing each day. For the French, conviviality is the most important aspect of the meal.

The French eat much less in between meals, which may contribute to how in the United States 26.9 percent of the population is obese, as opposed to 14.5 percent in France. The French consume more of their calories at lunch—37 percent for the French as opposed to 24 percent for the Americans.

So, to eat the French way and not get fat, all you've got to do is sit down three times a day at regular hours, eat a variety of food in small portions, nix snacking in between meals, and take the time when at the table to enjoy not just the food but the company and the conversation. Sounds French to me—a bit of everything with joy and in moderation. How hard can that be?

A Common Thread—What, Besides French Food, Goes into a Joyful French Meal?

A common thread runs through all French meals whether sumptuous or simple, whether a one-dish affair or a five-course extravaganza, whether *chez* the local librarian, a friend, or the in-laws.

That common denominator is that French hosts and hostesses "put out." *Haphazard* is not an adjective that goes well with *French dinner party*. More appropriate ones would be *well-ordered, well thought out*. They "put out" not to impress but to create an atmosphere in which everyone is comfortable and having a good time. It may sound simple, but a lot of work lies behind the "show" they produce.

First of all, the host and hostess pride themselves on making sure that the guests are at ease. Unlike the customer in France, who can do no right, the guest in France can do no wrong. In one of the best-loved apocryphal stories about true *politesse*, the host, upon seeing his guest mistakenly drinking from the finger bowl, picks up his own finger bowl and drinks from it as well.

Second, whether for friends or family or colleagues, considerable time and thought goes into the preparation of the menu and the table setting; for example, our friend's couscous meal was perfect for a cold, humid wintry evening. The couscous without anything preceding it would have been fine, but a tasty and colorful first course gave the meal a touch of finesse. Even when we had our improvised lobster feast, my husband made sure to serve a small starter. Once, in my early days in France, I asked why we had to bother with a first course, as we always did at his parents' place.

(And I mean always: in forty years, I cannot remember one meal without a starter.) I found this all well and good as long as someone else was thinking about it and doing it. But why all the fuss? Why not skip it and go on to the essential? Philippe patiently explained that the first course doesn't have to be fancy, but it's an *introduction* to what's coming. It takes the edge off the appetite, it's part of the ritual, it's refined. You don't want the famished hordes to gorge themselves and assuage their hunger immediately. Then what would you do?!

As for setting the table, my attitude was "Who, me?" It was the part I hated the most—maybe because I felt I deserved some kind of medal for actually getting three to four courses on the table, so why bother about the rest? I always left it to the last minute. And it looked like it.

Once again, the French knew more than I did. Well, how was I supposed to know that the table setting is capital, even crucial? Whether the glasses are Baccarat or Monoprix, the plates Limoges or IKEA, the idea is to showcase the food (no small wonder the French excel in *les arts de la table*) and please your guests (they can see that you made a special effort for them).

When I finally got around to emulating my in-laws and went beyond the bare bones of knives, forks, glasses, and plates, the result was as startling as it was unexpected. The food was the same, but suddenly I was getting compliments on my cooking. Odd? Not really. Totally *logique* (as the French well know). Served on an eye-appealing table, the food got noticed in a way it hadn't previously. I was thrilled— and baffled at how long it had taken me to scope this out. Something the French had known for centuries, and which my mother-in-law had gently been hinting about for some time, was a pure revelation to me—and I've never looked back since. One more little lesson in what makes up the famous French *art de vivre*.

Another point about these "typically French" repasts is that few Frenchwomen, or at least the ones I know, have help or ask guests to bring dishes. It's *their* show, from beginning to end. To make a similar four-course French meal in the States, an American host and hostess would need to ferry in the entire U.S. Corps of Engineers—or at least a neighbor girl or two for assistance. The French have this little art of making their dinner parties look effortless, as if they went to no trouble at all (giving me the urge to kill!).

Taking the Time to Enjoy

When you're at the table so long, the conversation counts as much as the food.

In Paris, whether at a simple dinner with friends or one of those stylish Parisian dinners where everyone is (supposedly) in the know and gossip about other Parisians is one of the main staples, the diners dine, but they are also talking, often interrupting each other in midsentence, which, as I mentioned before, to my Anglo-Saxon eyes seems impolite (but who asked me?). At a successful Parisian dinner, the guests gossip, prattle, hold court, and theorize until the end of the night, write the authors of *Une vie de Pintade à Paris*. And if someone gets offended by something said, it only adds a bit of *piquant*. The opposing parties may hold grudges that last centuries—or make up the next day. And who cares? What they do or don't do will be the subject of the next dinner party. Note: not all Parisian dinner parties end up in skirmishes. At most of them, the conversation turns around more mundane matters, such as the latest restaurant, latest great meal, latest fun place to go, or the latest scandal (invariably

the sex life of a current president or politician), all punctu-
ated by animated facial expressions, laughs, and sighs, and
much drinking of wine. Parisian dinner parties reach their
crescendo as they advance, so the later the hour, the better.

An American friend who moved to the States after living
in France with her French husband said that in the beginning
she had a hard time convincing her busy guests that they
could arrive later than they normally would and stay longer.
"When we were invited to people's homes, they'd always say,
'Come early,' the idea being that you would leave early as
well," she said. After living in France, she found this "strange,
kind of like an allotted time for fun." To the delight of their
crowd, she and her husband retained their French lifestyle in
the States. It did, however, take those companions a while to
get with the program.

"Our friends could not believe our dinners lasted three
hours. They'd say, 'We have to go home early, go to work to-
morrow.' Now they can't wait to be invited." She continues,
"The dinner parties we have are with well-educated people
with good jobs and strong political opinions. They know
we'll have a meal that lasts hours and will have plenty of time
to discuss, and I think that's why they are so delighted. Where
else but at the table can you talk with people in that way?
Sitting down to a real meal with a real conversation is so
civilized." (The Americans got used to the long meals, but her
French husband, like mine, still goes into acute culture shock
at restaurants when the American friends order a dish to
share or an appetizer as a meal. Blasphemy!)

Debra Ollivier, who lived in France with her French husband for many years and now lives in L.A., appreciates the
French talent for living and their ability to have a late dinner
party *and* get up in the morning to go to work. She told me
that on a recent trip to France she was at an *apéro dinatoire*
(a French version of tapas or an ameliorated cocktail party)

in which courses and courses of varied goodies, hot and cold, were served throughout the evening with good wine and champagne. What struck her, besides the food and the effortless and elegant way French hostesses carry off such occasions, was that "no one was rushed." No checking the watch or having a loud cell-phone conversation with the office. Work is work and fun is fun.

Julia and Julie and Joy

Which brings me to Julie and Julia. Much was made—in the States—of the blog that led to the book *Julie & Julia* and the ensuing film. In France, if you took a poll, you wouldn't find many people who know who Julia Child is. This only underscores that she is a uniquely American phenomenon. We bless Julia for bringing French recipes to the States in a pleasant and unpretentious way (even though I find her recipes complicated, but then I had a French mother-in-law to teach me firsthand), and we have to take our hats off to the persistence of Julie, who spent an entire year making every single recipe in Julia's cookbook.

This being said, Julia clearly had more fun than Julie. Rather than spend a year making every single recipe in anyone's cookbook, a normal French person would prefer to learn a few good recipes to make a few good meals to serve to a few good friends. "Learn how to make a handful of delicious dishes perfectly," my wise father-in-law advised me early on. "And don't serve guests something you're making for the first time." I thought that unexciting and odd, but knowing my genteel father-in-law, I understood what he meant. For him, you honor company with the tried-and-true, the best. A guest shouldn't be a guinea pig.

Making every dish in a cookbook is indeed a feat, a show

of prowess, a victory, but I wonder, Was it a pleasure? Did Julie sit down at a candlelit table to quietly eat and share the meals she made? Certainly not in the film, where she was harassed and harried and hysterical. In the end, the whole ambitious operation looked like a giant anti–*joie de vivre*.

Between Julie and Julia, I'll take Julia, whose *joie de vivre* was infectious. Because, as the French well know, the point of cooking and eating is . . . joy.

Entertaining—No Space Is No Excuse

An average Paris kitchen, at least in the apartments I've lived in, is about as big as an airplane cockpit. And in that cramped space, French hosts and hostesses turn out lavish meals. The French are experts at making do with what they have. This fascinates me, especially when I compare it to what comes out of some of the gargantuan, expensively equipped kitchens I've seen in American homes in which the only food in sight was the makings of a sandwich, if you got lucky (my apologies to all those who have immense kitchens and turn out full meals regularly—I'm just jealous of your spread!). As an American friend who is married to a Frenchman and has lived in both France and the United States observed, "In American homes there are all those kitchens with granite counters and brand-new appliances. There's all the beautiful crystal and silverware, but no ever uses it or invites anybody over. You have the props but no cast, no one playing the parts."

My kitchen's not bad for a Parisian kitchen, but no one would go so far as to say it's spacious—which is why I find myself dreaming of a monster kitchen and planetary living space when it's time to throw a big party. One December, for example, the entire family turned up from Paris, Marseille, and Montreal to celebrate Christmas. That meant a Christmas Eve dinner for thirteen adults and seven children. I fantasized about living in a enormous American house with a separate dining room and a huge kitchen and a pantry and counter space and machines for this and that and a breakfast nook where I could serve the wee ones—but soon landed on earth and realized that what I was up against was no fantasy: it was preparing the meal in my 70-square-foot kitchen with next to no counter space and serving all those people in my 250-square-foot living room. *Crowded* wouldn't begin to describe what it was going to be.

I timidly floated the idea of a buffet, but that didn't work because there wouldn't be enough places to sit comfortably. Next, I imagined serving a one-dish meal, maybe couscous or chili (I know—it's a weird idea for Christmas). My sons and their partners listened to me respectfully, but clearly, for this French contingent anything other than our traditional Christmas meal was going to be a shocking disappointment and major letdown. After much discussion, we decided on two services. The children, aged three to nine, had basically the same meal we did (including the oysters and the smelly cheeses) before Santa Claus appeared and they got down to the joyful task of opening their presents. We then cleared the table, pulled it out to its maximum size, put in three leaves, reset it, this time around with a large tablecloth, candles, and a centerpiece. Elbow to elbow, we gorged on oysters and foie gras, the Christmas goose, and a medley of fresh vegetables, followed by a salad with homemade vinaigrette and shallots, a flavorsome cheese plate that starred the Mont d'Or, from the Jura, which is at its apogee at this time of year, and as the finale, cakes from a top *pâtisserie* (no, I did *not* make the dessert, but in our family that's a tradition, and I defy anyone to do all the rest in a tiny kitchen—enough is enough!).

But as I said, the French entertain like this all the time and don't complain about lack of space. I will never forget Philippe's elegant aunt, slim and dressed all in black, stirring up the most fabulous food I've ever eaten in my life in a kitchen so microscopic only one person at a time could be in it. One young French travel specialist, Amandine Dubessay, told me she regularly does dinner for thirteen in her small apartment (70-square-foot kitchen and a 250-square-foot living room, just like mine). The same week I talked to Amandine, I was corresponding with an American friend who said she'd like to invite us to her Paris apartment to dine but it was too small. "How small is it?" I asked, and found that it was almost exactly the same as Amandine's and mine!

Amandine has no dishwasher, but does that mean she brings out the paper plates? Absolutely not. The *apéritif,* the main course, the cheese, and the dessert each is served in different dishes as between every course she changes plates. The butter goes in a butter dish, and if she buys sushi from the local Japanese caterer, she transfers it onto a pretty plate. Granted, afterward the apartment's in disarray and she's got a lot of cleaning up to do, but between that and paper plates or plastic glasses, she says she would rather have the work. And speaking of plastic glasses and paper plates, my husband agrees with his compatriot. He would rather spend all night doing dishes than use plastic. Plastic's for picnics, he says— and he hates picnics! (But he's just . . . himself; not all French people have such scruples—if they did, fast food would never have made the inroads it has.)

Time to Learn About Timing

My mother-in-law made the cooking and serving of meals look like such fun, such a pleasure, so *facile,* that I foolishly started thinking it was—that is, until one day when she was ill. In a well-intended but pathetic attempt to replace her in the kitchen, I put on an apron (hard to find as no one in the household ever wore one) and made dinner for eight. The hot course cooled while we ate the first course, so I had to go heat it up again. I'd forgotten to make the vinaigrette rather than doing what my organized mother-in-law did, which was make it and put the desired quantity at the bottom of the serving bowl, with the already washed and sorted lettuce leaves gently rested on top ready to be tossed with the serving utensils placed next to the bowl. I didn't have the cheese out on the serving plate ready to go, I didn't have . . . well, you get the idea.

I think I never admired my mother-in-law more than I did that day. *How* did she get everything so right and make it look so natural?

As the French say, *chapeau* (hats off).

The Thought Process of Meal Planning

To say I've come a long way is an understatement. I can pull off those French meals now, but you should have seen me in the beginning. It took me ages to get to the point where I felt at ease giving dinner parties in France. When I was a novice, even the idea of holding a French dinner party made me break out in hives. My husband is French, but that was different. He was my husband. But for his friends, what was I to do? How would I plan a menu? What would I give them? Would they laugh at me? After some initial faux pas (terrible, awful no-no's, such as *forgetting the bread* and *serving the cheese stone cold*), I at least got real familiar with what *not* to do.

Now, all these years later, I'm no longer terrified, but that's normal after decades of watching the experts and soaking up a few of their little French secrets like an American sponge.

In the beginning, when it was all too complicated for me,

I'd make a checklist. On that list: the starter, the main dish, the salad, the cheese, the dessert. You can skip some of them and have a one-dish meal with a starter or dessert (hence those formulas in restaurants with the either/or). My husband, as I said above, is big on first courses, so in the beginning I would run to my *belle-mère* for advice (after all, if he liked them so much, it was her fault, *non?*). *Au secours!* Please, Marie-Jeanne, something simple, *de préférence*. She always came to the rescue and instilled in me (forever) the idea that the *entrée* doesn't need to be a big, complicated deal you spend hours on, but rather something easy to make, pleasing to the eye and palate. (You can also get into things that are *très compliqué*—if you've got centuries ahead of you or help, which I don't.) For my beginner's purposes, she suggested a fresh salad of tomatoes, spring onions, avocado slices, hard-boiled egg, and hearts of palm drizzled with a homemade vinaigrette. Easy, yes? *However,* when my *belle-mère* makes even a simple salad, she gets the freshest tomatoes at the market and takes out the seeds and peels off the skin, she makes the vegetable guy swear on the Bible that the avocados are not too hard and not too soft, she presents her salad on individual plates on a bed of fresh lettuce leaves, not one of which would dare to have any visible defect. She would never in her life use a commercial bottled salad dressing. She doesn't even know they exist, so no problem. If she did, the one that would kill her would be the "French," which has no earthly resemblance to any real French salad dressing.

You can't imagine the things she taught me, things I didn't know, had no idea about, for example, taking meat out of the fridge an hour or so before cooking so it wouldn't be tough. She taught me that you use different eggs for soft-boiled than you do for other purposes. That was a revelation, believe me. I quickly rushed to my *fromager,* asked for *œufs coques,* and watched him take them from a place next to the "ordinary" eggs. Oh, so they *were* special. (It wasn't that I didn't trust my mother-in-law, but I had to see for myself.) Now I choose the *œufs coques* to make soft-boiled eggs, which (another learning experience) the French eat with *mouillettes,* finger-size, buttered strips of bread they dip into the yolk. I was taught this not by my mother-in-law, but my two-year-old stepson, who was upset to see me attacking my soft-boiled egg, and serving his, with a spoon. Even at age two, he set me straight on that one *tout de suite.*

While we're on food discoveries (but I'll soon stop because the list is so long), I learned that you don't have to buy an entire rabbit when you have a hankering to eat bunny but there are only two of you. You can buy a *râble* (saddle or lower back of the rabbit or hare). I buy one because they're big, baste it with mustard, then prepare it the same way as the chicken I describe later, and it's a feast for two. Armed with the precious basics my mother-in-law taught me, I was equipped to turn out savory home cooking, mostly *plats mijotés* (stews), which are my favorites. To this day I stick with what's simple and tasty and good. I admire complicated recipes and sometimes wish I could execute them, but then, I reasoned, that's what the great chefs and restaurants are there for. And they've got help and huge kitchens!

But back to my early days: Now give me an idea for the main course, I would beg my *belle-mère. Pas de problème, ma petite fille,* she'd reply. (I am not little or a little girl, but *petite,* as you've seen in the chapter "Small Is Good," is affectionate.) How about a tasty chicken with spring onions and *champignons de Paris,* diced bacon, and white wine? You peel and cut the potatoes (get the red-skinned ones that don't fall apart and turn into mush as they cook) in two and nestle them alongside the bird. She gave me a few little tips on braising that chicken so it would have a nice color, and on thickening the pan sauce. In the summer she would steam an entire hake, head and all, in a huge, oblong pan. When it was done, she'd gently extract it—I could never figure how she did this without it falling apart—let it cool, and carefully remove the skin. She would then place the beautiful white fish on a large oval serving dish and surround it with hard-boiled eggs, tomatoes, cooked and skinned potatoes, and her superb homemade mayonnaise. For the finale, she placed a sprig of fresh parsley in the mouth of the fish. Simple as it was, it was always a major hit.

Once I'd benefited from her advice about the starter and the main course, the cheese course was a cinch. All you had to do was choose a few *chez le fromager* and put the *sélection* on a plate—making sure to serve at room temperature by taking them out of the fridge at least an hour before the meal. The dessert: as I said, you don't even have to make it! French pastry shops offer a multitude of choices, and French sherbets are superb. You can keep your dessert simple or go upscale for *petits fours* or *tuiles* or *macarons* from Pierre Hermé or Ladurée, to take but two examples.

So you see? A French meal in courses isn't that hard (especially in France, I must admit, where it's so easy to buy savory cheeses and pâtés and other quality food). There's harder, *bien sûr* . . . sophisticated dishes, meals in which you make every single item, but if I learned a thing or two about *joie de vivre* in this country, it's "to each his own." Those who love spending their days in the kitchen concocting complex dishes do that, and so much the better for all the guests. Those whose skills lie elsewhere go the simple route. The main thing is that both hosts and guests enjoy the moment. I've heard some Americans say in shocked tones that they were astounded to discover that French hostesses will serve starters or desserts that are *bought,* not made. That doesn't shock me in the least. A dinner is not a cooking competition. A dinner, I learned from my in-laws, is gathering people around the table, and if you don't have time to make every single dish, it's no crime, especially in a country where the *charcuteries* and the *pâtisseries* turn out first-rate food you'd be proud to have on your table.

Part of the enjoyment of having a dinner party is in the shopping—but you've got to be willing to give the time to your excursion: the vegetable store, the butcher shop, the cheese shop, the *boulangerie,* and the wine shop. And the supermarket? I didn't move across the ocean to shop for food in a supermarket. It is indeed a convenient two-minute walk from my apartment, and I buy staples such as flour and sugar and mineral water and laundry soap there. But why would I come to France to buy industrial cheese, packaged bread, and meat under cellophane? And with no conversation other than "hello" to my favorite cashier. On the other hand, if I walk a mere ten minutes, I'm in a street with a cheese shop, several *boulangeries,* and *boucheries* where I buy my heart out and come back home laden with succulent seasonal raw-milk cheeses, baguettes still warm from the oven, and meat the butcher cut right in front of me all the while telling me how long to cook it and at what temperature. It takes more time, but when I've finished my shopping expedition, I've had a cheery discussion with each of the shopkeepers, procured special food instead of standard fare, and am in a good mood. A nice way to spend time if you ask me!

Reality Check

Now that I've painted a picture of France that might have given you the misleading impression that every owner of a French passport sits down to a four-course meal twice a day

and people spend their time palavering with their food pur-
veyors, let's get real.

I'll be frank. It was my luck to marry a man who comes
from a family of cooks. Not professional cooks, although
Philippe's maternal grandmother worked for a time as a chef
in a restaurant in her native village in Périgord. No, they're
what I'd call "natural" cooks. They love food, they love com-
posing a menu, they love going to the market, they love preparing and serving, and they love having company. It's in
their genes.

However, I could have married a man whose family is
indifferent to food and would rather be anywhere else in the
world than in the kitchen. For while many Frenchmen and
Frenchwomen cook and prepare meals, many don't. One famous French fashion designer amusedly told me that she
raised her kids on the Laughing Cow (which, if you didn't
know it, is French). My butcher told me that the younger
generation doesn't come to his store during the week, when
they eat packaged stuff from supermarkets They do, however, show up on the weekends, when they have more time
to devote to *la cuisine*. I know Frenchwomen, especially in-
tellectuals, for whom it's a point of honor *not* to cook (so
bourgeois . . . puhlease).

Life is brief; people work, and they don't have time to turn
out elaborate meals daily. Many French people, young, old,
men and women, are regular clients of the frozen-food giant
Picard, which has eight hundred stores scattered throughout France. Frozen food? you may say. *Ce n'est pas possible.*
But Picard products are haute couture compared to the frozen
TV dinners found in most U.S. supermarkets. I mean, how
about a *tartare de saumon* (minced salmon) or *coquille aux
noix de Saint-Jacques, à la Bretonne* (scallops) or *bouchées
aux ris de veau* (sweetbreads in a puff pastry)? Picard is frozen food with flair; until it became so ubiquitous, many a

French hostess would surreptitiously slip in a Picard product among the "homemade," unbeknownst to her unsus-
pecting guests. My sister-in-law, who's a highly skilled cook,
would do this when short of time. The main thing to say
about that is not that she did it, but that *she didn't announce it.* Blunt American that I am, I would have made
some comment about not having had time to do a whole
homemade meal. A French hostess wisely figures that what
went on in the kitchen is her affair. If she does own up that
she didn't make the cake or the pie, it's because she feels like
doing so, not because she feels guilty. So she takes a shortcut—
big deal.

When I walk from my place to the metro, I pass a French
café-restaurant, serving typical French fare; a chain restaurant called Indiana, serving cheeseburgers and fries; a McDo,
with same but less expensive; a typical French *boulangerie,* in
which a long line of people await their turn for the various
sandwiches and salads; a Greek restaurant; a Chinese takeout; and a kebab stand.

In France today, there's a mix of everything—French restaurants, foreign restaurants, fast food, takeout, people who
know how to cook and how to serve, people who have no
idea, people whose mothers passed on their recipes, people
whose mothers wouldn't go near the kitchen, people who frequent fast-food joints, people who wouldn't touch fast food
with a ten-foot pole.

That's for the reality. The famous eighteenth-century French
gastronome Brillat-Savarin coined the phrase "Tell me what
you eat, I will tell you what you are." I'd love for him to return from the grave to tell us what the French "are" today
when it comes to what they eat. I think he'd find a thousand
different stories, with, still, one common thread—eating is
enjoyment. But what about the younger generation in France?
Do young people know how to cook? Do they care?

On Passe à Table *with the Younger Generation*

For thirty-year-old Déborah Dupont, the owner of the Librairie Gourmande, a well-known culinary bookstore near the trendy rue Montorgueil, the French expression *on passe à table* describes a typically French relationship with the meal— the expectancy of what's going to happen *at the table*. She compared that with what she saw in the States when she spent a few weeks with her husband, who was studying at Stanford, and whose roommates were another Frenchman, an American, and a New Zealander. "He and his French friend found recipes, made food, and sat down at the table to eat. The New Zealander and the American looked at them with astonishment because they themselves were eating a quick sandwich standing up."

The contrast was even greater, she noted, when the French students got together for a dinner party. "Their conversation at the table was about the meals they had before, how their grandmothers cooked, the meals they would have in the future."

This being said, although the younger generation still loves to talk about memorable meals and loves to get together around the table, that doesn't necessarily mean they know how to cook the way Maman or Grand-mère did.

Many young Frenchwomen barely know how to boil water. Their mothers were too busy flinging cobblestones at cops in the 1968 riots. That's one reason so many young French people flock to cooking classes now. They're getting from a chef what Maman didn't transmit. Déborah is an exception. "I learned how to cook from my mother," she told me, modestly revealing in the conversation that she can make a *mille-feuille,* flaky pastry and all. Now, *that* is impressive.

"But," she continued, "I have friends whose feminist mothers on purpose refused to pass on their recipes and their secrets because they didn't want their daughters to be subject to their husbands." Déborah paused. "Except that when my friends started having their own children and the pediatrician explained to them how bad the ingredients in store-bought products are—too much sugar, too much salt, too much bad palm oil—they realized they didn't even know how to make a simple cake." They also realized they didn't know what to buy. "Food shopping for our generation has become a totally psychotic activity," she claims. Actually all of this is good for her business because the members of what she calls this "lost" generation are avid for knowledge and on the prowl for cookbooks.

Faire à Manger and Faire la Cuisine

What's new in this generation, Déborah told me, is that people make the distinction between the routine making of a meal every day (*faire à manger*) and making a special meal (*faire la cuisine*). In the first case, generally the mother in France gets home earlier than the father, so she has to rack her brain about what to serve her little family, usually one simple main dish followed by, perhaps, a yogurt and fruit, and that's it. "I'm an exception—my friends look at me as if I'm from outer space when I tell them I serve my children a first course of raw vegetables or salad, a main dish, cheese or yogurt, and a dessert." (Well, perhaps not as far out as all that: see my comments about our grandchildren.)

When the weekend comes, the men, who haven't been around much of the week due to long office hours, take over the kitchen and, instead of doing the routine, make something exceptional. (When you think about it, if there are so many male chefs, it's because they haven't been bogged down in the humdrum daily stuff.) Times are changing: I know quite a few young French couples in which the woman works full-time and comes home late, while the man takes care of the children and the cooking. Lucky women! In our case, Philippe generally got home around eight-thirty or nine p.m.; during the week, I turned out the meals. On the weekend, he did. You can guess whose food was more creative.

On Sunday, Déborah told me, many young people with families have adopted the American tradition of brunch. I find this funny. Philippe, being traditional, never liked the concept of brunch, which he said was both too late and too early and you ended up being hungry in any case. So we never did brunch either at home or out in spite of my being American— and now here are all these French young people doing it. Weird.... They like it, Déborah said, because it's informal, because they can sleep later, because the children can participate and not have to stay at the table, but can move in and out of the meal. All very American, if you ask me.

Still, when all is said and done, the French remain French. Déborah told me about inviting an American friend for "an informal, no-fuss" dinner. What did they serve him? Among other things, a *blanquette de veau*. That typical French dish of veal in a white sauce, which was one of my mother-in-law's specialties and *really* good but long to make by American standards, is a "major meal" and, even by French standards, hardly "no fuss."

So if I understand what she's telling me, this new generation is in a sense a lost generation, but not as lost as all that. They're not necessarily going to serve elaborate meals in courses, but they're making an attempt to eat healthy food and learning to cook when they feel the urge.

And being French, they don't raid the refrigerator or eat standing up. *Ils passent à table.*

Regional Specialities and the Joy of a Joue (Cheek)

The French, let's face it, lucked out. They live in a country whose mountains, rivers, seas, and plains yield an astonishing variety of produce. Place names are important because they denote the region the product comes from. Little French children learn early on that *rillettes* come from Le Mans, *cassoulet* from Castelnaudary, *escargots* from Burgundy, *aligot* from Auvergne, *sole* from Dieppe, *tripes* from Caen, *Camembert* from Normandy—and those are only a few of the specialties linked to specific regions.

Even the way people cook depends on the region they come from. Northerners use butter; southerners, olive oil. My mother-in-law, who is from the Dordogne, uses goose fat. I salivate to think of her sautéed potatoes and onions and *lardons* (bacon) cooked in goose fat. (Did cooking this way make her fat? What a question. No, not at all, for heaven's sakes, she's French.)

French journalist François Hauter chose the village of Saint-Julien-du-Sault in Burgundy, where Japanese chef Keigo Kimura presided over the kitchen of Les Bons Enfants (Keigo Kimura has since moved on to a Paris restaurant), to reflect on the combination of gastronomy and a great chef. He described some of the dishes on the twenty-one-euro lunch menu: *gougères chaudes* (cheese puffs), foie gras and *ratafia* (sweet aperitif), *bœuf en selle en terrine* (saddle of beef in a terrine) . . . But, as usual when it comes to the French culinary experience, there was more than that. "The clients . . . were laughing as they left the restaurant. They look like rainbows. . . . Delight has made them fraternal and beautiful." Note the lyric description. The Frenchman eats, but the Frenchman also speaks, describes, relives the meal and its effect on the company.

Hauter says that when he was living in China, he assiduously followed a French TV food program called *Les Escapades de Petitrenaud*, in which bon vivant French journalist Jean-Luc Petitrenaud hits the road in a jalopy to interview merchants in the markets and chefs in their kitchens in every part of France. Brimming with enthusiasm, Petitrenaud gently prods cheeses, lift lids, and pokes a finger into whatever's cooking. He may go a bit overboard, but you can't help but wish you were with him. Hauter said his Chinese friends, like him, watched the program with their tongues hanging out and tears in their eyes. What's so special about French cuisine, wrote Hauter, is the "push toward excellence, the sublimation of something as daily as what the rest of humanity calls 'eating.' " And, I'd add, the love and pride of the people in each region for the products of their specific *terroir*.

In Washington, D.C., my friend Dorie's French husband, Jacques, happily does all the shopping and cooking—for him it's a joy. Sometimes, though, his projects are foiled. One day, Dorie told me, he wanted to make a *pot-au-feu*, that long-simmering traditional dish of meat and vegetables. Since an important part of the *pot-au-feu* is marrow bones, he ordered them at the meat counter, as he would in France. "The what?" asked the butcher. "Marrow bones," Jacques repeated with his charming French accent. "We don't have them. We throw them away," the butcher replied, apparently mystified that anyone would even ask for them. Jacques was equally perplexed. Dorie said she could hear him five aisles away where she'd taken refuge from the "conversation." "No marrow bones?" Jacques replied. "But what do you do with this part of the cow? In France we eat everything in the animal." Dorie laughed at the scene of cultural differences: one, the idea that for the French it's normal to eat everything in the cow and for the Americans it's normal to throw all that yucky stuff away, and two, that the butcher may have thought

Jacques was arguing when he was in fact having an "impassioned discussion" *à la française.*

But thanks to marrow bones, dishes take on a tasty twist. And thanks to that rich *terroir,* eating in France is not boring, and you can change your menu every single day. You don't have to stick to simple chicken or steak or veal or lamb if you live in France. The French eat almost every part of the animal—they eat blood sausage, tripe, heart, tongue, sweetbreads, cheeks. One of the reasons former president Jacques Chirac was so popular was because he loved food and it showed (not on his waistline, he was slim, but in the obvious enjoyment he took in tasting). His favorite dish was veal head (*tête de veau*). Can you imagine an American president wolfing down a nice little veal head *à table*?

When Chirac was president, every year at the Paris International Agricultural Show, TV reporters would follow him, zooming in on his tall silhouette amid the admiring farmers, where he'd be smiling and and joking and biting voraciously into a piece of mouthwatering *saucisson,* followed by a big swig of beer. A diminished Chirac, aged and hard of hearing, continues to attend the show and is as popular as ever with the farmers, who revere a man who obviously knows what's good and respects their work.

The *agriculteurs* were much more reticent about former President Sarkozy, who couldn't tell a cow from a cat, eats with little gusto, and doesn't drink a drop of alcohol. No wonder the French voted him out of office!

Eating It—Dead or Alive

At the Salon, which is held every year in the spring, the attitude the French have toward the food and the land, what they call *le terroir,* is on high display. As Jean-Benoît Nadeau and Julie Barlow write in *Sixty Million Frenchmen Can't Be Wrong*, the French don't bother to be hypocritical about what they are ingesting. Arriving at the show, the authors saw "no hot dogs," but they did see "cattle pens . . . decorated with huge posters of raw steaks and sausages . . . a stand with live ducks right beside another one selling their livers in jars." The unsettling juxtaposition of the live animal with the "dead" product almost ruined their appetites at first, but they rapidly ditched their qualms as they tasted the wine, the cheese, the *saucisson,* and a Savoy *tartiflette.*

I laughed as I read this passage, recalling the moment the daughter of American Francophile friends, having bravely eaten one oyster at a dinner with a French family of oyster growers, curiously poked at a second one with her fork—and saw, to her horror, that it *moved.* "Mom," she asked, her eyes opening wide, "is it alive?" The French hostess proudly answered, "Of course it is"—at which point the friend's daughter rushed from the table to be sick. The cultural gap went both ways. Although the hosts were sympathetic and served grilled fish during the rest of their guests' stay, they were startled when my friend suggested they bake the oysters. For them, *that* was positively unthinkable.

Strong Tastes, Strong Smells

It's normal that foreigners might cringe at the sight or smell of rather horrid-sounding foods such as *museau de porc* (pig's snout), not to mention cheeses that smell like old socks. The French, on the other hand, have grown up in a culture of strong tastes and strong smells. In this not totally antisepticized country, you've got Guerlain and Chanel as well as the Urine Packed Parking Lot and the Deodorant Deprived Metro.

Ever bought a ripe Camembert and driven around with it in the backseat of your car on a hot day? I did—and thought I would probably expire before the Camembert and I got back home.

As for *andouillette* (pig's intestines), well, let's just say that it's an acquired taste . . . and an offal (pardon the pun) smell.

I didn't really think of onions or garlic as being particularly potent so was rather surprised when our lovely German *au pair* girl informed me she could not abide either of them, a problem considering we were on vacation in the south of France, where they are staples. I tested her by making a ratatouille and not telling her that both of her loathed ingredients were in it. She loved it and asked for seconds. When I confessed, she gamely replied that what she didn't like were *raw* onions or garlic. *Touché.*

Camembert and the Crèche (Day Care)

It's natural that little French children don't shy away from robust tastes and smells. They're used to them. Our children and grandchildren attended French schools, where they ate the French way, and where cheese, and not just "mild" cheese for children, is served at almost every meal. French school lunches don't feature sandwiches at all. Children are expected to sit at the table with knives and forks and eat the meat or fish and vegetables and yogurt on the *menu du jour.* I'd almost forgotten about cheese at the *crèche* until one recent day when our eighteen-month-old grandchild was having lunch *chez nous.* What should I give her? I asked her parents. "Whatever you're eating—she eats like we do now" was the reply. I hardly thought I'd try her on kidneys or brains, so offered her steak and green beans, which she gobbled up. Then she spied the cheese and pointed at it. I followed her gaze to the plate, which had Camembert and a sheep cheese and a comté. She lapped up the Camembert. Then her mother suggested I give her some of the *brebis*. "Sheep cheese?" I asked. "Are you sure? It's kind of an acquired taste, isn't it?" "Try it and you'll see," my son said, smiling. I sliced off a tiny piece and gave it to her. She took it with her baby fingers and popped it in her mouth, eating it all. She pointed for more, and we had to stop her before she ate the whole thing.

Even Five-Year-Olds Eat Mussels

Globalization is trotting along at a fast clip, and now I see French people gobbling burgers and fries, not just at McDonald's but at sit-down restaurants. Not to mention snacking on nachos! Good Lord! *L'Amérique* has come to France! So should I or should I not fear that our grandchildren will shun strong tastes and smells and never taste an *escargot*? That they'll raid the fridge rather than sitting down to the table? Frightening. Frightening.

I don't think I should worry. In spite of the creeping industrialization and standardization of food throughout the world, the French are still extraordinarily interested in what they eat and drink. They've elevated even the simplest dinner party to an art form, and the highest compliment they can give is to invite you to their table. Sure, you see young people snacking on sandwiches in the metro, but I have the sneaking suspicion that when they go home at night, they eat a "regular" French meal. (It's more than a suspicion: statistics say that almost 90 percent of the French population has a sit-down dinner in the evening—in other words, kids and teens and students may take to Starbucks and McDonald's like gorillas to bananas, but that doesn't mean they've totally abandoned their French ways.)

I write these lines while on vacation with our grandchildren aged five and nine. We have three sit-down meals a day, which, with the exception of breakfast, consist of three or four courses. The children eat everything from fresh asparagus to *pâté de lapin* (rabbit pâté) to aged comté, chèvre, and Roquefort, which they devour. But in case you think they're poster children, rest assured, they did solemnly inform us of their dislike of any form of cabbage. Other than that, though, they are French through and through and polish off provender that would surely disgust most American kids their age. When Judith was six years old, we were on vacation in Normandy and took her to a restaurant where she tucked into an entire plate of mussels with cream sauce. I watched her in amazement. On a recent trip to Brittany during school vacation, I sat on the terrace of a restaurant in Le Croisic and curiously checked out what the various families were eating. At the table in front of me, a young father sat opposite his son who was probably twelve. The father ordered a crêpe, the traditional Breton pancake; the son ate what I was eating, an enormous bowl of mussels accompanied by French fries. Only a few tables away from them, an even younger boy was expertly delving into *his* bowl of mussels. I don't know about you, but for me that's French. (The other French aspect of that scene is that those children weren't squirming or monopolizing the conversation or complaining about the food. That's normal.) French children aren't asked what and when they want to eat. The French would relate to Fran Lebowitz's sage one-liner: "Ask your child what he wants for dinner only if he's buying."

Even though I'm American, when it came to meals, our sons grew up in a French household. Naturally I made brownies and chocolate chip cookies and barbecued spareribs and all my favorite American foods and would not on my life miss Thanksgiving, the one day of the year, according to the late humorist Art Buchwald, that Americans eat like the French do every day. However, when it came to the daily serving of meals, the modus vivendi in our Franco-American family was definitely French (logical: we live in France). This had its advantages: when we had company, the "treat" was that the kids got to drink Coke and eat sandwiches.

Now, even though our sons have left home and have their own families, when they come back, they expect the full monty. (That will teach me to have gone so native.) Fortunately my husband gets in there and often does all the cooking. I told him he does it better than I do, and that's not only so I won't have to do it. Mine's fine, but his is better. He's got the French touch.

Le Hamburger (Ahm bür gair)

I realize I've made several allusions to hamburgers, and you may be wondering why. (Are they evil? Do I have a hang-up?) The reason is that when I first came to France, the hamburger didn't exist, whence my authentic anecdote in *French Toast* about serving a homemade one to my father-in-law, who was absolutely astonished. "Why don't we throw bones over our shoulders while we're at it?" was his comment. He was shocked not by the food (after all, if you deconstruct a hamburger, it's bread and meat and tomato and lettuce, all of which are components of a French meal), but by its being all of a piece and eaten with the hands.

That was then, and I still smile when thinking back to the scene. Since then, the hamburger has become commonplace, served not only at McDonald's but even in bistros and brasseries. It's caught on like brownies and muffins and cheesecake.

(But not to worry, the French have always adopted food from other cultures and incorporated it into theirs—couscous from North Africa always rates among the most popular "French" dishes.)

One Frenchman who adores hamburgers decided to make his living from them. A graduate of a prestigious French business school who lived in Santa Monica for four months (presumably eating every hamburger in sight), Victor Garnier is the twenty-five-year-old owner of a tiny restaurant named Blend in the trendy Montorgueil area. Blend's hamburgers are garnished with onion compote and Emmentaler, and, yes, there are even veggie burgers. (Good Lord, I can assure you that you didn't see veggie anything when I first came to France!) All the burgers come served in a basket, and the clients happily eat them with their hands (when I think that a few years ago I wrote that the French eat everything, including bananas, with a knife and fork . . . It's true, though. Philippe cuts the shell off his shrimp with knife and fork!). I was so fascinated by the idea of fancy French hamburgers that I hopped over to the restaurant—where I had to wait in line for twenty minutes. Once seated, I glanced around the minuscule room, trying for the life of me to figure out why in the country of haute cuisine all those young French people were chowing down on American food. I asked my tablemates, forty-year-old Mickael de la Selva, the director of public relations and marketing for the Buddha Bar, an Asian fusion-food restaurant, and thirty-five-year-old Cornelia Oswald, who works in e-marketing, if they ate that way all the time or if they actually made French food. Cornelia, who asked the waiter for a knife and fork to eat her *ahm bür gair* with (ah, something French at last . . .), told me that her mother taught her how to cook and that she pays attention to what she eats and shops at markets. However, she pointed out, "These days the difference between young people who make and eat traditional French food is often a question of social class. Some young people don't even know what an avocado is." (How depressing!) Mickael, who lived in New York for ten years, cheered me up when he noted that there's still a key difference in eating habits. "In the States even the president of a company eats a sandwich—you wouldn't see that here." And, they both agreed, there's a huge difference in time. "In the States," Mickael observed, "people wolf down their sandwiches anywhere. Here, even if it's a sandwich, we take the time to eat it." For example, they told me they were planning to spend an hour at Blend eating and talking—and for them an hour was even minimum. Cornelia, lively, pretty, and slim, thinks this is healthy: "Since I eat well at lunch and take my time, I don't take a break every couple of hours at work to snack." She added that when she has to eat lunch at her desk, she definitely sees it as a "constraint."

Why No Doggie Bags?

When an American woman one day asked me why the French have such a "thing" about food, I realized I had never given much thought to the question. But I did manage to come up with a few answers. One is that at many moments throughout the country's long history there was little to nothing to eat. During the Franco-Prussian War in 1870, the people of Paris were reduced to eating rats. In World War II, the legal ration was 1,150 calories a day per person (2,500 to 2,800 are considered necessary to survive in average conditions of life). Philippe, who was a toddler, still remembers the oranges his uncle tracked down for him and the chocolate and the chewing gum distributed by the GIs. The generation of French people who grew up during the war do not throw away good food. This explains why, if you leave a substantial amount of food on your plate, it is a faux pas. Of course, it's not much of a compliment for the host or hostess, but it's mostly shocking because it's wasted food.

As for leaving a restaurant with your unfinished food in a box . . . If the French don't have this custom, it's because of the cultural expectation that you'll finish what's on your plate, portions being small enough for a normal human being to consume right then and there at the table. Coming from Midwestern cow country, where steak is a serious (and delicious) matter, I was used to eating T-bone steaks that overlapped the plate. When I served a similar-size steak to my mother-in-law, she didn't know what to do; she thought that her portion was for the entire family. Finishing what's on your plate goes hand in hand with another strong cultural expectation: that you haven't grazed all day long, snacked in between meals, or stuffed so much in your mouth at the *apéritif* that you're no longer hungry.

Allergies and "Food Issues"— Leave Them at the Door

For the French, food is more than calorie units you cram into your body to keep the machine running. Food and wine are objects of joy and desire to the French, and the conviviality of a shared meal is a hymn to life. Pardon my eloquence, but I do feel that the French attitude toward food—they love it and don't fear it—is the reason they have so few "food issues" and that dinner parties are such joyful, pleasant, stressless experiences. Sharing a meal is supposed to be pleasurable, and the cultural expectation is that you eat what you're served. My sister-in-law, who entertains a lot, told me that if she's serving oysters and she's got a guest who doesn't like oysters, "the person will just have to sit it out until the next course." I asked her what she'd do if she'd invited a person to dinner and he told her he was a vegetarian. "I'd uninvite him!" she replied. To Americans, who are attentive to everyone's special needs, food allergies, and issues, this probably sounds cruel. And I think my hospitable sister-in-law was kidding about not inviting the person. But for sure she wouldn't make a special menu. French people view the table as a place for conviviality, not a place where each person does his own thing and brings to the table personal food requirements.

I once threw a party and made the mistake of asking the guests if there was anything they didn't eat—oysters, shrimp, foie gras. The French guests predictably said they liked everything—and were obviously surprised to be consulted. The non-French guests furnished a laundry list of their allergies and food preferences. It made me tetchy, but it was my fault. How were the non-French to know about the "invisible social contract": when invited to dinner, guests leave their food issues at the door.

In four decades in France, I've never once heard a French person mention the word *allergy* at a dinner party. Most likely because, according to etiquette expert Marie de Tilly, "It is completely impolite to talk about them. If you have real food allergies, you don't accept a dinner invitation."

I once asked a French friend if she had allergies to anything I'd be serving—and she could hardly believe I'd asked. She didn't want to tell me but eventually confessed that, yes, she did have an allergy to mushrooms. Not a light allergy, but a serious one where she kind of blows up and horrid things happen. "But," she said cheerfully, "serve whatever you want, of course." I *love* it.

Why this discussion about food issues and allergies? Because allergies can be serious, even life-threatening (in which case, as Marie de Tilly advises, you simply don't accept the invitation), but also because "allergy" is often used as a substitute for "I don't like" or it's a cop-out. A clear case of the cop-out happened many years ago in Nantes, where we were in contact with a group of American students whose leader lived with us. One night one of them called him from the hospital and, when he arrived, reported that she'd been violently ill because she was allergic to champagne. The French doctor, my husband, the group leader, and I admired her creativity. "Young lady," the doctor said with a smile, "you're not allergic. You had too much to drink."

American Susan Herrmann Loomis, who runs On Rue Tatin, a cooking school in France, thinks, "Americans are afraid of food. They generally want it processed, packaged, tamed, and antiseptic. The idea of live bacteria in food, what an American might call 'dirt,' is unthinkable. This plays out in the preponderance of our food allergies and food-related illnesses. The French eat a lot of live bacteria because their food is closer to the source and less highly processed, so their systems are healthier and food allergies are nearly absent." I saw her theory confirmed during a trip in Turkey with some Americans and French. Guess who became violently ill? The Americans, myself included. The French ate the fresh fruit, the vegetables, probably even drank the water, and were fine. The French were also comfortable with the fruit that was bruised, whereas the Americans were leery.

In a country where unwrapped baguettes are passed from hand to hand and people encounter more germs, the French seem to, at least, have fewer food allergies. Little French children eat raw-milk cheeses the way little American kids eat candy bars.

As far as not liking what's served, the (polite) French will take a minuscule portion, which they'll push around their plate so that it looks as if they've eaten at least half. Do not ask me how they do this, but they do. I know—my husband has a severe esophageal malfunction that means that he can choke on anything, and I mean anything, from a grain of rice to a steak. The absolute worst-case scenario is when we're invited to a dinner party where a big *côte de bœuf* (beef rib) is the main course. He smiles, takes a *small* piece, does *something* with it, and makes it look as if he's eaten. "Why don't you say you can't have this or that?" I asked him. "We're invited to dinner, not a pharmacy," he replied.

Our American friend Alan Kors, a history professor at Penn and firm Francophile, says that he never informs hosts that he has certain food requirements, things he can't eat, and a few strong dislikes. "It wouldn't be polite," he says, as he recounted the repercussions of his policy one long-ago day in France. The Frenchwoman he was interested in invited him to dinner, excitedly telling him she'd spent the entire day on a stew he was going to love. It did indeed look and smell delicious. As he lifted a forkful to his mouth, he casually asked what the meat was. "Rabbit," she replied, to his astonishment and despair. "You've got to understand," he says, "that I grew up in New Jersey. For me, eating rabbit was like eating kitten." But—*toujours* polite—in a ruse he asked her to get him a glass of water and, during her absence, hurriedly picked pieces off his plate and stuffed them into Kleenex "in my pockets, in my pants, everywhere." When the meal was finished, he asked her if he could help take the plates to the kitchen. *"Non, non, ça ne se fait pas en France"* (No, that's not done in France), she replied, leaving the table to do some fast cleanup before, presumably, more interesting things happened. Which they never did. Apparently our friend hadn't done a good enough job of eliminating the morsels of the dreaded rabbit. (He needs lessons from my husband.) As she scraped the plates, she discovered the subterfuge and, he said, "became very cold." End of budding romance.

The Dining—Now the Wining

When I first came to France, what I didn't know about wine would fill a big book. It would still fill a book, but, I hope, a slightly smaller one. I knew then that wine came in three colors: white, red, and rosé. It made food taste a lot better, it made conversation more animated, it tasted "good" or "bad." The French drank a lot of it, but curiously, Frenchwomen stayed sober and never seemed to go overboard.

Not wanting the above to be the extent of my knowledge, I enrolled in a wine-tasting course offered by the City of Paris for an affordable price. Along with one Frenchman and a group of fellow foreigners, we learned (in French) about the various wine-producing regions of France, how to read a label, how to see, smell, and taste the wine in our glass, and some of the vocabulary describing that experience. We studiously jotted down information about the different soils and grape varieties—and let me tell you I never knew there were so many. Like most everyone, I knew the names pinot noir and Syrah, but I'd never heard of Tannat, Cinsault, Carignan, and Mourvèdre. Never too late.

Before I signed up for the weekly three-hour course, I prided myself on what I considered my fine-tuned sense of smell. I can sniff out a wet dog a mile away. If someone lights up a cigarette, even in the windiest spot on a cliff overlooking the sea, I'll detect the smoke. Whether it's a gas leak or rancid butter or a heady perfume or the succulent scent of a *bœuf bourguignon,* my nose is twitching.

Which is why I had initial pretentions of being rather gifted when it came to describing the various scents in a glass of wine.

Pride goes before a fall, and my pride—and delusions of grandeur—took a tumble after lesson number one.

When it came time for our professor to introduce us to identifying smells, she passed out numbered vials filled with mysterious liquids with characteristic odors we supposedly know from everyday life.

The English fellow picked up one receptacle, ran it under his nose, then picked up another and another, closed his eyes, opened them, passed all the containers under his nose again— and almost committed suicide on the spot.

"I can't identify *any* of them," he said in despair.

The lone French fellow sniffed away while seriously scribbling his impressions.

The Italian gaily shuffled the little vials around, picking them up, setting them down, picking them back up again, inhaling each one like a madman. The expression on his face could only be described as puzzled.

I picked up vial number 48 and confidently wrote down *grilled almonds*. Vial number 52 was dark and had a familiar smell. I wrote *nuts*. Then I assigned *vanilla* to number 13, *musk* to number 34, and *cloves* to 42.

It turned out that the grilled almonds was in fact toast, and that what I thought were nuts was coffee. My vanilla was raspberries—talk about being totally off—and my musk was cedar.

Cloves, fortunately, were cloves. Score: one out of ten.

As I said, a true lesson in humility.

My classmates didn't do much better, but this didn't stop any of us from swooning over a marvelous 1999 Hermitage, whose fragrance, we concluded, with *beaucoup de* hints and prodding from our teacher, consisted of cherries, leather, prune, and peonies.

Leather? Peonies? I admit I didn't get all that the first time around—or even the second.

But was the wine good?

Délicieux.

I like the taste of wine, I like learning about the various regions of France in which the wines are made, I like to experiment with the pairing of food and wine, especially cheese and wine. I like what Sanche de Gramont writes about wine and France: "The ability to develop a wide range of wines suited to every kind of food is often used as a metaphor for French civilization and its qualities of patience, good taste, and judgment" and "Against the French tendency toward suspicion, wine provides a bond of fellowship, and against tightfistedness, something which it is natural to share." Wine as a testament to the French qualities of patience, good taste, and judgment? Wine as an antidote to the French defects of suspicion and tightfistedness?

Frankly, what's not to like?

Winespeak

Writing and talking about wine is a strange thing: normally talkative people fall silent, and the otherwise silent become eloquent. The person you thought was a normal sort suddenly becomes pretentious, eager to show off all he knows. The person who admittedly doesn't know that much dares not utter a word. And most of us limit our impressions of the wines we drink to "good" and "bad." Of all the delightful areas of eating and drinking in France, wine seems to be the one that's hardest to talk about.

Talking about wine is one problem. Choosing a bottle of French wine is another. Look at the label: there's a château with a beautiful name from a place in France you may or may not know. Most of the time you have no idea of where it is nor from what grapes the wine has been made. This is all very complicated, and the reason many people prefer New World wines to Old World wines. In the New World, the United States, South Africa, Argentina, it's easy. The wine is called by the name of the grape variety: Chablis, chardonnay, merlot, pinot noir.

In the Old World, the wine is called by the name of the *terroir,* the exact place in which the grapes were grown. So then you get names such as Pouilly-Fuissé and Moulin-à-Vent, and unless you've lived in France a long time or are a crack at geography, you wouldn't know that the former is a chardonnay and the latter a gamay. (Or maybe you would.) The idea of *terroir,* says Elisabeth Villeminot, a young Franco-American wine broker, is that the position of the vines on the slope, the sun, rain, and wind will all affect the final product. "You taste chardonnay from one *terroir* to another and you see the way that particular plot of land affects the wine." For Elisabeth, the Old World wines are "still the benchmark of what real quality is," whereas the New World wines are easy to understand and ones people feel less intimidated by.

Intimidation: that's the word. And until or unless you get an interest in or a passion for wine, you are exactly that . . . intimidated.

Not to worry. Plenty of people in France know next to nothing about wine. Olivier Magny, the young founder of Ô Chateau, a wine bar in Paris, goes so far as to say the French are "clueless." He does, however, give them credit for not giving in to a logic of "utter simplification" and buying a bottle of wine from a château they know nothing about rather than requesting a generic name such as Chablis or chardonnay. "Putting the name of the grape on the label makes business sense," he admits. "But is that what we want? We need to show people that diversity is not a threat." (I agree, in case my opinion means anything.)

As for knowledge, yes, some wine connoisseurs know

exactly what they're talking about and what they want, but many people befriend their local wine merchant and ask him to suggest a bottle for what they are serving. Many go to the supermarket—not a good idea for Elisabeth. "Those wines are filled with chemicals and you have no idea of what you're getting." Plus there's no one to give you any advice!

Le Sommelier

In ordering wine in a restaurant, things can be fine—or dicey. If you're unlucky, you'll get a pretentious, overbearing, know-it-all sommelier who force-feeds you his "suggestions." One worldly French gentleman told me that even he let himself be "convinced" by a *sommelière* who imposed her own choices on the terrified table. "She spoke with such conviction and force that we all caved in," he said, adding that the wines she suggested were fine but bore little relation to their initial choices.

Better to fall upon a *sommelier* or *sommelière* who is attentive and open-minded and reads people well, the ideal combination. M. F. K. Fisher, in her book *Long Ago in France*, tells a charming anecdote about arriving in France, not knowing anything about wine, and going to a well-known restaurant in Burgundy where the wines were fabulous and the waiter's "tact was great, and touching." He didn't present them "the incredible wine book" on that first visit but instead suggested they might enjoy the simple house wine. It was the only time he did it, she writes, and she blessed him for it, as the fine wine the establishment was known for was expensive and "would have been utterly wasted on us." Afterward, when the couple became more familiar both with French food and wine, things moved to a different level. "Charles started us out right," she writes, "and through the months watched us with his certain deft guidance learn to know which wine we wanted, and why."

Maybe you'll get lucky with a wine steward like Charles or like Jean-Michel Deluc, who was head sommelier at the Hôtel Ritz for ten years. Deluc, a fifty-six-year-old native of the southwestern region of Gers, a land known for its Armagnac and rugby teams, indeed looks more like a solid sportsman than the stereotypical image of the cold, forbidding, haughty sommelier. The day of our interview he had on a pink-checkered, short-sleeved shirt and chuckled as he thought back to his "costumed" days at the Ritz. In those opulent surroundings, he recalled, clients were often "scared" when they saw him arrive at the table in his uniform with golden grapes on the lapel bearing a thirty-six-page book with the wine list. Deluc says he tried to "make things more relaxed" and smiled as he recalled the "American I loved who said, 'Here's fifty dollars. Do what you want and give me something nice for the money.'" No Frenchman would ever do that, he said, first of all because the French have a problem talking about money, and second, because nothing would be that simple—"They'd want to discuss choices, argue."

A wine consultant and instructor at Le Cordon Bleu and other prestigious venues, Deluc says he'd rather see the young generation "drink a chardonnay from Mr. Dupont [the equivalent of Mr. Jones in English] than Coca-Cola. It's a way to bring them to wine and educate them progressively." For him, wine is about pleasure. If he has any criticism of young sommeliers, it's that they sometimes get "too serious" and forget that the meal should be "a moment of *joie de vivre*." For this professional, who tastes thousands of different kinds of wine a year, *joie de vivre* counts. His goal is clearly to select wines that correspond to the pleasure of the ordinary consumer.

When friends invite him to dinner, he says, they're frightened about what to serve him. "Relax," he says, reassuring

Some Joie de Vivre Wine Tips

From Jean-Michel Deluc, wine consultant, Le Cordon Bleu instructor, former head sommelier at Le Ritz:

- Trust the person in charge of the wine, whether it's the waiter, owner, or sommelier. The person should be there to make you happy.
- Unless you're an expert (which most of us aren't), don't be afraid to admit you don't know much or anything.
- But . . . don't let that admission keep you from giving an idea of the kind of wine you'd like—red wine, white wine, heavy wine, light wine—and stating the price beyond which you do not want to go.
- If you get a bottle of corked wine in a restaurant, tell the sommelier immediately. It will be replaced. If you bought it in a wine shop, take it back—but don't tarry.
- Other than corked wines, don't send back a wine you "don't like" unless there's been a major misunderstanding. Try to make things clear from the beginning, says Deluc, remembering a client who insisted on a Sauternes to drink with his meal. Knowing it wasn't a judicious choice but not wanting the client to look bad in front of his family and friends, Deluc acquiesced. When the bottle came and the client tasted the wine, he proclaimed the obvious: "But it's too sweet." A good sommelier has to know how to advise and not offend, but as this case shows, sometimes it requires phenomenal tact.

- French wine-bottle labels can be confusing for those of us used to seeing the name of the grape variety (merlot, for example). A French label will tell the name of the region, the category, the name of the person who put the wine in the bottle (owner of the vineyard or negotiant), the amount of alcohol, whether or not it contains sulfites, and a compulsory warning for pregnant women. The year is generally marked but is not obligatory. The label won't necessarily tell you the name of the grape varieties. Reading a French wine label is a wonderful way to get to know France, but arm yourself with patience and a good map.
- Wine is conviviality. Says Deluc, "A simple wine in good company in a good place outside with a beautiful sky can be great. With people you don't like, even a very expensive wine won't taste that good."

them, "and tell me what you're making. I'll bring the wine." Or if he doesn't bring the wine, he drinks what they serve and. even if it's not that good, says nothing. That's because he's polite, of course. But above and beyond that, for this ebullient wine lover and expert, the company, not the wine, is the point of the evening.

As always in France, when it comes to eating and drinking, it's the conviviality that counts.

Quality Food, Ritual Meals, the Beautiful and the Good

A real Frenchman is deeply attached to his food and wine as well as to the rituals surrounding it. An American friend told me that at Christmastime one year she and her French husband found themselves in Santa Fe with "no oysters, no foie gras, no salmon," and that her husband, a world traveler, was practically desperate. He couldn't believe it. She wasn't surprised: "He practically cries because I don't drink wine and appreciate cheese the way he does."

She reflected on this cultural difference that she also sees with her French in-laws: "The first time I was with his family, they spent eighty-five percent of the meal talking about food, the meal they had three years ago and the meals they're planning to have—and yet they don't get fat. They're really French—everything has to be beautiful and taste good. They buy only the best-quality food."

That phrase, *quality food,* mystified a Dutch student of mine whose French host family told her that if she bought food on her own, she should aim for quality by going to markets, not supermarkets, because the market produce would be superior, albeit more expensive. She looked at me with questioning eyes: But what's the difference? My mother-in-law could have taken her in hand on that one: the meat, the fish, the vegetables she served had to come from the market and be of the best quality. I'm paraphrasing and I don't know what French chef it was (but logically it would be any of them) who said that you can have the best recipes in the world but without excellent products the dish can't be good. The product is primary.

Protecting the French Gastronomic Meal

The focus on and requirement of quality produce, the combination of good food with good wine, the attention given to the serving and presentation, the time spent savoring the meal in a convivial atmosphere—all add up to that specific French way of wining and dining, specifically "the gastronomic meal of the French," which in 2010 was inscribed on the UNESCO Intangible Heritage List.

The activists behind the demand for classification say their motivations were to honor the specific French tradition, not to be snobbish or exclusive about French food. Still, for some skeptics, the initiative inspired doubts when not cruel mockery. One critic, Michael Schuermann, the author of the guidebook *Paris Movie Walks,* wrote sardonically, "So, it's official. French cuisine is now a part of the world's 'cultural heritage.' Hurrah and congratulations to French cuisine for joining the illustrious ranks of the art of Croatian throat warbling and the Peruvian scissor dance." Others openly wondered why the age-old tradition of the gastronomic meal needed to be defended. What's the threat?

"What's threatened," wrote Jean-Robert Pitte, president of the French Mission for Patrimony and Food Cultures, a Sorbonne professor of geography, and food lover, "is the joy of living we get through what we eat and drink." While some saw the UNESCO move as representative of the smugness of the French, Pitte sees it as a way to do everything in his power to help protect the country's powerful gastronomic heritage. How do I see it? Here's how: If you've got to put world treasures—monuments that might collapse or landscapes that could disappear or intangible food traditions that are menaced by uniformity—on the UNESCO list to protect them, then . . . why not? It can't hurt. As to whether it can help, the jury's out. Like all of us who love French food and as one who's had the privilege of four decades of conviviality and joy at the French family table, I hope the French will realize what they've got—and never let it go.

The Joy of Living

I agree with Pitte that what we get when we're eating and drinking in France is not mere sustenance, but the joy of living. I feel this every single day in France when I:

- Jump out of bed in the morning, rush to any one of the three bakeries surrounding me, and buy an absolutely perfect baguette (either the classic one or the *tradition*) to eat with real salted butter from Normandy.
- Trot over to my local cheese shop to discuss what cheese is in season and get ready to describe how I want my chèvre or my Camembert or my Brie.
- Ask my local wine merchant to recommend what wines I should serve with my dinner menu and get some interested, thoughtful, pertinent, and unpretentious advice.
- Make daily trips to buy fresh fruit and vegetables at the numerous fruit and vegetable shops near me, where I tell the vendor when I want to eat the kiwi or the avocado—tonight or in three days—so he will select it accordingly.
- Splurge every once in a while on a sweet, light pastry, the kind only the French can create.
- Invite family or friends to dinner and think about the hundreds of possibilities of things to serve because there's such a vast variety (marrow bones, raw oysters, quenelles).
- Am invited to dinner and know that no matter how simple the occasion, something will be special— maybe the unusual plates, maybe the flowers, maybe the silverware, maybe an out-of-this-world cheese

plate or dessert, maybe the scintillating conversation or, maybe and most probably, all of those and more.

- Go to a restaurant, stay as long as I like, and not have a waiter asking me if I am working on my meal (answer: no, I am *enjoying* my meal).

Joie de vivre. That's the key word, the word never to forget when it comes to wining and dining *à la française,* whether in a French person's home, at Le Bristol, tasting three-star Michelin chef Eric Fréchon's chicken cooked in a pig's bladder, in a trendy bistro, or at a *pique-nique* of your own making. For the latter, venture into a cheese shop, and even if your French is nonexistent, point at those you'd like to taste. Be sure to include at least one that's unpasteurized (*au lait cru*) to get the real experience. Then head for a wine store and ask what would go best with your cheese. Go into a deli (*charcuterie*) and buy some *pâté* or sausage to eat with a still-warm, fresh baguette from the bakery. Then take your feast to savor on the banks of the Seine, watching the boats go by, or on a bench in one of Paris's many beautiful parks.

If that's not a moment of *joie de vivre,* I don't know what is.

French Cheese, Please
A Day in the Life of a Cheese Shop Owner

A dessert without cheese is a one-eyed beauty.
—Brillat-Savarin

I don't *like* cheese. I *love* it. Which is why my local cheese shop on the rue des Pyrénées is my favorite

(continued)

hangout. It's one of three owned and run by François Priet, who when he's not selecting and selling *fromage* is salmon fishing in Ireland or stalking boar or deer in Poland.

What's a day in the life of the owner of a cheese shop?

On a typical day, by five a.m. he's already at the giant wholesale food market in Rungis, thirteen kilometers south of Paris near Orly Airport, making the rounds, talking with suppliers, placing orders for the cheese he'll put in his shops. By ten a.m. he's back in the first *fromagerie* he opened in 1991 in the working-class but slowly gentrifying twentieth arrondissement of Paris. Sandwiched between a butcher shop and an Italian delicatessen, the boutique is small but stacked with a dizzying array of carefully arranged cheeses, artisanal for the most part.

The first thing he does when back in the shop is fortify himself with a strong cup of coffee and a piece of cheese (what else?). Camembert or Brie, he specifies.

Bear in mind that when François Priet says Camembert or Brie, he's talking about a raw-milk cheese redolent of the pastures the cows grazed in, a Camembert or Brie he has lovingly chosen for his customers and which has no resemblance to the standardized Camembert or Brie in the nearby supermarket. "Supermarkets," says Priet, "don't have the same cheese or the same *clientèle*."

After the Brie break, Priet removes his work outfit, a dark blue, knee-length coat with FRANÇOIS PRIET, VOTRE FROMAGER stitched in light blue on the left-hand pocket, and goes to check out his other two stores. Having started the day so early, after lunch he tries to slip in a well-deserved siesta before reopening the shop at four p.m. He stays open until eight p.m. When the last customer has left, he's still not finished. Only after he's attacked the inevitable paperwork does he leave the premises around nine p.m. No thirty-five-hour workweek for him.

"I work thirty-five hours a week," he jokes, "in two and a half days."

Working hard is nothing unusual for this forty-seven-year-old Norman who represents the third generation of a cheese family. Priet's grandmother had her own cheese shop in Normandy in the fifties when there were no supermarkets—and not as many cheeses. "In those days," says Priet, "there were perhaps fifteen to twenty cheeses which were produced locally."

His father carried on the family tradition with seventeen shops scattered among Normandy, Paris, and various markets. By the time Priet decided to set up his own business, the world of cheese had changed. "Cheese people know much more about their profession now, and there are many more new cheeses all the time."

Priet took advantage of this new tendency to change the stock in the shop he'd purchased from a *fromager* who offered a standard choice of industrial cheeses and mostly young goat cheeses. Priet brought in tasty raw-milk cheeses, new cheeses with shapes and odors his clients hadn't seen—or smelled—before. Part of the pleasure of his job, he says, is explaining where the various cheeses come from, how they are aged, and how old they are. He takes pride in noting that his clients, many of

(continued)

whom he knew when they were tots, are "informed amateurs." Many know exactly what they want—a Camembert not too ripe or very ripe, a comté that is young and fruity, or, on the contrary, an aged comté with a sharper taste.

Whether customers are in the mood for a Sainte-Maure, Saint-Marcellin, Echourgnac, Chabichou, Camembert, Mont d'Or, Petit Fiancé, Abbaye de Citeaux, Fougerus, Soumaintrain, Langres, Roquefort, or Fourme, they'll find them in the store (depending on the season, of course), along with the discovery *du jour,* artisanal cheeses from small producers that sit proudly with their more traditional brethren.

"I'm always interested in finding new cheeses as long as they are artisanal and made with raw milk," Priet tells me, remarking that on any given day up to two hundred different varieties of cheeses are in the shop. The day of our conversation, he made a quick count, scanning the shelves with the eye of a master. "Today we've got about one hundred and fifty different cheeses," he concluded, "of which one hundred twenty are raw-milk." In his quest for artisanal cheeses, Priet keeps an open mind. "One day a fellow who looked like a beggar came to the store. I was going to give him a piece of cheese when he told me he was a shepherd in the Pyrenees and made his own sheep cheese. He'd been at the hospital near my shop and stopped in to talk." Priet agreed to taste his cheese and was surprised and stunned by its uniqueness. The shepherd has since become one of his regular suppliers.

Priet's preference for raw-milk cheeses is not surprising, for, he explains, they are the cheeses that are living entities and hence have the most authentic tastes. "A pasteurized cheese will always be the same, whereas a raw-milk cheese can attain excellence one day and might be not as perfect the next—but when a raw-milk cheese is at its height . . ." He raises his eyes to the sky with the expression of a true gourmet and connoisseur.

What is Priet's favorite cheese? He smiles and shakes his head. "That's a horrible question." Then he replies, as would any self-respecting *fromager* who knows his stuff, "It depends on the season. Comté and Beaufort in the winter, goat and sheep cheeses in the spring, goat again in summer, a good mozzarella." But for Priet, the best cheeses come in autumn, when they take on their full flavor and are, in his words, *"formidables."*

I love to consult with François or his experienced helpers. One day my daughter-in-law told me she was bringing us a bottle of wine for dinner and that she had been told that the cheese to serve with it should be "strong, but not overwhelming, with character." The least one can say is that the field was wide-open. I took the challenge to François Priet, who pointed me to a cheese I had never before tasted, but which has become one of my absolute favorites. It's called Soumaintrain and is from Burgundy. I proudly brought it home, and when the cheese course rolled around, we all served ourselves and . . . it was a smashing success with the wine. Priet, I thought, not for the first time, is more than a shopkeeper. He's a one-man advisory board.

Is French Food in a Free Fall?

Many observations food lover Michael Steinberger, the author of *Au Revoir to All That: Food, Wine, and the End of France* (no less), makes about the decline of food in France are true. You can't deny that fewer French people know how to cook, that more and more people prefer supermarkets to outdoor markets, and that certain kinds of cheeses are dying out. McDonald's is extremely popular, fast food has carved out a permanent niche, the French are taking less time for meals. The business lunch no longer takes three hours, and *les Français* now drink more mineral water than wine. The number of cafés is dwindling seriously. Are you depressed yet?

Steinberger's book unleashed the tongues of doubters, gave the green light to foodies (a word I so dislike—it sounds like such a *job*) everywhere to share stories about the disappointing to downright dreadful meals they had on their last trip to Paris. Whether this is because the Paris food scene has really changed or because people have become more sophisticated is hard to tell. Thanks to Steinberger's book, the frustrated, the distraught, and all those unhappy with their last meal in Paris could at last stand up and be counted.

One of them, Zofia Smardz, writing about "the decline of French cuisine" in the *Washington Post* in September 2009, said she was "relieved" when Steinberger's book appeared on her desk. After a trip to Paris with "not one fantastic feast" in the week she was there, she was beginning to think that she'd built up fantasy memories of the great meals she'd had on her previous travels when she gorged on "wonderful, cheap food."

She acknowledges that nothing's cheap any longer. But, she asked, "How could the food be so . . . awful?"

I sympathize with her, even though her example of a watery onion soup left me with a doubt. When I see onion soup on a menu, unless the restaurant's known for it, I order something else. Onion soup, sadly, has become "food for tourists." No wonder it was awful. This being said, I have to agree that, sadly, the chances of getting a mediocre to bad meal in a Paris restaurant are greater than they ever were before. And do you know why?

One out of two restaurants in France no longer serves food made in the kitchen. Instead, the establishment's "director" or "manager" orders *bœuf bourguignon* or other specialties from industrialists who produce the signature French dishes in quantities and deliver them in vacuum-packed containers. All the "kitchen manager" or "chef" (if there is one) needs to do is open them, heat them, and dash on a bit of parsley to make them look "homemade."

The restaurants resorting to this technique don't trumpet it, and the industrialists furnishing the goods don't give the names of their clients. The food isn't "bad"—but it isn't homemade, that's for sure, and do you really want to part with twenty to thirty euros when you could have exactly the same thing by buying it and microwaving it at home for one-quarter of the price? I don't know about you, but in my opinion it's a valid reason for another

(continued)

French revolution. The French, who are so good about striking, should stage mass demonstrations. They should wake up and smell the coffee.

If they do, I'll join them.

In the meantime, I'll go back to eating my delicious baguette with a dab of nice salted butter from Guérande, I'll whip over to La Maison du Chocolat for a taste of real chocolate, I'll dream of the mussels and muscadet I'll have on my next trip to Brittany, I'll keep up those conversations with my next-door wine merchant about what wine goes best with what dish. I'll take the best from this country and not despair, because France is a bounteous land with a superb variety of food. And you, as a tourist? You too can frequent the small food shops, the *charcuteries* and the *fromageries* and the *pâtisseries*, where you'll find some truly delicious food to taste. As for restaurants, brasseries, and bistros, there may be so-so ones, but that's not the whole picture. I'd even say that France has an increasing number of creative, hard-working, talented chefs. Get a good guidebook and go find the places that excel, not only in good food, but in *joie de vivre*. That's what your French experience should be all about, *n'est-ce pas?*

Epilogue: How I Became a
Little Bit French

Only in France: things you can buy—French jewelry, scarves, perfume, food, and wine. And things you can't—taking to home and heart the best of France, not only French objects, but some special "French ways."

On the days I'm strolling in Paris, whether on the gilded Pont Alexandre III or in the gardens of the Palais-Royal; on days I'm at the seaside downing plump, briny oysters and drinking a glass of crisp white wine at a restaurant with starched, white tablecloths; or on days in any hamlet or city in any region admiring the local museum, church, or historical monument—I'm proud to be a part of France, an observer of French history, an admirer of French art, a lover of French food and wine, and a willing participant in the ever-unfurling *joie de vivre* this country offers. In sum, I'm delighted to be an American in France and even more so because . . .

I am also French! In 1996, when the U.S. government allowed its citizens to take dual nationality, I rushed to the nearest city hall to fill out the necessary papers. I now have French nationality and a French identity card and a French passport.

One word from my lips will tell you, however, that the French accent didn't come with the territory, more's the pity. Moreover, even though I have now lived longer in France than I lived in the States and, as I hope you've seen from this book, enormously appreciate the French and their culture and have tried to take the best from it, I'd need a brain transplant to "think French." My brain is American-wired (put me in any French meeting for more than two minutes and that's immediately apparent).

I'm an "American in France" just as I would imagine that a French person living in America for forty years, speaking perfect English and fitting in, remains at heart a "Frenchman in America." Unless your goal is to totally reject your culture, and you succeed, you generally remain who you are. You can't undo your heritage, your education, your behavior, your outlook, your values, your culture. And you wouldn't want to, for they are what and who you are.

You can, however, "annex" what's best in your adopted culture. And in France, the good things to add on are legion.

The Contradictory French

But first of all, what is it to be French? Jean d'Ormesson, a writer and member of the Académie française, answered that question in a special issue of the magazine *Le Point* devoted to the subject: "In a garden where the water from fountains is running between 18th-century statues and borders of well-trimmed boxwoods, you say 'that's very French.' Looking at an incredible mess where no one understands anything, you say 'that's very French.' In the face of a strike carried out with useless panache, you say 'that's very French.' . . . Pascal is very French and Cyrano is very French. Montaigne is very French and Pasteur is very French. . . . To be French, is to love tradition and love the revolution. To be French is first of all a contradiction."

It's this contradiction, the complexity of a country that's neither fully north nor south, that permeates every aspect of life in France. French admirer Edith Wharton put it this way: "Between the Swiss snows and the icy winter fogs of Germany on the one side, and the mists and rain and perpetual dampness of England on the other, her cool mild sky shot with veiled sunlight overhung a land of temperate beauty and temperate wealth. Farther north, man might grow austere or gross, farther south idle and improvident: France offered the happy mean which the poets are forever celebrating, and the French were early aware that the poets were right."

And yet . . . tell a Frenchman he's living in the land of milk and honey and he'll most probably look at you as if you're crazy. Modesty? Taking it for granted? Pessimistic? As I said earlier in this book, and as polls have shown, in fact the French are "delighted pessimists." They are pessimistic about "life in general," life "out there"—and contented and optimistic about their personal lives.

The same person who will tell you how bad the economy is and how disastrous politicians are won't tell you about all the good things in his life, of which are there plenty. Is it because the ever-present spirit of *critique* is practically poured into baby bottles? Or that at school teachers focus on what's wrong, not what's right? Hard to know, but one thing is sure: someone who talks about what's good is generally seen as naïve (even if everyone else believes what he says). As proof, the French flocked by millions to see the film *Amélie Poulain,* with Audrey Tautou. They were enchanted with the postcard rendering of Paris, the whimsical and touching Amélie, her generosity, her simplicity, her heart on her sleeve. And yet some reviewers panned the film for being too idealistic, unreal, Pollyannish. Bah! Yet another contradiction, this time between the intellect and the heart.

Le Plaisir

In this book, I've purposely skirted around the numerous contradictions, focusing on a simpler, more evident side of France—the pleasure and the *joie de vivre* for which it is famous the world over.

When we come to France, that pleasure delights us and makes us dream. I may live here, but it's impossible to become jaded. To say I feel joyful as I descend into the odiferous metro might be a stretch, but getting *out* of the metro to enter a cozy café or wander around an eighteenth-century garden is a pleasure. One rainy day in a café I watched a group of Japanese tourists, two men and two women, snapping pictures of each other taking fingernail-size bites of macaroons from a distinctively wrapped Ladurée package. They took turns reverently extracting the macaroons one by one, delightedly examining the colors of greens and pinks and bordeaux, before tasting. Ah, what would the flavor be? Pistachio? Mint? Raspberry? Strawberry? When they go back to Japan, they'll take out those photos of themselves in that French café with the variously colored macaroons grazing their lips, bringing happy smiles to their faces. Who knows? They may even remember the tastes. For a small purchase, they got a big moment of pleasure.

Things You Can Buy

So, what do people take home from France with them? I interviewed a few Francophile friends on the subject of what's typically French for them, what things they like to buy when they come, what they find in France that they don't find "back home."

The consensus was that times have changed, that in the age of the Internet, you're only a click away from your desires. I used to ask my mom to bring chocolate chips and peanut butter, both of which I now find on my next-door supermarket shelves—along with Oreos and Philadelphia cream cheese. The day the Oreos and the cream cheese materialized, not at a specialty store but at my local grocer's in the twentieth district of Paris, where there are hardly any Americans, I realized the jig was up: we really are living in a "globalized world."

The French buy Oreos or Philadelphia cream cheese and muffins and hamburgers because they represent America. For the same reason we buy Dior or other French name brands. They become symbols, the tangible representations of the essence of a culture. Paris resident and Scottish businessman Kris Mackay told me that for him Chanel is emblematic, and that one of the only things he ever paid full price for was the Chanel bag he bought for his wife in New York as a gift after the birth of "the most important gift," a baby girl named Lily. "My wife was ecstatic," he said, smiling at the memory. He lives in France and his wife is French, but when asked what he thinks it is that motivates people to come to France, what they are looking for, what they want to take back home with them, this man, who knows all about retail, answered, "People don't come to France for material reasons only. I think they come to

France to adopt another lifestyle they don't have, to be inspired in some way, or to learn and educate themselves at the same time. Fine wines and cheeses and cognac and other wonderful French products give you something more than eating and drinking: they give you an emotional attachment."

My college roommate, Meril Yu, who often comes to France with her Chinese husband to enjoy the wine and food but also to get on their bikes for some impressive rides, said the same thing in a different way. "You can find most things in the U.S., but marc brandy, Armagnac, patchouli-scented soap, *verveine*-scented soap, dark chocolate with hazelnuts, are easier to find in France. The selection of nice jacquard fabrics is better in France. Nevertheless, I think the real reason we truck things back from France is not for the stuff but for the memories."

One of my supershopper American friends, a food writer and ardent Francophile, takes advantage of regular trips to Paris with her husband, a French professor, to stock up on all the things she loves. Among them: Mariage Frères teas (hard to find in the States and packaged so exquisitely in their shiny black boxes or cans) and *fleur de sel*, which she says you can now get in the States but at a much higher price. Pâtés and foie gras in tins, cheeses that are vacuum-packed, and, of course, wines and spirits are all at the top of the list for many travelers, she says, noting, "Even if we can get some of these items at home, they are usually less costly or the selection is better on this side of the pond." Hermès is always a hit: "I don't personally buy there, but on a weeklong tour we led through the city for a university group, the men bought three Hermès ties and showed them off to everyone. There is a real cachet in being able to say that you bought your Hermès tie in Paris." Same for women's clothing. "Who doesn't want to say, 'I got it in Paris'?" she asked. "On every visit I look for the perfect French purse, shoes, scarf, or sweater to take home so I can nonchalantly whisper that phrase, 'Oh, I found this in Paris.' On the high end, I like Sonia by Sonia Rykiel, Vanessa Bruno, and Ventilo. For real bargains, I look for things from Zara (now in New York and Boston) and Kookai." And to finish her Paris wish list, she added "antiques and artwork, and old silver and linens at the flea markets."

Another Francophile friend, screenwriter Diane Lake, ticked off a list that included chocolate and perfume and foie gras, *bien sûr,* but also Pont-Aven butter cookies and a line of cookies found in cheap supermarkets ("fabulous to serve with coffee"); large coffee-cup bowls with or without handles; linens if only pillowcases; scarves, even at Galeries Lafayette for only nineteen euros (I can second her on that—I've made some fabulous finds there); Clairefontaine notebooks with grid paper, little notepads, pens, pen/pencil boxes (that's the writer talking); baby clothes (amen, from the expensive Bonpoint to Monoprix's Bout'Chou line); glass perfume bottles; bincoculars. She also loves old magazines of Paris in the forties and Paris museum shops. Plus, "I've taken home a forty-cent *Pariscope* just to show people all that's going on in Paris. I can't wait for Wednesday when it comes out." She admires shop windows as she wanders around Paris. "Everything," she observes, "is a work of art, from the bakery shop to the flower shop. This city is one giant sculpture."

And Things You Can't

The list of things you can buy is interminable. So is the list of the things you can't: the French lifestyle, *art de vivre, savoir-faire,* and *savoir-vivre.* The French appetite for pleasure, joy in the moment. Even the Gallic shrug. Wouldn't we like to wrap them up and take them with us?

There's also what Edith Wharton calls "French continuity,"

objects from past generations. Much of the enjoyment of a piece of silver or a beautiful piece of furniture comes from its having been in the family and the memories attached to that. Philippe and I inherited a two-hundred-year old *lit Directoire* (daybed from the Directory period, which lasted for five years after the Revolution) from his aunt. It's no ordinary bed; in fact, having it in the room makes me feel as if I were living in a history book. We wonder who slept in it two hundred years ago, but of course we'll never know. However, we do know its fate once it got in his uncle's clutches. At the time of purchase it had its original paint from the eighteenth century. The uncle covered that with the thick paint you use for boats. *I kid you not.* Obviously, the value of the bed is now *nyet,* but we still like it, and when I see how cleverly it's assembled, it's obvious that bed makers haven't made much progress. It's now going on 220 years old, and who knows how many people will have reclined on it and will continue to in the future? Philippe did when he was a little boy, our children did when they were little boys, friends have slept on it, grandchildren have slept on it. I like the idea of having a piece of furniture with a story. Philippe's family has quite a few stories about their furniture because his father was in the wallpaper business but was also an amateur oil painter with the eye of an *artiste.* After World War II, an *antiquaire* friend of his, who found many treasures from noble families living in ruined castles and manors, usually gave him a first look. So he bought a Flemish Renaissance buffet that is a work of art plus other unique pieces, each of which has its own history. I can and have lived with IKEA (oh, those Billy bookshelves!), but living and being around furniture with a deep past has given me an idea of and immense appreciation for the "continuity" Edith Wharton refers to.

Sometimes I imagine that I am returning to the States to live, which, after living in France for most of my adult life, would almost be like moving to a foreign country. What would I take with me?

First of all, my French husband.

Then . . . one of those pieces of furniture, those mementos of history, I mentioned above? I remember visiting our French friends Madeleine and Micheline in their Minneapolis home. The minute they opened the door, you were in France. Part of that was their French reserve and *élégance* and hospitality and sparkle, part the precious antique furniture they had brought to America with them right after World War II.

So, yes, maybe one of the antiques. Beyond that, I'd take back a few intangible, easy things, ways of doing things and spending my time that evoke France.

What would those be? An enjoyment of the moment, a heightened appreciation for aesthetics—in daily life. If I had a dinner party, I'd ask my guests to come at eight for a three-hour sit-down meal at a table with a linen tablecloth, pretty plates, and candles. The dinner party would not be before or after an activity—it would *be* the activity. I'd write notes on French notepaper or in those little Clairefontaine notebooks with grids that I adore, and I'd write with a beautiful French fountain pen. I'd make an effort to look put together all the time (you don't have to be French for this—my mother's my model on that), including when all by myself at home. Like the French, I'd keep things simple: a family brooch, or special scarf, one little black dress, a pair of *très* chic black heels. I'd take along my love of "impassioned discussions" and be ready to quarrel and quibble *à la française* but fear I wouldn't get far on that one (and yet, I told you, verbal sparring is good for the heart!). Every once in a while, I'd take a blue- or red-checkered tablecloth, a bottle of Bordeaux or burgundy, two glasses (real glass ones), a hunk of cheese (good French, raw-milk cheese), some fine sausage, and good bakery bread to the banks of any river anywhere, spread out my feast, close my eyes, and pretend that I am in France. I'd reread *The Three Musketeers* to get a dose of French panache and maybe Houellebecq to get properly depressed and a little morose (that's good for *joie de vivre*). I'd finish up my *pique-nique* with a small, strong espresso and a tiny taste of the finest dark chocolate. In general I'd go for quality, rather than quantity.

I'd do all those things and anything else I could dream up, but I would miss France because it's the country that makes it possible for these things to happen easily and all the time. It's the place where people revel in the moment, appreciate the long meals, the time spent in making and enjoying a perfect feast. It's a country where history envelops you and doesn't become toast immediately. And it's a country in which, indeed, you don't strike up friendships fast, but when you make a French friend, it's for life.

Now there's one more thing. When wearing that special scarf, I'd need a man's compliment on it and how I look. I would appreciate it and say, *"Merci."* Remember the Finnish journalist's comment—if Frenchwomen are well dressed and well turned out, it's because Frenchmen show their appreciation. *Mais oui.*

For the moment, I'm in France, never taking this *joie de vivre* for granted. How could I? Chinese writer Chongguo Cai, who was exiled in France for twenty years and now lives in Hong Kong, asks rhetorically, "What would the world be without the philosophical thought of France? What would it do without your obsession of taking to the streets for whatever reason? Who other than the French turned Europe upside down in 1789? . . . Thank you, France, for showing us that the happiness of living, and of loving without afterthought, is possible on this Earth."

"All the French look like they're acting in a French film," Bruce McCall wrote in the *New Yorker*. I so agree. I wanted to be in that film. And now I am.

Joie de Vivre—*What It Is, What It Isn't*

I love the expression *joie de vivre* and am happy that although the French invented it, we can all have it. Here are a few things I learned about *joie de vivre* from living in France, mainly a way of thinking that can be transported anywhere I go. *Merci, les Français!*

1. *Pleasure isn't sinful*—and pleasure isn't planned. "Play dates" for your children and your obligatory gym session are not necessarily *joie de vivre;* in fact, they might just be *le contraire*! A moment of serendipity with your child is *joie de vivre,* as is a rollicking, impromptu gab and gossip session with your best friend or an unplanned tête-à-tête with your lover. You can't schedule happiness!

2. *Time is not money. Joie de vivre* is having enough money to spend time with family and friends, as opposed to lots of money and no time. Just ask the French, who prefer lots of family and vacation time to huge salaries and little vacation. A no-brainer!

3. *Work is not your life.* Work is important, but family, friends, human relationships, a passionate avocation come first, not last. The French philosophy fits well with the words of Oscar Wilde, who is buried in the Père Lachaise Cemetery: "I put all my genius into my life; I put only my talent into my works."

4. *Expressing yourself is good for the heart!* When we foreigners see the French gesticulating and going ballistically verbal with each other, we're taken aback. What we don't know is that they're having a whale

(continued)

of a time, an intense moment of *joie de vivre*! They evacuate their emotions and then move on to more important things, such as feasting on foie gras and drinking Sauternes.

5. Here's what I learned from Philippe and his mother and sister: when it comes to pleasure, *the French think of the pleasure for others* and "put out" for them in a way I've rarely seen elsewhere. That can range from dressing nicely just to sit in a café (give other people something pleasant to look at) to arranging a pretty table for their guests to serving them good food and keeping the wine and the conversation flowing. The French are big on pleasures that please the palate but also pleasures that please the eye. Their style, their panache, their attention to the little things in life, is their *joie de vivre*.

En Guise d'Adieu

Should the French succeed in shaping the world to their liking . . . every minute of life would be a drop of exquisite pleasure for man to enjoy.
— Salvador de Madariaga, *Englishmen, Frenchmen, Spaniards*, 1929